The European Rupture

UNU World Institute for Development Economics Research (UNU/ WIDER) was established by the United Nations University as its first research and training centre and started work in Helsinki in 1985. The principal purpose of the Institute is policy-oriented research on the main strategic issues of development and international cooperation, as well as on the interaction between domestic and global changes.

UNU World Institute for Development Economics Research (UNU/ WIDER) Katajanokanlaituri 6 B, FIN-00160 Helsinki, Finland

The European Rupture

The Defence Sector in Transition

Edited by
Mary Kaldor

Sussex European Institute, University of Sussex, UK

Geneviève Schméder

Centre Science, Technologie et Société, Conservatoire Nationalé des Arts et Métiers, Paris, France

Edward Elgar
Cheltenham, UK • Lyme, US
United Nations University Press

Published jointly by
Edward Elgar Publishing Limited
8 Lansdown Place
Cheltenham
Glos GL50 2HU
UK

Edward Elgar Publishing, Inc
1 Pinnacle Hill Road
Lyme
NH 03768
US

United Nations University Press
5–53–70 Jingumae
Shibuya-ku, Tokyo 150
Japan

Library of Congress Cataloguing in Publication Data
The European rupture : the defence sector in transition / edited by
    Mary Kaldor, Geneviève Schméder.
        Includes bibliographical references.
        1. Economic conversion—Europe. 2. Defense industries—Europe.
    3. Post–communism—Europe. 4. Economic conversion—Europe, Eastern.
    5. Defense industries—Europe, Eastern. 6. Post–communism—Europe,
    Eastern. I. Kaldor, Mary. II. Schméder, Geneviève.
    HC240.9.D4E94 1997
    338.4'76233'094—dc21   96–49723

ISBN 1 85898 544 7   CIP

Available exclusively in Japan from United Nations University Press
UNU Press ISBN

Printed and bound in Great Britain by
Biddles Ltd, Guildford and King's Lynn

Contents

Tables

Acknowledgements

This book was a collective endeavour. The ideas and the research that went into it were planned jointly and the editors would like to thank Yudit Kiss and Ulrich Albrecht, in particular, for their contribution to the overall conception and execution of this project. In addition to the contributors, we would also like to thank Sean Horstead for providing a continuous and essential supply of documentation and for his background work on intervention; Yahia Said for organizing key interviews, collecting invaluable research material and developing arguments about the former Czechoslovakia; and Stephanie Baker for language editing a disparate set of chapters. We are especially indebted to Andrew Davis for rescuing the final manuscript. Finally, we would like to express our thanks to the John D. and Catherine Macarthur Fellowship for funding a fellowship programme at WIDER that enabled us to undertake this project. Needless to say, the editors take final responsibility for the contents of the book.

1. Introduction

Mary Kaldor

The end of the cold war marks a profound rupture with the past –
probably more profound than we can yet realize. It has revealed a
rupture, not only in international relationships, but also in forms of
economic organization and democratic representation. It has brought
to the surface deep-rooted changes that have been under way for at
least two decades.

In the East, the fragility of the economies became obvious. These
vertically organized autarkic systems, dominated by energy-intensive
mass production heavy industries, shattered under the impact of opening
up towards the West. It was also transparently clear that the ruling
parties had lost any shred of legitimacy that they once might have
assumed. In the West there were equally significant changes. Forms of
economic organization changed from nationally centred economies
based on mass production, the intensive use of energy, particularly oil,
and standardized consumer products towards a much more globally
interdependent economy based on new information technologies. This
transformation was accompanied by an erosion of the dominant institutions of the post-war period – the liberal world economy, the welfare
state, the commitment to full employment, and so on. There was also
a crisis of political legitimacy: the political parties that shaped the
post-war period no longer seem capable of representing the views and
interests of substantial segments of society; advertising images, 'sound
bites' and opinion polls seem to have replaced serious political debate
and organization; national governments have become increasingly ineffective, unable to implement policies in the new interdependent context.

The artificial framework of the cold war contained these developments. The cold war provided a sort of cohesion that preserved the
dominant institutions. The permanent confrontation, the imaginary war
atmosphere in which the threat of the 'other' constituted a continuing
source of legitimacy, froze the institutional structures of the post-war
period long after they had ceased to serve their purposes.[1] The end of
the cold war has exposed the weakness of those institutional structures

1

– their impotence in the face of new problems that confront post-cold war Europe.

The term used to describe the current period is 'transition'. It is, of course, a transition in the sense that it is characterized by dramatic change. But in so far as the term implies a transition from one way of ordering affairs to another – a temporary breakdown which we shall live through – it is misleading. Without awareness of the profound nature of this rupture, without conscious efforts at restructuring, this period could lead, not to some future new order, but instead to a long epoch of disorganization and chaos.

If we are to draw parallels with the past, which is always to some extent deceptive, then it could be said that this period more closely resembles 1918 than 1945. In 1918, politicians, by and large, did not recognize the need to restructure their own societies. Some adjustments had to be made in international relationships with the collapse of the Eastern empires and the largely cosmetic creation of the League of Nations, but it was hoped that it would somehow be possible to restore the pre-war world. It took a depression and another world war before new institutions could be established. In contrast, in 1945, a new generation of politicians came to power untainted by appeasement and collaboration; they emerged out of a sea change in popular political thinking that had characterized the preceding period and they offered and were able to implement transformative programmes.

In this book we focus on the consequences of the end of the cold war for the European defence sector. By the defence sector, we mean the institutions engaged in preparations for defence – armed forces, ministries of defence, defence industries, and so on. This sector represents the institutional connection between security and the economy. In theory, at least, the demand for defence preparations is determined by overall security policy, while the supply depends on the general level of technology and the availability of resources. But the sector itself is not neutral. How it is organized, the resources it absorbs and the vested interests it generates also shape both perceptions of security and the direction of economic development.

During the cold war, the defence sector was not only the institutional connection between security and the economy, it was also the institutional connection between East and West. A central argument of this book is that the economies of Eastern Europe were, effectively, cold war economies; that is to say, they operated, as a whole, in much the same way as the defence sectors in the West, as mini-command systems, with profound consequences for the market economies within which they functioned.

The implications of the end of the cold war are twofold. First of all, East European economies are not just undergoing a transition from centrally planned systems to market economies; they are also undergoing a transition from a cold war economy. Secondly, transition is not a problem for Eastern Europe alone – Western Europe also faces a post-cold war transition, even if this transition is not as pervasive as that experienced in Eastern Europe.

In the aftermath of the cold war there have been major cuts in defence spending, especially in Eastern Europe, in some areas of which the defence sector has disintegrated. But these cuts have not led to a 'peace dividend' or to a reorganization of the defence sector. A number of reasons can be adduced: the uncertainty about future security policy, the neo-liberal reluctance to introduce strategies for the conversion of the defence sector as a whole; vested interests within the defence sector. But perhaps the most important reason is inherited mind-set: a failure to understand that this is a transition for all of Europe and that choices about the future direction of economic development cannot be separated from choices about the future direction of security policy or vice versa.

Our approach is close to that of the 'regulationist' economists in France or the evolutionary economists in Britain. Both schools of thought emphasize the role of institutions in guaranteeing the rules of economic behaviour. They attempt to describe how different phases of economic history, distinguished by different patterns of production and consumption, are governed by different laws and different regulatory mechanisms. And they demonstrate that economic laws, in a given period, are determined by the institutional context. However, the missing element in these theories is the process of institutional change. Institutional change is, so to speak, the black box in these theories. These theories can provide indications of what has to change, what new regulatory mechanisms are required, but not how this is to be done. We think that security is a key ingredient in opening this black box. Institutions are profoundly shaped by wars or by the threat of war. Yet those who study security issues rarely consider the economic implications. They treat security as a compartmentalized activity and they treat political institutions as free-floating entities able to adopt appropriate security policies. They rarely take into account the influence of security arrangements on the overall regulation of the economy, or how economic factors influence the level of political violence. By linking the issues of security and economy through a study of the defence sector, we hope to gain some new insights into institution building that could make possible a new ordering of international relationships.

This book is the outcome of a programme of fellowships on the theme of security and economy at the World Institute for Development Economics Research (WIDER).[2] The first part of the book represents a summary of the general ideas we developed during this programme: Chapter 2 analyses the connection between security and the economy as if functioned during the cold war period and argues that the defence sector profoundly shaped economies, technologically, geographically, industrially and socially. Chapter 3 describes some of the new issues that have to be confronted in the transition period: in particular, some of the new challenges to our conceptions of security, changes in technology and problems of defence conversion.

The second part of the book consists of a series of case-studies in which we attempt to describe what has happened to the defence sector in particular countries. The first three studies, on Britain, France and Germany, attempt to describe the changes in the defence sector in the immediate post-cold war period in Western Europe. All the case studies have some trends in common: in particular, a tendency to nationalize security policy, combined with laissez-faire economic policies and a profound restructuring and transnationalization of the defence industry. There are also important differences. Only in Germany is it possible to identity significantly new approaches in security policies as well as genuine regional efforts, based on the participation of both the community and the defence enterprises and unions, to redeploy resources released from the military sector in socially useful activities, for example environmental technologies or public transport. Even in Germany, however, these new initiatives are overshadowed by more traditional economic and security approaches. In Britain and France, a preoccupation with an imperial past and an over-dependence of industry on defence orders have made change very difficult. Spending cuts have not been nearly so large as in Germany or Eastern Europe and there has been virtually no attempt to redeploy resources. There are some differences between the two countries, however. In France, the military–industrial complex remains more or less cohesive and contained. In Britain, Thatcherite deregulatory policies have speeded up the restructuring of the defence industry, characterized by a combination of privatization and transnationalization. In addition, one of the legacies of the British peace movement of the 1980s, as in Germany, has been strong local and regional pressure for conversion.

The last three cases studies deal with Eastern Europe. Chapter 7 discusses the problems of arms conversion in Czechoslovakia and how they contributed to the break-up of the country. The study shows how the initial internationalist policies of the post-1989 government failed both because of the difficulty of converting a rather heavily militarized economy, especially in Slovakia, and because of the unfavourable international environment. Chapter 8 is about the overall changes in the defence sector in Hungary, where some similar trends can be observed. As in Western Europe, the difficulty in coping with the effects of substantial defence cuts and the absence of an international security framework which Hungary could join have led to a growing renationalization of security policies. Chapter 9 considers the Russian defence industry and the need to rethink overall economic strategy in Russia as a problem of defence industry restructuring rather than merely as a problem of transition to the market.

The last chapter is more speculative. It reflects upon the need for new institutional arrangements and how these have to be structured in order to re-establish a system of international security and a system of economic regulation. In particular, this chapter puts forward proposals for the shift from national or bloc security policies, based on the anticipation of a World War Two-type conflict, towards a more internationalist security policy, and for appropriate measures of economic adjustment, especially defence conversion.

Our main conclusion is the need for a long-term cosmopolitan, that is non-exclusive and non-territorial, approach to both security and economic change. The cold war was a partial territorial solution; it applied to Europe. It is possible to envisage partial temporary arrangements. For instance, Russia might be held together by the military and an expanded NATO might regain its role of balancing Russia for a while. But this kind of arrangement could not last because it could not provide an institutional framework for solving a range of economic and social disorders which are both transnational and local. While it is not possible to establish a blueprint of institutions which could satisfy this condition, because institutions are the outcome of social and political processes, we can suggest some of the tasks that those institutions would have to be able to perform. There is no inevitability about the establishment of a new set of instititutions. Transition can be long-drawn-out. The current uncertainty could constitute a long-term condition. The institutions required to overcome uncertainty can only be constructed through conscious political efforts based on new ways of understanding our current impasse.

NOTES

1. For an elaboration of this argument, see Mary Kaldor (1991), *The Imaginary War: Understanding the East–West Conflict*. Oxford: Basil Blackwell.
2. We are very grateful to the John D. and Catherine MacArthur Foundation for financing the programme.

2. The Economic Legacy of the Cold War

Mary Kaldor and Geneviève Schméder

During the cold war, Europe was structured in a bipolar way by forces which were not only ideological and military but also economic. These forces were strongly interconnected, since the ideological division between 'liberalism' and 'communism' corresponded to a division between countries whose economies were respectively labelled 'capitalist' and 'socialist' and which belonged respectively to the NATO and to the Warsaw Pact camps. On each side, in spite of the persistence of distinct national traditions and trajectories, the integrative elements were very strong. The cold war provided a clear definition of a shared threat which held together both the security and the economic systems under the respective guidance of the USA and the USSR.

In each camp, the crucial element which moulded the global economic order and held it together was the military threat. The discipline of the cold war not only froze the military and ideological status quo, it froze the economic status quo as well. It was not just mere chance that, during the 1970s and 1980s, the structural character of the economic problems was systematically neglected or underestimated, especially by governments. Had these problems been properly addressed, it would necessarily have meant a reconsideration of the socioeconomic foundations of the security system elaborated after World War Two.

The fact that, well before the end of the cold war, the different pieces of the puzzle no longer formed a coherent ensemble could be masked or ignored as long as the two blocs linked between them the different countries. Even when the progressive erosion of the economic foundations of the post-war security systems gave rise to growing economic imbalances and social conflicts, the cold war provided a mechanism through which individual countries were able to overcome potential conflicts of interest and which prevented any radical institutional change, in spite of the growing inadequacy of the arrangements made after World War Two and the increasing need for new institutional configurations.

7

The situation changed with the end of the cold war and the removal of the military threat. It became clear that most of the difficulties of European economies, both in the East and in the West, were less the consequence of the transgression of economic laws or of mistakes in economic policies than the result of dynamic trends which had their origin in the institutional arrangements which were established after World War Two. The structural and far-reaching nature of the crisis, in the West and in the East, had to be related to long-term structural changes which have taken place since World War Two. It is in this context that the current situation of European defence sectors has to be understood. The end of the cold war, in the West as in the East, represents a major source of instability but opens the way for alternative organizational principles and institutional transitions. While the suppression of the previous federative elements replaced the old dialectic of integration with a new dialectic of fragmentation, the collapse of the Eastern bloc opened a process of restructuring within a larger Europe.

THE ECONOMIC LEGACY OF THE COLD WAR IN WESTERN EUROPE

In Western Europe, a new international order emerged under the technological, financial, diplomatic and military guidance of the USA and a new system came into being after World War Two. Its implementation and diffusion was partly the result of the immense distrust of pure laissez-faire theories after the catastrophic evolution of the 1930s, partly the outcome of major transformations in technology and new forms of social organizations and state interventions experienced during the war and partly the consequence of the new fascination for the 'American way of life' which originated in the USA in the inter-war period. The new system involved much greater state intervention than ever before and the style of that intervention was shaped, to a lesser or greater degree in different countries, by the experience of World War Two and the context of the new cold war. The former war led to the replacement of traditional European ruling classes by new elites more open to social and technological change and the emergence of new political and social forces which were urged to rebuild or modernize their national economies and put the design and implementation of an entirely new economic organization at the top of the agenda.

The new economic system implied three major changes. The first was a new social compromise, traditionally labelled 'Fordist': unions accepted scientific management methods which they had previously fought, provided wage-earners got the major share of productivity increases associated with the diffusion of new production methods, through direct wage increases and social benefits. This bargain led to tremendous improvements in both labour productivity and living standards, since production and consumption rose in parallel: substantial increases in real income allowed wage-earners to buy mass-produced consumer goods (cars, houses, appliances and so on) and this in turn spurred production, including that of capital and equipment goods. Hence there was a virtuous circle of cumulative growth which made possible the development of universal social security.

The second major change affected the forms of competition. The new type of capital–labour relationship was accompanied by a new monopolistic/oligopolistic type of competition, which was marked by a much higher centralization of financial assets and concentration of markets. The state provided subsidies to monopolistic and nationalized firms operating in key sectors and competition was based on compromises between firms on prices and productive capacities. The third change was a completely new approach to monetary and state management. A new financial system based on extensive use of credit was created, which allowed a lowering of the monetary constraint both at the international and the national levels. States were major actors in this process through permissive credit, countercyclical Keynesian economic policies and massive redistribution of income. Fields where state interventionism was particularly strong were infrastructure and social redistribution. The 'welfare state' ideal implied not only the support by the state of investment, growth and competitiveness, but also that the way the labour force was reproduced, through education, health, unemployment, retirement and so on, was given to the state. It was no longer left to the individual or family solidarity but was promoted through collective procedures. Hence there were high levels of social expenditure.

High government military expenditures played a major role in this paradigm shift. In the aftermath of World War Two, the defence sector became, for the first time, a major element in the organization of Western economies, at least those of the USA, Britain and France. Parallel to the welfare state was the so-called 'military–industrial complex', which is no less important in understanding the functioning of Western economies during this period. Military spending, which remained exceptionally high as a proportion of national output compared with any other previous peacetime period, helped to stimulate aggregate demand and had a 'multiplier' effect which lasted well into the 1950s and 1960s. Its macroeconomic impact was, however, less

important that its structural effects in terms of geographical location of
industries, provision of infrastructure, strategic choices in the field
of energy, development of certain types of skills, and so on. It helped
in particular to sustain a specific pattern of demand for such things as
cars, weapons, consumer durables, synthetic materials and oil.

Armed forces were much more capital-intensive and science-intensive
than ever before. Around 40 percent of defence budgets was spent on
equipment an around 10 percent on research and development. This is
much higher than expenditure on investment or on R&D in the civilian
economy. Equipment was produced by large companies that were both
private and state-towned, but which were nevertheless dependent on
the state for their market. These companies were 'national champions'
and became, whether consciously or not, instruments of industrial
policy, stabilizing employment and influencing geographical location
and technological priorities. Essentially, the defence sector was a
planned sector which could be used to shape the direction of market
economies.

Because of high levels of R&D, this was particularly important in the
field of technology. For the fist 20 years, high levels of military spending
helped to stimulate rapid technological advance. A number of major
manufacturing innovations had their origins in the 19th century in the
arms industry (development of machine tools at the Woolwich Arsenal,
interchangeability of parts at the Whitney and Colt factories, Taylorism
at the Watertown Arsenal) but military research had rarely been the
source of radical innovations. Instead it was mainly concerned with
adapting civil technologies to military needs. During World War Two,
scientific research was systematically used by governments as a regular
source of new armaments and a lasting cooperation between scientists,
universities, industrialists and armed forces was institutionalized, which
proved to be crucial for the outcome of the war and during the armed
peace that followed it. This scientific mobilization was prolonged during
the years of the cold war for the sake of security but also, it was
argued, of prosperity.[1] Besides its strategic utility, military research was
supposed to be a main source of technological spin-offs and progress
for the whole economy.

As a matter of fact, massive injections of military spending on
research and development in laboratories and *bureaux d'étude* in charge
of designing high-tech military systems had a crucial role in the development of new technologies. Nuclear reactors, integrated circuits,
supercomputers, laser X-rays, and composite materials are but a few of
the technological ideas stimulated by the military sector either as a
result of R&D or through procurement, thus creating an initial market

for new products. To the direct effects of military R&D in terms of new commercial products were added indirect effects like the maintenance in contracting firms of a critical mass of research staff or the progress of basic research.[2]

The Emerging Crisis

The adaptation to the European specificities of this new global organization was quite successful. The adoption of the same production and consumption norms and the adhesion to the international order under Pax Americana created a strong homogeneity among Western Europe countries and led to much higher rates of growth and milder cyclical crises than ever before. However, these successes were achieved at great cost. The most obvious consequence was permanent inflation, especially in those countries which were most engaged in the cold war. This was not only due to high military expenditures, but also to wage inflationary pressures and the restriction of competition. It was hard to believe, however, that this successful post-war model could fail and that the features inherited from World War Two would come to a deadlock in the 1970s and 1980s.

In Western Europe, the post-war model entered a long structural crisis in the early 1970s. This crisis manifested itself in a slowdown in productivity growth, accelerated inflation and a declining rate of profit. After the two oil shocks, the persistence of inflation during recessions was accompanied by worsening public deficits, balance of payments imbalances and upward unemployment trends. Keynesian therapies, when applied at the national or international levels, were no longer able to provide the expected results. However, restrictive monetary and conservative policies which were then adopted in some countries did not achieve any better results than social democratic alternatives.

The roots of this structural crisis lay in major changes which progressively challenged the post-war model. A first change was related to the nature of demand and the organization of work and production. To the increasing challenge by workers of the Fordist and Taylorist systems was added the loss of efficiency of traditional methods for reaping increasing returns to scale through standardization and mechanization. After 1973, the significant slowdown of the growth of labour productivity in all OECD (Organization for Economic Cooperation and Development) countries called into question the very principle of mass production of highly standardized goods. Big was no longer beautiful when the saturation of markets called for differentiation, flexibility and quality of products rather than increasing quantities. Another form of organization than rigid energy- and material-intensive mass production was now required.

A second change was linked to the growing impotence of the welfare and Keynesian state as a consequence of both the internationalization of national economies and the excessive costs of the welfare systems. The rapid development of international trade and competition, in a context of growing uncertainties about the world financial and trade systems, was a factor of governmental impotence and economic instability. In a context where even countries with a creeping protectionism could not prevent the share of external trade from increasing relative to national production and where wages were no longer the source of aggregate demand but of costs detrimental to external competitiveness, the development of multinational corporations destabilized the previous organization of budgetary and trade deficits. Production and income distribution operated increasingly at a transnational level, while economic policies were still elaborated at a national level.

The welfare state also experienced increasing financial constraints which exacerbated the problem of the allocation of public resources between alternative ends, especially between social and military expenditures. During the first phase of the crisis, priority was given to the prevention of domestic inflation. This led to unprecedented levels of real interest rates which checked credit and monetary supply, with negative effects on growth and employment. Strong state interventionism then tried to cushion these adverse effects for households and firms, with strong public deficits as a result. Finally, governments tried to reduce total public intervention: individual unemployment benefits were reduced and expansionary Keynesian policies replaced by restrictive and conservative strategies.

Policies of demand growth restriction had negative effects on the employment situation, which was already harmed by progressive saturation of demand for many 'Fordist' goods, competition from newly industrialized countries and the labour-saving character of the 'microelectronic' technological revolution. Unemployment grew from 5 million people in 1973 to 16 million in 1983 and 22 million in 1993. This put a heavy burden on public expenditures since social protection, which represented less than 15 percent of gross domestic product (GDP) during the 1960s, absorbed almost a quarter of GDP a quarter of a century later.

A third series of substantial changes took place in the technological field. The destabilization here came from the gradual exhaustion of the cluster of innovations which had launched the post-war boom and the emergence at the international level of a new technological system based on electronic and information technologies. While the typical technologies of the post-World War Two period, based on low-cost oil and energy-intensive materials, evolved along rigid trajectories with sharply diminishing returns and growing costs, the new information technologies which were developing allowed a shift in the productive paradigm.

It is remarkable that those economies most affected by these structural changes and least effective at developing the new generation of products and processes were those where the military sector operated in much the same fashion as in Eastern Europe, that is as centrally administered systems, where employment, until the 1980s, was more or less guaranteed, as systems characterized by soft budgets, with perpetual cost overruns, and as autarkic systems in which trade was relatively low compared with the rest of manufacturing. As in Eastern Europe, the benefits of this system outweighed the costs in the first 20 years after World War Two. In the 1970s and 1980s, however, the defence sector displayed many problems similar to those experienced in Eastern Europe. In those countries, especially the USA, Britain and France, where military sectors had a leading role in shaping industrial policies, these were plagued by shortage and inefficiency. Technical change took place but, owing to the rigidity of military organization, was confined to the trajectories that originated in World War Two. Sharply diminishing returns were reflected in sharply rising prices for defence products, which fed inflation and put continued pressure on defence budgets. Because budgets were fixed, this in turn forced periodic cuts in numbers of weapons, ammunition, stores and so on, thus reinforcing the tendency to shortages and inefficiency.

Military sponsorship did not only preserve and accentuate the typical technological trajectories of World War Two and contribute to inflation; it also tended to maintain specific labour relations. It thus became progressively an obstacle to economic, technological and industrial development. Technological devices developed or influenced by the military became less reliable and more complex and tended to use more energy and other resources than technological devices directed towards exclusively civilian ends. Finally, high levels of military spending became a structural obstacle to change and one factor in explaining the growing disequilibrium between the USA and Britain, on the one hand, and Germany and Japan, on the other.

THE ECONOMIC LEGACY OF THE COLD WAR IN EASTERN EUROPE

In Eastern Europe a new 'socialist' system also came into being after World War Two under Soviet control. Central to the definition of this system was the Communist Party's monopoly of power, but it was, according to Janos Kornai, nevertheless possible to distinguish, among economic and political systems which defined themselves as socialist, three system prototypes:[3] 'revolutionary–transitional systems' which existed in the 1950s in all of Eastern Europe except Yugoslavia; 'reform socialist systems', which were introduced in Yugoslavia and Hungary in the 1960s and in Poland in the 1980s; and finally 'post-socialist systems'. According to Kornai, only classical socialist systems could be considered as 'coherent' systems since reform socialism contains inherent contradictions which inevitably lead to the collapse of socialism.

This classification is useful in understanding the key role that war and the cold war played in European 'socialist' systems. Revolutionary–transitional systems were, by definition, war systems: they came into being or were consolidated under wartime conditions. The classic example of such a system is the period of 'war communism' in the Soviet Union. Party discipline and hierarchy, heroism and revolutionary fervour, and military priorities were all typical of war situations and left their inevitable imprint on subsequent systems. Classical socialist systems also could be defined as war or cold war systems: not only did they work *as if* the country were at war, but they operated more 'coherently' the closer the approximation to a wartime situation. Typical examples were the Soviet Union during World War Two and all of Eastern Europe during the 1950s, when the memory of the war was still fresh and the confrontation with the East most acute. By contrast, reform socialist systems were détente systems: the systems were still predicated on bipolarity but the sense of confrontation had been relaxed. Post-socialist systems are of course also post-cold war systems.

What were the central characteristics of a war or a cold war system? The first was centralized control of the economy, which included state ownership and the use of administrative methods of regulating economic activity. The second was the combination of harsh repression and ideological appeals to patriotism and revolutionary loyalty as the main form of labour discipline. The third was a system of priorities which ensured the fulfilment of centrally defined goals. One of the most important of these goals was preparation for war. During the 1950s, Soviet military spending may have been as high as 40 percent of net material product.[4] In Eastern Europe, military spending may have been between 10 and 20 percent of NMP. The priority of the military sector was also evident in other respects: for example, privileges for the military elites, what Vozlensky called the 'military nomenklatura'; investment priority; priority in supplies, that is the ability to cut through red tape and overcome shortages; and greater quality control than in other sectors.[5]

In addition, the defence industry ministries which also produced civilian goods controlled a very large part of the economy. In the former Soviet Union there were 15 defence industry ministries out of a total of 28 ministries.[6] Investment, especially investment in heavy industry, was also a priority, which was of course linked to the construction of a strong industrial base to meet wartime needs. Agriculture and consumption were relatively neglected.

The fourth characteristic of this war system was a combination of autarky and territorial integration. While closure to the outside world was very important, internally a territorial division of labour was established. Within the Soviet Union as a whole, a territorial division of labour was established. However, this was not extended to the whole of Eastern Europe, where each economy was established as a separate autarkic unit. In Yugoslavia, also, there was a tendency to territorial autarky within each of the republics. In both cases, however, the military sector served an integrative function and played a key part in territorial integration. In the case of the Warsaw Pact, a clear military and military industrial division of labour was established among the constituent members, which limited the possibilities for separatist political or economic actions.[7]

Such a system worked coherently only in wartime. The reason is that war imposes an external discipline, somewhat akin to the market. It was Clausewitz, after all, who likened war to business competition. War is a struggle for survival in which those who fail to measure up to its demands are penalized by defeat. The main goal of the first two five-year plans introduced by Stalin in 1928 was war preparation. Yakovlev, the famous aircraft designer, explained in his autobiography how mass production methods were introduced in the Soviet Union, not to meet the needs of consumption, but for war. Gigantic 'American-style' factories were built to manufacture armaments.[8] However, when the Germans invaded in 1941, these preparations turned out to have been totally inadequate and most of the newly built industry was destroyed. Within a very short period, industry was rebuilt in the East and the Soviet system went on to produce armaments of a scale and quality equivalent to those of the USA: American assistance in the form of lend-lease cannot explain this extraordinary achievement. During the

1950s, when the wartime atmosphere persisted, arms production became a feature of forced industrialization in all of Eastern Europe.

In the absence of war, the system lost its coherence. First of all, without external discipline, it was much more difficult to maintain a centralized system. In fact, in the absence of war, it was wrong to describe Socialist systems as centrally planned economies. They were vertically organized and bureaucratically coordinated, but not centralized: decisions taken at the top were the outcomes of a process of bureaucratic bargaining which incorporated all sorts of pressure from below. The plan was thus a mechanism for mediating different bureaucratic interests. The weaker the external imperative, the greater the subjective nature of the plan.

Secondly, it became much more difficult to sustain labour discipline. The appeal of patriotism is a less strong incentive when the external threat diminishes, or is perceived to diminish, and the case for harsh repression is weakened, especially since members of the apparatus themselves are subject to repression. Thirdly, it was more difficult to resist other priority demands, for example for higher living standards, or demands for less autarky and more territorial democratization. If the military sector retained its privileged positions as the priority sector and as a mechanism for territorial integration, it was not because of external necessity, but because of its powerful domestic role.

The classical system was a resource-constrained system, in contrast to a market system which is demand-constrained, which led to shortage and inefficiency. In wartime, shortage can be managed through the elimination of redundant production not required by the war effort. As the system becomes less coherent, the problems of shortage are magnified. Shortage is the consequence of the 'soft budget' which is the characteristic of a priority system. The priority sector always experiences a soft budget: there is no limit to the resources which can be demanded for a priority project. And there is evidence that, even now, the defence sector experiences the softest budgets. In wartime, however, non-priority systems experienced hard budget constraints, not because of the existence of a market, but because of discipline imposed by the state. In the absence of war, bargaining on investment and supplies of intermediate products is the rule.

A soft budget means that investment always exceeds planned targets, even when the planners try to anticipate this, and that expenditure always exceeds output. The consequence is shortage and bottlenecks. Moreover, because of the behaviour induced by shortage, that is the hoarding of supplies and supply networks, as well as the difficulty of eliminating redundant sectors and the perverse consequences of administrative directives, once all resources are employed, there is a tendency to stagnate. Because households experience hard budget constraints – fixed wages – and since they have no voice in the planning system, there is a tendency always to squeeze consumption.

Furthermore, in a system of centralized incentives, firms are not motivated to introduce innovations corresponding to user or consumer needs. The incorporation of technical change in production is thus very slow, especially since the greater part of technical resources is mobilized in the defence sector. The result was a continuous productivity slowdown in the consumer goods sector, and a vicious circle of shortage and chronic underproductivity.

The reform system[9] modifies some of the characteristics described above. First, administrative directives are replaced by financial indicators; more private property is tolerated; a large part of the economy is formally or informally regulated by market means. Second, repression is much less harsh and ideological statements become forms of labelling or methods of expressing loyalty as opposed to genuine incentives. In other words, the reform system continues to operate as if there was an ideological struggle, but everyone knows that this is a deception – necessary perhaps for the functioning of the system and one's own position in it. Third, military spending remains a priority but levels of military spending are reduced. There is a greater emphasis on light industries and consumption. Indeed, higher living standards are a substitute for greater freedom, a way of dealing with with public discontent when repression is weakened but democratic forms of expression are not allowed. Fourth, there is less autarky in the sense of greater opening to the West, but the military territorial division of labour remains. In some countries, such as Yugoslavia, there is great decentralization leading to the nationalization of party structures. In fact, the opening to the West applied to most of the former socialist countries during the 1970s when Western credit was extended to these countries, as a result of détente and of the effort by Western banks to recycle petro-dollars.

The reform system magnified many of the problems that follow from the incoherence of socialist systems in the absence of a genuine external confrontation. Some improvements in efficiency were achieved, but the most overwhelming consequence of reform was indebtedness, which reached alarming proportions in the early 1980s. Chronic shortage leads to import hunger and export aversion and these tendencies were self-reinforcing as bureaucrats overestimated their import needs and underestimated their export capacity in order to prevent further shortages. The consequence was debt-induced austerity policies and a return to repression, exhibited in a most extreme form in Romania in the early 1980s. The new cold war of the early 1980s was linked to this necessary reversion to some elements of the classical system.

Post-socialist systems are post-cold war systems. The most funda- mental change has been the ending of the monopoly of the Communist Party and, in most cases, the removal of the Communist Party from power. This has removed the main mechanism through which the state exercised control over the economy. Changes introduced by new post- cold war governments include the dismantling of administrative controls over domestic and external trade and over labour; a much bigger role for the private sector, although the privatization of state-owned property is extremely slow; the abandonment of repression and ideology in favour of the discipline of the threat of unemployment;[10] big cuts in state budgets in order to stabilize deficits and prevent inflation; the creation of a modern banking and credit system, and the giving up of the 'passive money' which characterized the old system; and an even greater opening to the West and the total collapse of the territorial system of military integration, with the collapse of the Warsaw Pact and the disintegration of the JNA (the army of the former Yugoslavia) and the Red Army, exposing fissiparous tendencies both among the East European coun- tries and within Yugoslavia and the Soviet Union.

In the immediate post-cold war period, the main effect of these changes has been a fall in gross national product (GNP), increased inequalities and the re-emergence of unemployment. The impact of unemployment in Eastern Europe is especially dramatic because full employment was formerly guaranteed and because most countries lack universal social coverage. Social benefits were usually linked to employ- ment; individual enterprises and not the state were responsible for child care, health, housing, pensions and even food rations. Unemployment seems to be a major source of growing nationalistic and xenophobic sentiment.

TOWARDS WHICH EUROPE IN THE FUTURE?

In *the Economic Consequences of the Peace*, which was written in 1919, Keynes emphasized the need to think about the peace and the future of the world in terms which were not only diplomatic but also economic. We now know the disastrous consequences that resulted from not taking this warning seriously. After World War Two, it was precisely the explicit willingness of the Western victors not to repeat the mistakes of the pre- war period that was the root of the establishment of a new international economic system. With the end of the cold war, the problem poses itself anew: what major changes have to be set in motion in order to restore the long-term stability of the economy and of security? The situation is in effect comparable to that of 1918 and of 1945: either new principles of economic organization and social cohesion will be negotiated and put in place at the national and international level or, as was the case in the 1930s, autarkic responses will simultaneously undermine the basis of international exchange and of peace.

There are, however, several important differences between the present situation and that of 1945. The first is that, if the last decades have been a period of war, this 'cold' war has been more imaginary than real. While the previous 'hot' wars destroyed a great deal, this one has left productive capacity intact, so that markets are saturated and competition is fierce. The second difference is that the cold war has produced neither a new hegemonic power capable of imposing its 'order' nor a true sense of urgency about the reforms that need to be undertaken. The burden of military spending, which contributed to a growing disequilibrium among advanced industrial countries and the progressive weakening of the global financial system, accelerated the decline of the hegemonic powers. The countries which emerge from the cold war the strongest are those which were least involved, while the race for military superiority weakened (some would say ruined) the economies of those countries which took part.

This situation represents a major source of instability, but also opens the way for real alternative organizational principles and institutional transitions. The end of the East–West confrontation, in allowing centrifugal tendencies to take over, has created a situation of great uncertainty and danger. Each country and each zone may from now on be tempted to declare its independence, to renounce former ties and to defend particular interests, with the goal notably of maintaining in its own area maximum employment and revenues. The return of right-wing exclusivist movements which feed on unemployment and social inequalities provides a further impetus to this particularist approach. In a difficult economic context where the exacerbation of international competition reinforces the difficulties of coordinating national policies, it leaves the field free for the doctrine of 'each for himself'. The return of the old mercantilist doctrine, which assumes that the cake to be shared is fixed and that it is only possible to increase one's share to the detriment of others, means that economic competition could be transformed into open commercial warfare and confrontation for the conquest of markets into nationalist confrontation.

These centrifugal tendencies are of course counterbalanced by tendencies in the opposite direction. In the economic domain, the main factor slowing down the evolution towards fragmentation is interdependence, which as established itself globally and can no longer be bypassed. Growth is from now on inevitably linked to the enlargement of markets, itself a necessary condition for better organization of work, new forms of distribution, a re-evaluation of the role of the state, new rules of competition, and so on. Nothing guarantees, however, that the opening up of markets will bring the hoped for results. In 1989, the collapse of the economic system associated with the Pax Sovietica seemed to open up extremely favourable prospects for growth. Several years later, the disappointments of the East European countries remind us that institutions, including markets, cannot be decreed but result from a long process of social construction.

The multiplication of frictions increases today the urgency of putting in place profound changes but also the difficulties of negotiating the principles of change in a world which has become multipolar and where no major catastrophe as yet acts as a catalyst for the relevant actors. On the other hand, the fact that no hegemonic power is capable of imposing its 'order' could allow the establishment of a new order to be negotiated rather than imposed. In other words, socio-organizational innovations which could break down the vicious circles and recreate the virtuous circles which we lack today could be based on explicit consent of the participants and the formal expression of compromise agreements, rather than on diverse forms of leadership, coercion and manipulation of initiatives.

One of the main challenges of the post-cold war period is the establishment of alternative principles and institutions to the ones which characterized the cold war period. This goes well beyond the restructuring of the military sector, implying a new productive organization, new rules of income distribution based on new types of compromise between capital and labour, a new definition of the role of the state and new articulations between national economies and the international economy. Without such new institutional arrangements, the world may face either a major crisis caused by the collapse of the international credit system or a slower process of economic disintegration provoked by the introduction of new forms of protectionism. In other words, vicious circles of deflation, unemployment and social and regional inequality may result in the spread of conflict and the rise of individual as well as organized violence.

Decisions about security will profoundly influence this process, since choices about the future direction of security policy cannot be separated from choices about the future direction of economic development.

Whichever economic, technological and strategic paradigm follows the cold war, its emergence will not be accompanied by a miracle allowing the easing of the new economic and budgetary constraints. Public budgets cuts due to the economic slump will thus exert strong financial pressures against continuous militarization. This represents a unique opportunity for a much broader cosmopolitan approach to security that encompasses new forms of economic cooperation and political dialogue. Only such a broad approach, which requires considerable vision, energy and thought to implement, could lay the basis for a new set of transnational and regional institutions which could also provide a framework for resolving economic and ecological problems. But there is also a real danger that Europe, especially the eastern part, will degenerate into small, closed-in militarized and contested nation-states facing a myriad of economic difficulties and conflicts.

The end of the cold war is the beginning of a difficult period of trial and error, a search for alternatives compatible with the legacy of the past. Nobody can predict where this search will eventually lead. One historical lesson is that a new international order generally comes after a major war and is imposed by the 'victors'. Is the end of an imaginary war the same as the end of a real war? Do European societies have enough vision and energy to introduce the necessary social and institutional innovations? Will the end of the cold war undermine the foundations of the ideology of armament which has influenced public policies and shaped industrial and technological developments for the last four decades? In the following chapter, we will examine some of these issues.

NOTES

1. The US government spent $4 million per year on military R&D between 1920 and 1935, $2 billion between 1985 and 1990 (E. Rothschild (1989), 'L'économie de la dissuasion. Les armes nucléaires sont-elles chères?', in J.J. Salomon (ed.), *Science guerre et paix*, Paris: Economica. In 1940, only 0.8 percent of the US federal budget was devoted to R&D, of which 3.8 percent on military R&D (the Department of Agriculture spent more on R&D than the Department of Defense). In 1960, these figures were respectively 10.1 percent and 90 percent.
2. D. Mowery and N. Rosenberg (1990), *Technology and the Pursuit of Economic Growth*, Cambridge: Cambridge University Press.
3. Janos Kornai (1992), *The Socialist System: The Political Economy of Communism*, Oxford: Oxford University Press.
4. Official defence expenditures, estimated on the basis of dollar equivalent exchange rates, amounted to between 20 percent and 25 percent of NMP, according to the Stockholm International Peace Research Institute. However, official defence expenditure only covered personnel and not procurement, investment and military R&D.
5. See Christopher M. Davis (1988), 'The High-priority Military Sector in a Shortage

Economy', in Henry S. Rowen and Charles Wolf, Jr. (eds), *The Impoverished Super-power: Perestroika and the Military Burden*, San Francisco: ICS Press.

6.   See Julian Cooper (1991), *The Soviet Defence Industry*, London: RIIA. Examples were the Ministry of Aviation Industry, the Ministry of Atomic Power and Industry, the Ministry of the Electronics Industry and the Ministry of Machine Building.

7.   See Gerard Holden (1987), *The Warsaw Pact*, Oxford: Basil Blackwell.

8.   Yakovlev (1972), *The Aim of a Lifetime*, Moscow: Progress Publishers.

9.   Of course the term 'reform' covers a wide range of changes, including measures that are intended to improve the efficiency of the classical system, such as the creation of Kombinate in the GDR, for example. Here the term applies to those systems which are moving away from the classical system.

10. Cf. Kalecki on the difficulty of organizing an economy without the discipline of the sack.

3. New Issues

Mary Kaldor and Geneviève Schméder

In the previous chapter we tried to show that, despite the sudden way in which it ended the post-World War Two period, the fall of the Berlin Wall represented the outcome of a long evolution during which social transformation, the growing interdependence of economies and technical change progressively outgrew the socioeconomic models and arrangements established at the beginning of the period. We also tried to show that, without awareness of the profound nature of the changes and conscious efforts at restructuring, this period could lead, not to some future new order, but instead to a long epoch of disorganization and chaos. In this chapter we focus on two other aspects of the 'rupture' in Europe – security and technology – which will also strongly influence military demand and the future of military sectors.

One of the most unusual features of the current situation is that the paradigm of the cold war become obsolete as the result of any military confrontation. On the strategic side, what destroyed the 'vision' of the last three decades was the collapse of the USSR, which was ruined precisely by its military drift. The falling apart of the former Soviet Empire and the reunification of Germany demolished the myth that nuclear weapons were going to maintain the post-World War Two geopolitical order forever. Nuclear as well as conventional weapons proved to be absolutely useless in preventing changes (which do not fit any of the prevailing scenarios). Hence the immense disarray of military and strategic planners. Whereas the previous situation was based entirely on the possibility of an East–West confrontation, the new situation is completely open.

On the technological side, the end of the cold war also signified the end of the military–technological style which went with it. Even though the obsolescence of big platforms (tanks, bombers, carriers and so on) and other baroque monsters of the cold war became obvious even before the political changes, as the arms race moved away from weapons of mass destruction towards weapons of high precision and made possible the accurate delivery of missiles[1] (improvements in precision made possible by the use of electronics and microprocessors in the guidance systems of missiles made battle tanks, combat aircraft and warships much more easy to locate, track and attack), with the disappearance of any clearly identified 'enemy' in the West as in the East, other types of security problem have emerged. Failure to take account of these changes in the security environment, a continued insistence on preparation for the next World War Two-type conflict, constitutes perhaps the biggest obstacle to constructive change.

NEW CHALLENGES TO SECURITY

We use the term 'security' to refer to protection from violence. It is customary to distinguish between external and internal security. External security refers to defence against external threats; internal security refers to the job of policing, maintaining law and order.

During the cold war period, external security was more or less synonymous with defence. The main threat to security in Europe was the danger of a 'high-intensity' East–West conflict in which advanced, sophisticated weapons would be used, including weapons of mass destruction. Such a war was envisaged as World War Three, more or less on the model of the two previous wars in Europe in the 20th century. In Western Europe, the threat was defined as Soviet aggression, while Western imperialism was officially defined as the main threat to Eastern Europe. This model of security could be located within a Clausewitzean logic in which war is defined as a conflict between states which is always pushed to extremes both because of the absolutist character of states and because of the inherent escalatory tendencies of organized violence.

This model no longer fits the new, post-cold war, situation. Indeed, in certain respects, it had begun to unravel even before the end of the cold war. The danger of high-intensity war in Europe has receded. In the aftermath of 1989, no-one in the East regards the West as a threat. The Soviet threat has collapsed. Even for those East Central European countries bordering the former Soviet Union, the risk is not one of external attack but rather of implosion, perhaps on the Yugoslav model, elements of which are already apparent in the process of disintegration as well as conflicts in the Transcaucasus, Chechen, Moldova or Crimea. Although it is possible to anticipate border conflicts in Europe, for example in the Southern Balkans or where Hungarian minorities are involved, a high-intensity pan-European war on the World War Two model is much more difficult to envisage.

The new challenges to security have to do with a continuum of violence ranging from the growth of violent crime, at one end, to full-scale war, as in Bosnia-Herzegovina and Croatia, at the other. These wars are often described as 'low-intensity civil wars'. The terminology is misleading, however; it implies that these are purely domestic national affairs and have a lesser priority for defence planners than 'high-intensity international' wars. In fact, these wars do use modern weaponry and technology, especially modern communications. They involve high levels of physical destruction, high levels of casualties, especially among civilians, widespread atrocities including systematic rape and torture, and, a characteristic feature of these wars, large-scale population displacement (ethnic cleansing). The shock waves are experienced throughout Europe and beyond via refugees, the spread of criminal networks and the 'knock-on' effect of minority politics. They represent a much more immediate threat than what is conceived as 'high-intensity war'.

The new forms of violence can be contrasted with World War Two-type conflicts which would be said to represent the epitome of nation-state wars, on the Clausewitzean model: they were centrally administered, involving total mobilization and, despite the importance of lend-lease, more or less self-sufficient. The new forms of violence are fragmented, dependent on the outside world for humanitarian assistance, military supplies and so on; they involve only partial mobilization – large numbers of people are unemployed. Far from being organized by a powerful state, they could be said to be symptomatic of the disintegration of state structures. We use the term 'laissez-faire' to describe the new forms of violence. Laissez-faire violence is linked to the erosion of national control of organized violence, a process which gained impetus from the dismantling of military machines after the end of the cold war. What one might describe as the reprivatization of violence includes the following:

- the mercenarization of former soldiers, officers and military scientists;
- the sale of surplus weapons through legal and illegal channels;
- the sale of services by the armed forces and by Ministries of Defence;[2]
- the privatization and contractorization of defence manufacturers and defence services.

In other words, there are more and more non-state mechanisms through which criminals and paramilitary groups as well as governments can acquire military experts and hardware. Moreover, these markets in violence are transnational. One reason why it is misleading to describe the new wars as 'civil' is the extensive international involvement in these wars, ranging from international humanitarian agencies, journalists and non-governmental organizations (NGOs) to Diaspora support and transnational criminal networks.

Weber defined the state as the organization that successfully upholds the 'claim to the monopoly of organized violence'. It is not just that we can observe the proliferation of private armies and non-state fcrms of violence; it is also that no single political unit seems to have the legitimacy to reimpose control over the means of violence. With the discrediting of communism and dissatisfaction with the experience of transition, many groups have sought legitimacy through nationalism and other exclusivist ideologies. This has tended also to generate fragmentation rather than unity. Of course, the tendency towards laissez-faire violence already existed before 1989, but after 1989 such tendencies became more visible and were, of course, accentuated by the cuts in military budgets, the immediate economic and social consequences of transition, and the loss of cold war identities, among other reasons.

Not only have the forms of violence changed, but the nature of the political response has changed also. Long before the end of the cold war it was recognized that avoiding war in Europe was as much a problem of politics as of defence. This was formalized in the Helsinki Agreements of 1975. Nowadays it is widely recognized that security can no longer be equated with defence, that protection from the new forms of violence has to be undertaken through an array of instruments which include diplomacy, economic sanctions and/or cooperation, and human rights monitoring.

An equally significant change is the fact that security policy can no longer be purely national. In fact, the two blocs already represented an internationlization of security; apart from the United States and the Soviet Union, no individual country has the capacity to fight a prolonged war. In the aftermath of the cold war, the process of internationalization has speeded up. Along with privatization, it also represents an erosion of national control over organized violence. There has been a proliferation of international security organizations – the Conference for Security and Corporation in Europe (CSCE) has been institutionalized as OSCE (Organization for Cooperation and Security in Europe); the West European Union (WEU) is revitalized as the security arm of the European Union; both NATO and WEU have developed partnerships with Eastern European countries; the United Nations now plays a much more active role. Arms production is increasingly internationalized, thus breaking up national military–industrial complexes. Joint exercises, inspections under arms control regimes and multinational military units all contribute to the multinationalization of armed forces.

What do the changes in the security field – laissez-faire violence, the broadened conception of security and the internationalization of security – imply for the defence sector? One might expect that the defence sector will be smaller, a less important component of overall security, that it will be less self-sufficient, that is that individual nations will ensure their security through their contribution to multinational efforts; and that armed forces will be less oriented towards traditional 'high-intensity' war fighting and more towards a new form of peace-keeping which might range from policing to more robust forms of military intervention.

Our case-studies suggest that these implications of the new situation have not yet been grasped. Although some countries have begun to adapt to the new realities in certain respects, there is a contradictory tendency among defence planners towards the renationalization of defence sectors. In our view, this cannot ensure security; rather, it could contribute to insecurity.

NEW APPROACHES TO TECHNOLOGY POLICY

The military–technological style of the cold war was in many respects strongly influenced by the legacy of World War Two: the technological paradigms involved were nuclear physics and electronics; nuclear weapons were to be employed in offensive ways which were very reminiscent of that war (as an extended form of strategic bombardment in the West, of artillery in the East); the emphasis was on big weapon platforms – tanks, aircraft, submarines, surface ships, large missiles – incorporating increasingly sophisticated secondary equipment; conventional forces were configured for mobile operations very much along the lines of the blitzkrieg. There was nothing extraordinary in that. In order to be integrated into military theory and practice, technical change has to conform to a certain vision of warfare, which generally changes only during a major war, often prolonged, in the course of which some technological breakthroughs or conceptual innovations appear which fundamentally transform the very conception of the war.[3] Between these periods of promotion and adoption of radically new military solutions, military strategies and technologies tend to develop following established trajectories and are based on a view of warfare that is directly inherited from the war which provided the previous turning point.[4]

The main difference during the cold war was that the stress was now put on the continuous improvement of products rather than on the improvement of mass production processes and devices. In a field where any delay can mean obsolescence, the stake was to integrate into traditional heavy platforms (tanks, bombers, submarines, carriers and so on), product innovations with the highest possible level of performance. The result was a 'high-tech conservatism' characterized by a mixture of high-tech and traditional concerns in the approach of technology. If big military programmes of technological promotion aimed at major technological breakthroughs, it was in order to improve traditional overall systems which tended to be more and more elaborate and expensive, ending in 'baroque technologies'[5] and 'technological follies'.[6]

During the early 1970s, at the time of the Vietnam war, there was much debate about the implications of new electronics technologies for strategy and the military–technological style, since the combination of new forms of communication and sensing (lasers, microwaves, sonar and so on) and new forms of control or data-processing, based on microelectronics, had enormously increased the ability to identify and hit targets and thus the vulnerability of big weapon platforms. Some people thought that these new technologies would bring about fundamental changes in both strategy (to the advantage of the defender) and the military–technological style (with a greater decentralization and a reduction in the scale of equipment). Other people argued that weapons systems had, on the contrary, to become still larger and more expensive: they had to incorporate complex electronic countermeasures and protection and to use decoys, jamming devices and area destruction munitions in order to increase survivability and ensure the continuous success of the offensive.

In practice, the second argument prevailed, although there was no rational debate or experiment. 'Deep Interdiction', the Follow-On Forces Attack, AirLand Battle, the Maritime Strategy and the Strategic Defence Initiative were all presented in the early 1980s as new strategic concepts arising out of emerging technologies. The first ones, which put particular emphasis on the importance of offence and manoeuvrability, required complex and expensive weapon platforms to improve existing missions. Though it used the language of defence, the SDI also reinforced the use of big weapon platforms (long-range anti-ballistic missiles, high-velocity space guns, laser-firing satellites, brilliant pebbles and so on). None of these concepts altered the characteristics of the post-war military–technological style. Quite to the contrary, they augmented and reinforced the emphasis on mobility and offence, the reliance on weapon platforms and the continuation of intensive use of energy.

Since the end of the cold war, however, new factors have made the cold war paradigm definitely obsolete. The first is the new dimension of security and the broadening of the spectrum of what constitutes warfare. On the one hand, it is increasingly clear that problems associated with terrorism, drug-trafficking, the spread of weapons of mass destruction, the self-determination of national territories or intercommunal conflicts cannot realistically be solved through military means, that is with the use of weapons. On the other hand, the reorientation of military strategy from the NATO theatre to missions 'out of area' of the NATO Treaty has created new threat scenarios which have significant consequences in terms of specifications for future weapons. Military sectors, as a consequence, will have to adapt to new functional demands such as mobility or interoperability.

Unfortunately, nobody is actually capable of identifying even short-term needs when weapons have development and lifecycles which are decades long. In the current period of uncertainty, the only certainties of military planners essentially relate to what future weapons systems should *not* be, which makes it possible to identify by contrast some theoretically desirable attributes. The first of these requirements is 'flexibility', given the unpredictable nature of future threats and the delays involved in the making of new weapons. The fact that it takes between 10 and 20 years to develop and launch highly specialized systems, which are then supposed to be used for a further 15 or 20 years, makes them much too rigid to adapt to future requirements of military demand. Weapons have to become much more modular, in order to be produced and adapted with reduced delays and costs.

Another radical departure from the cold war situation, when perfect information on both sides was crucial in order to avoid the 'accidental' launching of a nuclear attack, is the importance now attached by military experts to organizing opacity on the battlefield. Perfect bilateral information is no longer needed when the possibility of taking the enemy by surprise and making him blind is, on the contrary, considered a crucial element of military superiority. As an American expert put it, the 'transparency revolution' will make future warfare no longer a 'struggle between offensive and defensive military forces', but 'a competition between the visible and the hidden – between transparency and stealth'.[7] Transparency implies not only knowledge and surveillance functions – search, location, identification, interception, control and verification – but more generally all detection and transmission functions.

Military planners thus attach a high value to 'automation', both because of the speed and magnitude of performances required, which

far exceed human capacities, and because of foreseeable military manpower shortages and the increasing lethality of the battlefield.
Automation affects not only the decision-making process, with the transmission of decisions to the people or computers controlling the weapons
to be used, but also the process of command, control and communication (in military language, C3) and the functions of collection,
provision, supply and delivery of intelligence and information. Security
depends more than before on efficient C3 systems and information
handling.

The idea of automated warfare is not actually new. It was described
quite accurately by General Westmoreland in 1969, at the time of the
Vietnam war:

> On the battlefield of the future, enemy forces will be located, tracked and
> targeted almost instantaneously through the use of data-links, computer-
> assisted intelligence evaluation and automated fire control. With first-round
> kill probabilities approaching certainty, and with surveillance devices that can
> continuously track the enemy, the need for large forces to fix the opposition
> physically will be less important . . . I see battlefields that are under 24 hour
> real or near real-time surveillance of all types. I see battlefields on which we
> can destroy anything we locate through instant communications and almost
> instantaneous application of highly lethal firepower . . . No more than ten
> years should separate us from the automated battlefield.[8]

Although military scientists have made less rapid progress than
expected by General Westmoreland, the Gulf War, which was welcomed
by military planners as both a guide-post and a laboratory for ideas
and materials, showed in 1991 that high-tech conventional warfare has
already become a reality. It showed that satellites and computerized
airborne radars could see far into enemy territory, that remotely piloted
vehicles and laser or television-guided bombs could destroy from a great
distance and that long-range anti-tank, anti-aircraft and anti-personnel
munitions were very accurate and tuned to extremely tight command
and control. It also showed, however, the extreme destructiveness and
lethality of such a war, which was only accepted by Western public
opinion because of the unequal nature of the losses,[9] and its outrageous
cost which makes its repetition quite unlikely, since the only country
which had the military and technical means for it could not afford it
economically and had to ask other countries for financial help.

The last, but not least, factor of obsolescence of the cold war paradigm
is precisely its economic cost, both at the macro and micro levels. At
the macro level, the alliance between science and power during the
cold war was structured around a series of analyses which credited a

high level of military spending, in particular on science and technology, with beneficial effects on both security and the economy. On the strategic side, what was pursued was less the preparation of a real war to be fought than the maintenance of a constant scientific and technological lead over the 'enemy'. On the economic side, military R&D and procurement were supposed to be a powerful engine of growth and to speed up technical change.[10] Indeed, combined with the enthusiasm of technologists, the rise of large public or quasi-public defence companies dependent for their survival on the defence budget generated considerable innovative energy and led to innovations which could be applied to the civilian sector.

Spin-offs in terms of technological products were especially important in sectors like aerospace, energy and telecommunications, whose markets were close to military markets. They were also decisive, even constitutive, in industries where the 'military trajectory' of technical change happened to be similar to the 'civilian trajectory' (that pattern of technical change which emerged as the dominant one in the independent market sector of the industry), as during the 1950s and 1960s in aeronautics and electronics. In aeronautics, similarities in airframe design were sufficiently pronounced to reduce substantially development and tooling costs for commercial airframes. An example of this was the Boeing 707, the airframe design of which followed so closely that of the KC-135 (a jet tanker previously developed by Boeing to provide in-flight refuelling for strategic bombers) that the first prototype 707 to be rolled out of the Seattle factory did not have windows in the fuselage.[11]

In the semiconductor industry most of the features of technical change – increased reliability, lower energy dispersion, wider range of frequency (later, with integrated circuits (ICs), ability to carry out more functions) and above all miniaturization – corresponded almost exactly to the requirements of both military and civilian demand. This close match was missing only in one regard: the lowering of costs, which was not relevant in public purchases but absolutely crucial for the expansion of non-military markets. However, this divergence was corrected by two other trends which were moving in the right direction: the interrelatedness of products and process innovations, on the one hand, and the mass character of military demand, on the other.

This overlap between civilian and military trajectories was pure chance, since they had completely different determinants. While the former was shaped by the existence of some actual or potential commercial market, the latter was dependent on political and military choices and the prevailing military–technological 'style'. As early as the 1960s, however, the large share of military R&D in the total R&D budget led some economists to examine with a critical eye the contribution of military R&D and procurement to overall economic performance.[12] Critiques were developed on their opportunity cost (in terms of diversion of resources), their contribution to productivity and their role in the decline of international competitiveness.[13] International comparisons tended to show that countries which spent most on military research were not the most efficient technologically. The success of Japan and Germany, which put the objective of economic vitality well above the objective of strategic independence and invested in civilian technologies, demonstrated that gearing innovation towards mass production and commercialization was no less favourable to high-tech developments than the impulse given by military programmes.

At the micro level, similar studies tended to show that military demand, because of its special characteristics, introduced biases which were very unfavourable in a long-term economic perspective. Whereas civilian products were geared to rapidly changing demand on large competitive consumer markets, weapons systems were produced in small series[14] for highly protected captive markets which put the objective of optimizing product performances well above that of cost reduction and production rationalization. While civilian consumers were 'unwilling to pay the high price of slightly pushing back the technological frontier', the military was ready to 'spend a lot to achieve marginal improvements'.[15] The result was that civilian technologies developed rapidly and efficiently, while military ones experienced weird trajectories and tremendous cost increases.

It is in relation to costs that, as war became increasingly a contest of information rather than one of firepower, the growing divergence between the military and the civilian technological bases became progressively intolerable. Indeed, in many industries, the patterns of technical innovation in the military and civilian sectors began to diverge significantly during the 1970s. This was particularly true in the semiconductor industry. While the military demanded almost absolute reliability, miniaturization close to the limits of semiconductor technology and resistance to extreme environmental conditions, the civilian market required further cost decreases and extension of applications and functions. As military orders, in spite of their rapid growth, represented a continuously declining share of the total output of industry,[16] the process of generating technical change became more endogenous to the 'normal' process of competition and to the interactions between producers and users. The gulf widened between firms working for the

military and firms working for commercial markets and military policies
ceased to dictate technological developments.

The same evolution was observed in the aerospace industry. As military fighters moved into the world of supersonic speed, they acquired
performance and cost characteristics that were increasingly inappropriate for the much more cost-conscious world of commercial travel.
The market failure of the Franco-British *Concorde* aircraft was an
illustration of these contradictions, which were also observed in communication satellites: while civilian applications use geosynchronic
orbits, send to the earth powerful signals and are expected to perform
many different functions, the secrecy demanded by military communications leads to completely opposite requirements: random orbits, very
low-level signals and narrow specialization.

These growing divergences progressively cancelled out positive spill-
overs, when they did not totally reverse them. The process of 'spin-off'
was, indeed, progressively reversed and new technologies pioneered in
the civilian sector were pressed on the armed forces in a new process
of 'spin-in'. In other terms, innovations required by the military now
have their roots in the civilian sector,[17] the precise opposite of what
was previously supposed to be the rule. Thus, whereas the major preoccupation of policy makers of the 1950s and 1960s, was to maximize
the spin-offs of military R&D to civilian R&D, their main objective
now is to organize in the best possible way the technological dependence
of military R&D on civilian R&D.

The development of new military systems is, however, a seesaw
between two opposing trends. It is not enough that technologies of
components, microcomputers, sensors and memory units which are
developed in the civilian sector improve from year to year in cheapness
and reliability if the designs of the overall weapons systems continue
to become more and more elaborate and expensive. In a context where
public budgets cuts due to the economic slump exert strong financial
pressures against continuous militarization, the fact that each improvement in performance is accompanied by exponential increases in cost
leaves reduced resources for increased purchases and makes inevitable
the need to hold in check in the future the endless tendency of designers
to improve and embellish new weapons systems.

DEFENCE CONVERSION ISSUES

At an economic level, the reduction of military budgets has repercussions on all areas associated with the military: armed forces, military

bases and arsenals, industrial and research establishments linked to defence and so on. The ramifications of these adjustments are particularly weighty as regards industrial armament activities, where the export markets have for some time now been affected by growing debt in the third world and the increasing importance of new producers.

Even if arms production is not a particularly vast sector when viewed in relation to European industry as a whole, it nevertheless represents a considerable part of production and manufacturing employment: between 1.5 and 3 percent in Germany, Italy, Switzerland, Sweden, Austria, Spain and Greece; between 7 and 8 percent in France; nearly 10 percent in Great Britain, and much more in Eastern Europe, especially Russia. The global economic impact of military industries is, however, far greater than the figures lead us to believe, on the one hand, in terms of employment, revenues and industrial and technical capacities and, on the other, because even in those countries with a smaller arms industry, the regions in which it is concentrated are placed in a position of strong dependence.

In view of this, the future of military industries deserves particular attention, especially regarding the reorganization of the military industrial base and the 'conversion' of some defence-related industrial activities into civilian industrial activities. However, if a global conversion process is possible, what methods can be used? Unfortunately, experience and reflection on the matter are sadly lacking from a historical point of view. The main experiences of conversion of arms industries, those which took place after the two world wars, provide few lessons for the current situation.[18] In terms of military spending, recent decades have certainly constituted a period of war, but this 'cold' war was more imaginary than real so, whereas the 'hot' wars brought physical destruction, the 'cold' war left capacities and materials intact. One of the major costs of conversion now is the 'de-activating' and the destruction of obsolete equipment – 'peace dividends'.

However, the situation was not the same in 1945 and 1918. Straight after World War One, industrial mutation was experienced by all the warring countries in extremely difficult conditions. In France, for example, difficulties of reconversion experienced between 1919 and 1923 explain the large enterprises' lack of enthusiasm for rearmament in the 1930s. The main pre-1914 producers had undertaken large-scale conversion of their factories, relegating military manufacturing to the position of a second priority, or in some cases totally abandoning it. At the end of World War Two, conversion was a major problem in the warring countries which had not suffered damage to their production capacities – Great Britain and the USA.[19] Whereas in Britain defence firms vegetated painfully until the Korean War, the USA transferred 30 percent of the GNP from war industries to civilian industries in one year, between 1945 and 1946, without unemployment ever growing higher than 3 percent. This bears witness not only to the flexibility of American industry, but to the planning done at local level by the Committee for Economic Development.[20] The American war effort was concentrated in a much shorter time scale; the rapid rise in importance of the American involvement in the war had obliged a large number of civilian firms to throw themselves into military production, and so, at the end of the war, it was simply a question of returning to former activities. All the employees of these firms, from production and maintenance workers to management and engineers, were used to working for civilian commercial markets. Moreover, and this is a crucial factor, the conversion process of the American industry had been carefully prepared beforehand.

As early as 1943, the vice-president of General Electric, David Prince, wrote to the War Production Board that

> there is a very great inclination to underestimate the length of time it takes to proceed from the conception stage to the cooling stage for any product. The very least time during which a new product can be conceived, models made and tested and pilot plant production initiated, is of the order of two years ... Priorities of the very highest order must be given to a very limited amount of work for long-range things. I am probably talking about a good deal less than one-tenth of one percent in terms of the effort of the country but that one tenth of one percent will make the difference of ... anything up to two years in making the conversion back from war to peace in those industries affected.[21]

The current situation is altogether different, for at least four reasons: conversion was not even envisaged, let alone prepared; the macro-economic context is much less favourable; markets are saturated and competition is raging; enterprises working in the defence sector have been doing so for decades and the fact that they are very specialized makes them much less suitable for any type of 'civilization' process. In one respect, the present circumstances are much closer to those of the post-Vietnam period. Between 1968 and 1978, the absence of adequate positions to withdraw to saw US defence material constructors dispersed in all directions: Boeing turned to monorails and jetfoils, Raytheon to computer terminals and business aeroplanes, General Dynamics to commercial shipbuilding and asbestos mining, Grumman to vehicles for public transport – experiences which, for most, ended in economic and commercial failure.

It remains difficult to consider as real experiences of conversion these attempts at diversification made by large defence groups whose long-term logic remained obstinately centred on the military. Their incursions into civilian commercial markets correspond to a tactical withdrawal allowing them subsequently to restructure into military activities, by liquidating their most traditional industrial activities in favour of more technologically intensive activities. Their objective was not in any way to 'civilize' their factories and arms producing facilities, but to diversify the risks they ran by implementing a conglomerate-type strategy. Even the rare firms, such as United Technologies – for which the acquisition of existing civil activities was a huge success – resumed armament activities as soon as the opportunity arose.

Generations of management, engineers, scientists, production and maintenance workers have had no experience outside the arms sector and have become conditioned to certain practices which are often aberrant when compared to classic commercial activity. It is not simply by chance that, in enterprises which produce both civil and military products, the types of production are usually carefully kept well clear of each other and are separated as far as sales and acquisitions are concerned.

Today armament is in every way a sector apart. In *The Defense Industry*, Gansler outlines more than 30 'imperfections and gaps' compared to a market situation: the existence of one sole buyer; very few salespersons; production of single pieces or small series; monopoly prices; orders placed regardless of price; barriers hindering both entry and exit; surplus capacities, and so on.[22] This situation is a result of the privileged relations that the defence industry has always had with the state, due to two specific factors which are traditionally acknowledged to be theirs: their strategic role, on the one hand, which means that they are not judged according to their contribution to national industrial performance,[23] and, on the other hand, their particular technological and financial needs linked to the length of time necessary to develop and produce new arms systems and the uncertainties of budgetary decisions as well as to the necessary cyclical nature of military markets. This special relationship with the state as guardian and banker has accustomed them to having a captive market and a situation whereby sales are guaranteed, whereas 'normal' enterprises are confronted by market restraints.

This is proved by the existence of very strong barriers which stop the enterprises from leaving the arms industry: market barriers, linked to the fact that an enterprise can keep its share of the market even when the overall market is shrinking;[24] financial barriers – dependence on the state, which is reinforced by scepticism in financial markets, while few enterprises have sufficient resources to develop new product lines; technological barriers, stemming in particular from state-financed R&D which encourages firms to continue defence activities; organizational barriers, linked to work and management procedures mentioned previously; and the limited production range.

The most decisive barrier comes from the specific nature of the workforce, composed essentially of high-level engineers and technicians, who are not predisposed by either mentality or know-how to practices conditioned by cost and profitability concerns or marketing experience. Coupled with the lack of flexibility already mentioned, a lack of experience and motivation on the part of top management as well as the 'base' of engineers and technicians, the only 'conversion' possibility is the pure and simple closing of sites.

The particularly constraining nature of the barriers to leaving is illustrated by the reactions of arms industries faced by the current situation. Confronted by the decline in orders, the initial reaction of the defence enterprise is to throw itself into a frantic quest for export markets. This desire to export at any price, which even leads some firms to sell their goods outside any governmental control, is nevertheless unable to restore profitability ruined by the shrinking of domestic markets which compromises both scale economies and the trust of foreign buyers.

Another immediate reaction is to make redundancies on the pretext of improving productivity. As a matter or fact, in both East and West, the main consequence of defence cuts has been unemployment, especially in particular regions where defence enterprises often represent a pole of economic activity. In the West, the scale of lay-offs has been more than proportionate to the cuts; this is because defence companies have used the excuse of defence cuts to justify far-reaching restructuring around the high-tech divisions. In the East, the scale of lay-offs has been less than proportionate to defence cuts; this is because the chain of activities associated with defence production is much more localized and the enterprises which are responsible for a range of social functions, such as housing, energy supply and child care, have an historical reluctance to lay off workers – instead they adopt measures like short-time working or obligatory holidays and the result is an alarming growth in the indebtedness of defence enterprises.

In both East and West there has been a tendency to conserve highly qualified manpower, a greater reluctance to lay off engineers and scientists than to lay off blue-collar workers. And in both East and West defence cuts have been used to run down the older traditional sectors of the arms industry while retaining the high-tech sectors. This has had important regional consequences, which is illustrated in the Czechos-lovak and British cases, where high-tech enterprises were concentrated in the Czech Land and South-east England, respectively. Moreover, the local effects of running down traditional manufacturing are much greater than for the more modern parts of the industry. This is because high-tech enterprises tend to be integrated into transnational networks and have fewer links with the surrounding localities than the more traditional sectors.

The directors of these enterprises proclaim that rationalization and modernization are necessary in order to satisfy a dual objective: to adapt firms to the new technological and strategical deal and to improve their profitability and competitiveness in the perspective of the Euro-pean market.[25] These demands accelerate the process of fusion concentration, at both a national and European level, of national enter-prises which were traditionally rivals, and branches and subsidiaries of groups from different countries. This process can be observed at the level of the most 'nationalistic' producers, right down to the tank manu-facturers. These formal alliances go on to include multiple collaborations.[26]

The last, but not least important, reaction of defence firms is to demand more state intervention. However, the days when state support guaranteed the overall survival of the military sector seem to be over. Concentration, by abolishing the national character of the markets, admittedly creates more powerful lobbies, capable of exercising strong pressure on the governmental and supranational authorities, but it also wipes out the obligation to keep (surplus) national capacities in all domains. In a process whereby the question of economic efficiency is becoming fundamental, the objective is to approach market realities rather than artificially support an administered sector.[27]

Does this mean that all conversion policies are impossible? From the moment a government reduces its armed forces, defence budget, mili-tary orders and arms exports, it can hardly ignore the consequences of its decisions. It is possible, moreover, that the main risk associated with the reduction of military budgets is not so much a rise in unemploy-ment[28] but the loss of scientific and technological potential incorporated in a workforce highly qualified in these respects. This fear is at present the major obstacle preventing more drastic reductions in military pro-grammes. The concentration of this personnel in certain regions and certain high-tech sectors makes the potentially disastrous consequences of making redundancies even worse.

There are differences and similarities in the experiences of defence conversion in East and West. In the West, defence cuts have been much smaller than in the East and there have been no state-sponsored conversion strategies. A few regional authorities have attempted conversion strategies, very often under pressure from local trades unions and peace movements, and there has been some limited support from the European Union through the PERIFRA programme for regions and, more recently, through a specific programme called the Konver initiative. In so far as individual enterprises have adopted successful diversification strategies, this has usually been as a result of market substituting policies, that is through undercutting other producers in existing markets and without creating additional employment.

Most defence companies see the main opportunities for conversion in large civil projects, financed by the state, which are similar to military projects. A certain number of gaps exist in the fields of energy, environment, telecommunications and transport where the market is far from being saturated. Particularly important are projects in what is known as the 'disarmament economy', that is new technology for scrapping weapons and in cleaning up military bases which are often heavily polluted. These technologies could have important applications in the civil field; up to now, the technology of destruction is much less developed than the technology of production and is still largely craft-based. Both civil and military demand in these areas is potentially enormous. There is in particular considerable potential for restoring areas laid waste by industrialization. Another potential market given considerable emphasis, particularly in Germany, is non-military threats to security: disaster prevention or reaction, control of immigration, accident control, and so on. This promising path is linked to the growing notion of security, which is being extended further than just military security, to encompass protection against accidental or pollution-related 'menaces', for example, which are largely left to improvization or charitable organizations.

The stopping of military orders does not mean the end of state orders, as long as the state reorients its objectives and beneficiaries of its support, notably as far as research is concerned. However, if the preceding analysis is correct, support policies reach their limits rather quickly, as conversion is not made 'to order' but appears as an overall result and in some respects as a secondary result of the numerous primary processes of 'creative destruction'. What needs to be encouraged in this respect is not the maintaining of acquired advantages, but an individual and collective initiative at local and regional levels, nearer to the grass-roots level, which would be more capable of identifying the microeconomic initiatives and small job-creating enterprises. The possible forms of intervention are multiple and not only finance-based:

training and recycling programmes, technical assistance, technology transfers, industrial restructuring, social and environmental measures and so on.

In the East cuts in military spending have been much larger and Central European countries have also been hit by a dramatic fall in exports owing primarily to the collapse of the former Soviet and East German markets but also to the decline of third world markets. In the former Czechoslovakia, for example, defence production has fallen by 70–80 percent since 1987, while it has been virtually wiped out in the former East Germany. Immediately after 1989, and even before, several governments introduced conversion strategies and in some countries, such as Ukraine or Russia, these policies are still in operation. Essentially, they involve finance for civilian projects proposed by the individual enterprises. The problem with this approach is that it is supply-oriented; that is to say, the projects are designed by defence engineers and scientists with little or no thought given to prospective markets. Moreover, they are designed to suit existing structures which are often characterized by obsolete and wasteful management practices. The end result is often the development of unsaleable products, the preservation of existing structures and indirect subsidies to continued military production. As a consequence, the word 'conversion' has acquired an unfavourable connotation, being understood as defence cuts and lay-offs.

Where there are successes in conversion, and there are a number of examples, especially in Russia but also in other countries, they are typically in international markets for medium technology products where defence enterprises can capitalize on cheap, highly qualified labour, for example in the field of optics or engines. Successful examples are very often associated with dynamic individual entrepreneurs who are motivated less by profit than by a social commitment to employees or to the locality.

Thus, in general, in both East and West, conversion has been very limited. The consequence in both halves of Europe, although it is much more serious in the East, is a rise in unemployment, especially in particular regions, the loss of valuable scientific and technical manpower and, often, renewed pressures for rearmament often associated with nationalist ideas. Our studies show that alternative approaches are, however, possible.

NOTES

1. The capability of massive destruction has been markedly improved, both in lethality and in area covered, so that conventional weapons today approach small nuclear weapons in destructive power.
2. In Hungary, for example, the post-cold war budget was insufficient to cover the costs of the armed forces. Therefore the Ministry of Defence began to engage in independent economic activities. The army undertook forestry and construction work and was even responsible for the laundry services of expensive hotels in Budapest. Military bases and barracks were rented out; an airbase, for example, was used for tourist flights to Lake Balaton. The Ministry of Defence actually engaged in financial speculation.
3. Examples of such qualitative changes were the mass offensives of the revolutionary and Napoleonic wars, the domination of artillery and trench warfare of 1914–18, and the mobile, rapid and offensive operations of World War Two.
4. This distinction between phases of breakthrough and phases of continuity in the military field can be compared to the distinction introduced by Kuhn in the scientific field between 'scientific revolutions' and 'normal science', which develops in the framework of the prevailing scientific paradigm, or by the 'evolutionary' theorists of technical change between the emergence of a new technological paradigm and the development of technical progress along established 'technological trajectories'.
5. M. Kaldor (1982), *The Baroque Arsenal*, New York: Hill and Wang.
6. F. Dyson (1984), *Weapons and Hopes*, New York: Harper & Row,
7. Quoted in Frank Barnaby (1986), *The Automated Battlefield*, London: Sidgwick & Jackson, p. 38.
8. Ibid., p. 1.
9. In fact, lethality is a cause as much as a result of the automated character of the war: as the battlefield becomes more dangerous, the objective is to minimize the number of people on it or near it. Hence the interest of military planners in what they call 'non-battle technologies' (*sic*), which are supposed to be able to prevent the battle (especially a surprise attack) or, if this proves to be ineffective, to win it with minimum losses, by destroying enemy targets with the highest degree of precision.
10. As the French Minister of Defence put it in 1987: 'Armament programmes create employment. They irrigate most of modern industries, their laboratories, their prototype workshops, their plants, feed research and innovation, intellectual competition with other countries. It is a true locomotive of economic development' (quoted in 'L'industrie militaire, une locomotive du développement industriel français?', in F. Chesnais (ed.) (1990), *Compétitivité internationale et dépenses militaires*, Paris: Economica).
11. D. Mowery and N. Rosenberg, 'The Commercial Aircraft Industry', in R. Nelson (ed.) (1983), *Government and Technical Progress*, New York: Pergamon Press.
12. R. Solo (1962), 'Gearing Military R&D to Economic Growth', *Harvard Economic Review*.
13. It is impossible to give a full account of the enormous literature on the subject. See, for instance, on R&D: in the USA, F. Lichtenberg (1984), 'The Relationships between Federal Contracts R&D and Company R&D', *The American Economic Review*, **74**, (2), and (1988) *The Impact of SDI on US Civilian R&D Investment and Industrial Competitiveness*, New York: Columbia University Press; Z. Griliches and F. Lichtenberg, 'R&D and Productivity at the Industry Level: Is There Still a Relationship?', in Z. Griliches (ed.) (1984), *R&D, Patents and Productivity*, Chicago: University of Chicago Press; M. Schankerman and A. Pakes (1986), 'Estimates of the Value of Patent Rights in European Countries during the Post-1950', *The Economic Journal*, **96**; in the UK, M. Kaldor, M. Sharpe and W. Walker (1986), 'Industrial Competitiveness and Britain's Defence Commitments, *Lloyds Bank Review*, London;

in France, B. Haudeville, 'Leadership technologique et R&D militaire: les politiques américaines des années 1990', in F. Chesnais (ed.) (1990), *Compétitivité internationale et dépenses militaires*, Paris: Economica; M. Odden (1988), 'Les incidences négatives des dépenses militaires sur la sécurité nationale', *Problèmes Economiques*, no. 2102.

14. The production of the Exocet missile, which was one of the 'bestsellers', was around three thousand units.

15. F. Lichtenberg, *The Impact of SDI* (1988).

16. This share was 50 percent in 1960, 30 percent in 1966, 24 percent in 1972 (quoted in G. Dosi (1984), *Technical Change and Industrial Transformation*, London: Macmillan, p. 44).

17. Examples include semiconductors, which represent virtually all of the so-called microelectronic devices for processing, manipulating and displaying information that currently exist, very fast microelectronic circuits and multiple sensors sensitive to light, sound, magnetic fields or infrared radiations, and more generally generic information technologies including telecommunications, radio-electric spectrum, treatment of signals, optronics, software, improvement of the calculation power and space technologies.

18. Exceptional conversion efforts undertaken by the British government in the 1970s (following the Labour government's promise to reduce defence spending in 1974) do not constitute a true precedent, as this promise was never sustained: interest shown in conversion evaporated with the defence boom of the 1980s.

19. Imposed on the vanquished countries, Germany and Japan, conversion was quick and far-reaching under American guidance ... and was to benefit their economies in the long term.

20. K.E. Boulding, quoted in L.J. Dumas (ed.) (1982), *The Political Economy of Arms Reduction: Reversing Economic Decay*, Boulder: Westview Press and the American Association for the Advancement of Science.

21. The War Production Board was created in 1942, several weeks after Pearl Harbor, in order to ensure the mobilization of industry for war. Letter dated 28 April 1943, in Dumas, *Political Economy* (1982).

22. J.S. Gansler (1980), *The Defense Industry*, 2nd edn, Cambridge, Mass.: MIT Press.

23. If contracts are awarded on a cost-effective basis, the desire on the part of the governments to maintain national capacities for the production of a given product or piece of equipment is a typical bias of a planned economy, and is what Alec Nove (1986) calls the 'conservatism input-output' (*The Soviet Economic System*, London: Allen & Unwin), 3rd edition.

24. There is no sharing of the market in the true sense of the term: an enterprise either is or is not included in a programme.

25. As a matter of fact, growth in productivity has been spectacular. In Great Britain in the 1980s, 155 000 jobs were suppressed in the defence industry while production rose in real terms.

26. As a traditional division of tasks founded on the principle of *juste retour* was not always compatible with a rational division of labour and contributed to the escalating of prices, cooperation projects have, until now, remained marginal, in spite of much verbal support since the 1960s.

27. However, it is not easy to transform a non-market into a market, as demonstrated by the vain efforts undertaken by the Thatcher government to establish a more 'Darwinian' process: 'At the heart of our strategy is the need to promote wider competition in defence procurement' (*White Paper*, Statement on the Defence Estimates (SDE) 1984).

28. In France, for example, the planned reductions are in the region of 50 000 jobs, which represents an increase in unemployment of less than 2 percent.

4. Britain

Mary Kaldor

World War Two was a defining episode for Britain, both politically and industrially. The cold war reproduced the experience of World War Two through Britain's role as number two in the Western alliance. With independent nuclear weapons and more military roles and command positions than any other NATO country apart from the United States, the British were able to hold onto a view of themselves as citizens (in fact subjects) of a great power. Because of the key importance of defence procurement, the cold war sustained the geographical and sectoral composition of industry for many years. The cold war, in the words of the Conservative MP George Walden, 'inflated our international influence' and resulted in an 'artificially large military burden'.[1]

The popular self-perception of Britain as a superpower has been periodically challenged by the left and by the peace movement. During the early 1980s, in common with other West European countries, Britain witnessed mass demonstrations against the deployment of cruise missiles and the purchase of *Trident* missiles from the United States. As a result of a wide-ranging public debate about defence issues, both the Labour and Liberal parties adopted a non-nuclear stance. The opposition to nuclear weapons generated a major rethink in large parts of society about Britain's role in the world.

After the 1987 election, however, both the Labour and Liberal parties concluded that the opposition to nuclear weapons was not popular or credible and, accordingly, they reversed their positions and tried to play down defence issues. The end of the cold war came at a time when all three political parties, for different reasons, were anxious to avoid debates about defence. The end of the cold war offered Britain an opportunity to break free of the legacy of World War Two and to face up to some of the realities of Britain's domestic and international situation. But this has been very difficult to achieve in the absence of a far-reaching debate. What is needed, according to George Walden is

> an imaginative and constructive approach ... to get people to understand that the good life and a proud, prosperous and influential Britain cannot be

43

bought by an overblown defence establishment.... The alternative is a country that simultaneously loses its will for self-reform and its empire of influence, a sour and shrunken island so insecure in the new world that it resorts, like our legendary football hooligans, to aggressive insularity to sustain its sense of identity.[2]

This chapter is about the implications of the end of the cold war for Britain's security policy and economy. The first section is about Britain's security and defence policy and the current choices. The second section describes the scale of Britain's defence effort and the third is about the defence industrial sector, how it functions and how it is changing. The fourth section assesses the impact of defence cuts so far and possible alternatives.

BRITAIN'S SECURITY AND DEFENCE POLICY

Background

Traditionally, British foreign policy has been defined in terms of what Churchill described as three overlapping circles: Britain's role as a post-imperial power with a number of post-colonial responsibilities and close relations to Commonwealth countries; Britain's special relationship with the United States, through which it was able to act as a minor super-power, viewing itself as second only to the United States and differentiated from the rest of Europe; and, finally, Britain's role as a European country and member of the European Community.

There was always some tension between these three roles but all three were predicated on the assumptions of the cold war and the notion of a more or less permanent Soviet threat. Periods of confrontation were generally associated with a tendency to emphasize the British and Atlanticist roles, whereas periods of détente, of efforts to accommodate the Soviet threat, tended to be associated with an emphasis on Britain's European role.

Throughout the 1960s and 1970s, under the governments of Wilson, Heath and Callaghan, there was a shift of emphasis towards the European role. The empire was replaced by the Commonwealth; colonial responsibilities, especially naval policing and far-flung land-based commitments, were phased out. In 1966, Britain took the decision to withdraw from east of the Suez Canal. Britain joined the European Community in 1973 and, on a number of issues (the US role in the third world, NATO strategy and so on), distanced itself from the United States and took a common position with other West European countries.

During the 1980s, under the government of Mrs Thatcher, this tendency was reversed. Along with President Reagan, Mrs Thatcher eagerly embraced the new cold war; defence spending rose and the government strongly supported the deployment of cruise missiles and went ahead with the purchase of American *Trident* missiles for Britain. By re-emphasizing the special relationship with the United States, the British government was able to rekindle populist notions of Britain's position as a great power. In addition to the Soviet threat, Mrs Thatcher, along with the US government, placed increasing emphasis on new threats in the third world, arising from the proliferation of missiles and weapons of mass destruction, the rise of regional dictators like Galtieri (Argentina), Gaddafi (Libya) and Saddam Hussein (Iraq), as well as the growth of terrorists, drug traffickers, fundamentalists and so on. The Falklands War substantiated this notion and provided an occasion on which to revive World War Two imagery and sentiments of Britishness.

In principle, the end of the cold war calls into question both the transatlantic relationship and the future of a specifically West European identity. On the one hand, Britain's national position has come to the fore once again; on the other, there is a need for a newly defined international role. In practice, a rethinking of Britain's foreign and security policy has been very slow to emerge.

Options for Change

In February 1990, in response to an oral question in the House of Commons, the Secretary of Defence, Tom King, announced that the government was examining 'Options for Change'. He explained that this exercise was different from the defence reviews which had taken place in 1957, 1966–8, 1974–5 and 1981, since these were driven by the need to make expenditure cuts whereas the 'Options for Change' were the result of changes in external circumstances. On 28 March 1990, he told the House of Commons' Defence Committee:

> We have an emerging situation – emerging is an understatement, a galloping situation – that has changed the prospects, changed the likelihood of our whole defence requirements, in terms of the threat as it was perceived – not entirely, but in many important aspects. I see the emerging situation ... as more dramatic and more comprehensive than people faced whether at Versailles or Yalta.[3]

On 25 July 1990 the government announced a framework for 'Options for Change', involving substantial cuts, especially in the British Army of the Rhine. Six days later, Iraq invaded Kuwait. It was not until after the Gulf War, in July 1991, that the government published details of 'Options for Change' in its first post-cold war White Paper (*Statement on the Defence Estimates 1991*, hereinafter referred to as SDE 1991). Considering that 'Options for Change' was supposed to be a considered response to the end of the cold war, SDE 1991 is remarkably coy about the security context. The threats to Britain which are now known as 'risks' were outlined in one paragraph. They included the residual threat from the Soviet Union (which then still existed) which was said to be an 'unstable superpower', 'instability in Eastern Europe and elsewhere' and 'events outside Europe, including the proliferation of sophisticated and destructive weaponry'.[4]

The government endorsed the NATO communiqué issued after the Rome Summit of 7 November 1991 which presented NATO's new strategic concept. This was somewhat more explicit about the new security context. According to the NATO leaders, Western countries no longer face 'the predominant threat of the past'. Instead, 'the risks to Allied security that remain are multi-faceted in nature and multi-directional, which makes them hard to predict and assess'. The communiqué refers to two kinds of risks: those that arise in Eastern Europe and those that arise in the Mediterranean and the Middle East. The risks in Eastern Europe

> are less likely to result from the calculated aggression against the territory of the Allies but rather from the adverse consequences of instabilities that may arise from the serious economic, social and political difficulties, including ethnic rivalries and territorial disputes, which are faced by many countries in Central and Eastern Europe. The tensions which may result, as long as they remain limited, should not directly threaten the security and territorial integrity of members of the Alliance. They could, however, lead to crisis inimical to European stability and even to armed conflicts which would involve outside powers or spill over into NATO countries, having a direct effect on the security of the Alliance.

The risks in the Mediterranean and the Middle East are said to stem from the 'proliferation of ballistic missiles and weapons of mass destruction capable of reaching the territory of some of the member states of the Alliance'.[5]

In practice, the 1991 White Paper defined Britain's defence roles in traditional ways and merely slimmed down each role. 'Instabilities in Eastern Europe' were, in effect, treated as a substitute for the Soviet threat. Hence the charge that the review was Treasury-driven had some substance. Through the cold war, Britain was said to have five defence roles: independent nuclear weapons; defence of the UK home base; defence of Germany, including the British Army of the Rhine; defence of the Eastern Atlantic and Channel Areas; and 'Out of Area' capabilities. The British Army of the Rhine and defence of the Eastern Atlantic and Channel Areas were Britain's contribution to NATO and accounted for the most substantial share of defence spending. SDE 1991 continued to emphasize these five roles, although the cuts fell most heavily on the British Army of the Rhine and the anti-submarine warfare role in the Eastern Atlantic (designed to protect American reinforcements in case of a war in Europe).

The 1993 White Paper (*Statement on the Defence Estimates 1993*, hereinafter referred to as SDE 1993) made an attempt for the first time to redefine Britain's defence roles. This redefinition is based on two significant changes of assumption. First of all, the government makes it clear that a 'major external threat ... is ... even more unlikely to re-emerge in the foreseeable future than seemed to be the case in 1991'; (para. 108). Secondly, the government argues that the distinction between capabilities for the NATO area and 'Out of Area' capabilities is no longer relevant. The main risks are new types of conflict such as Yugoslavia, Northern Ireland or Iraq, which may or may not involve NATO forces in a peace-keeping role.

On these assumptions, SDE 1993 defines three major roles for Britain:

1. the defence of Britain and its dependent territories;
2. Britain's contribution to NATO – 'to insure against a major external threat to the United Kingdom and our allies' (para. 103); and
3. Britain's contribution to international peace and security, including peace-keeping.

The government has introduced an extremely complicated system of earmarking military forces for different roles so that it is difficult to estimate the resources devoted to each role. The government estimates the gross costs of each role and then calculates a set of incremental costs to allow for the fact that some forces can be used in several different roles. Given the remoteness of the external threat and the immediacy of new types of conflict, defence role two would seem to be rapidly declining in importance. Nevertheless, this role still accounts for the largest share of defence resources, whether calculated in gross or in incremental terms. One argument that the government makes is the importance of multinationality:

The stationing of national forces on the territory of other member nations and the maintenance of multinational formations provide a visible demonstration of the Alliance's commitment to the visible security of its members. Its force planning process aims to achieve interpretability and co-ordinated planning, but it also gives useful transparency in the regular exchange of detailed information on national defence planning and military capabilities. In this way, it contributes to political stability and discourages the *renationalisation of defence*. (Para. 402, emphasis added)

This is an important argument. But, in the absence of a major external threat, there is no a priori reason why it should apply only to members of NATO.

Defence Capabilities

In terms of actual defence capabilities, SDE 1993 does not mark a radical departure from the past. This is partly because the structure of the defence sector is rather difficult to change. The budget is dominated by major projects like the *Trident* submarines or the European fighter aircraft which have very long lead times and around which a constituency of vested interests in industry, the civil service and the armed forces develops. In effect, existing capabilities have been attributed to new roles. What does each role entail?

Defence role one

Under the heading of Defence Role One – the defence of Britain and its dependent territories – are included Britain's nuclear forces which can also be attributed to defence role two; Northern Ireland; and the stationing of forces in dependent territories, such as Hong Kong, Gibraltar and Belize, which can also in theory be attributed to defence role three; and the security and integrity of the UK in peacetime.

Britain's strategic nuclear forces consist of four *Polaris* submarines which are soon to be replaced by *Trident* submarines, each of which will carry not more than 128 warheads. In addition, Britain maintains *Tornados* and *Buccaneers*, naval vertical take-off and landing (VTOL) *Sea Harriers* and *Nimrod* bombers which carry free-fall nuclear bombs. Naval depth bombs and ground-based nuclear weapons (short-range missiles and artillery) are being phased out.

Unlike French nuclear weapons, British nuclear weapons are committed to NATO. The main rationale for their possession is the 'second centre of decision making' – the notion that the enemy, that the Soviet Union or now perhaps Russia, will be more likely to be deterred if it is more uncertain about a likely response to an attack. In practice,

Britain's independent nuclear weapons are associated, both in popular perception and in statements of politicians, with Britain's role in the world as a former superpower.[6]

One of the interesting features of the new definition of defence roles is that the military role in Northern Ireland has become much more transparent. Some 19 000 servicemen and women are stationed in Northern Ireland on tours of duty ranging from six to 30 months. Given the need to rotate forces and for long breaks between tours of duty, nearly half the arm is, in fact, earmarked for Northern Ireland, even though the same forces can still be earmarked for other purposes. Out of a total annual defence budget of £23.5 billion, some £4 billion is spent on nuclear weapons and £1.6 billion directly on Northern Ireland.

Defence role two

During the cold war, Britain's main roles in NATO were twofold. First of all, Britain had responsibility for defending 200 kilometres of the intra-German border, and, in addition, maintained a military presence in Berlin. The British contribution to the Central Front was considerably larger than any other non-German partner except the United States. Land and air forces in Germany were structured or rapid offensive operations with an emphasis on tanks and strike aircraft for deep interdiction along the lines of classic World War Two-type warfare. Secondly, Britain had a significant naval role. Britain still has the largest navy of any European NATO country, which before 'Options for Change' consisted of three aircraft carriers, about 50 destroyers and frigates, 30 submarines and 40 mine countermeasures vessels.

Until the late 1960s, the navy's role was primarily related to Britain's post-colonial responsibilities and, even today, those who prefer to emphasize Britain's national role tend to favour expenditure on the navy as opposed to the army. In fact, after the decision to withdraw British forces east of Suez, the navy's role was redefined. At that time, NATO was shifting its strategy from the doctrine of massive retaliation to the doctrine of flexible response. Under the former doctrine, the NATO response to any Warsaw Pact attack was to be a strategic nuclear response. The strategy of flexible response implied that NATO would initially respond to the Warsaw Pact attack with conventional forces (or at any level deemed appropriate) and this opened up the possibility of a long war in Europe and the arrival of reinforcements from the United States. Hence there was perceived to be a need for a naval role in the Eastern Atlantic and Channel areas to protect reinforcements in time of war. In theory, therefore, the role of the navy was a NATO role, primarily directed towards the defence of Europe.

In this respect, the role of Britain's aircraft carriers is particularly interesting. The 1966 White Paper announced the decision to phase out carrier-borne aircraft. This decision was taken, according to Denis Healey, then Minister of Defence, for the following reasons:

> It was obviously necessary to see whether it was really essential to spend these enormous sums of money on so limited a capability. It emerged rapidly that the role of the carrier in support of land operations could, in most cases which concerned us, be carried out more cheaply and effectively by land-based aircraft; and that if we renounced the strategic option of landing and withdrawing troops against sophisticated opposition outside the range of friendly land-based aircraft, this would have little important effect on our commitments. . . . While it was a difficult judgement to decide against a carrier force for maritime operations East of Suez, once we had decided to withdraw from major military responsibilities in that area in the middle seventies, I do not believe that the decision was easy to contest.[7]

Subsequently, the decision came up against resistance from the Navy and from shipbuilders. The Conservative government of 1970–74 took the decision to go ahead with a replacement for aircraft carriers after all. They were to be called Anti-Submarine Warfare (ASW) Cruisers, and their role was ASW and not intervention. There were criticisms of the cost of such ships in an ASW role, since they tie up a considerable number of destroyers and submarines in their defence. They are at least as vulnerable as cheaper ships and the aircraft could operate from shore.

The 1980–81 defence review undertaken by John Nott took the decision once again to phase out aircraft carriers. However, in the 1982 Falklands War, the ASW cruiser HMS *Invincible* played a crucial role and it was decided to retain such ships. Even though the role of aircraft carriers has been rationalized in European/NATO terms, like independent nuclear weapons they have a symbolic (and real) function in establishing Britain's global identity.

After the end of the cold war, most NATO members took the decision to reduce drastically forces allocated to NATO. Forces in the Central Region (Germany) are to be reduced by 45 percent and there are also substantial cuts in naval forces. The British Army of the Rhine (BAOR) is to be halved, a number of bases are to be closed and RAF Germany is also to be cut substantially. Aircraft carriers are to be retained and a helicopter carrier has been ordered. The number of destroyers and frigates is to be reduced to 35. Conventionally powered submarines are to be phased out, on the grounds that the Soviet submarine threat to the East Atlantic has disappeared, and 12 nuclear-powered fleet submarines will be retained. These forces are to be deployed according to NATO's new strategic concept to meet the 'multi-faceted and multi-dimensional risks' which replace the Soviet threat. Forces stationed in Europe are now known as 'reaction forces', ready to react to different risks. Hence Britain's contribution has been relabelled as maritime, land and air reaction forces. The reaction forces are said to be designed around the characteristics of flexibility, capability (maintaining the level of sophistication of equipment) and multi-nationality. A key element of the new force structure is the multinational Rapid Reaction Corps.

In practice, the strategic concept amounts to scaling down and relabelling. As SDE 1993 points out: 'The reaction concept calls for forces that closely resemble the British force structure as it has developed over the last 30 years for both national and NATO purposes. The characteristics include high readiness in key areas, modern equipment and sufficient strategic and tactical transport to provide mobility' (p. 37).

Because the spectrum of risks as defined by NATO still includes 'high-intensity' conflict, which is a label for a modern World War Two-type conflict, there is no significant change in the types of equipment and force structure that were required during the cold war. The main difference is the emphasis on mobility. (Earlier, forces could all be stationed in readiness on the German border.) Hence the new emphasis on helicopters and the new lease of life for carriers.

Defence role three
Defence Role Three – Britain's contribution to international peace and security – includes capabilities for intervention, as in Iraq, peace-keeping forces under international auspices, military assistance and exercises with other countries, and inspection and implementation of arms control treaties. The intervention role bears some relation to the high-intensity plans developed in NATO, although whether this sledgehammer approach to intervention was justified in the case of Iraq can be questioned. But the most rapidly growing component of Defence Role Three is peace-keeping which potentially has radical implications for force structures. UN peace-keeping increased dramatically in 1992, from 12 000 to 60 000 troops engaged in UN operations. Britain was the second largest contributor, with contingents in Cyprus, Cambodia, Western Sahara, Iraq/Kuwait and Bosnia-Herzegovina.

Although the government claims an 'increasing congruence' between forces designed for Defence Roles Two and Three, in fact, there are important differences, some of which are highlighted by the contrast between the Gulf War and the Yugoslav war. Forces for Defence Role Two are structured for rapid offensive operations. The aim is to maximize casualties on the enemy side and minimize casualties on the allied side and to achieve objectives quickly. Hence the emphasis is on high performance, destructiveness and survivability. Especially important are long- and medium-range land or sea-based strike capabilities.

In peace-keeping and peace enforcement operations, on the other hand, forces have to be structured for long-term defensive and policing operations, such as protecting aid convoys or safe havens and disarming paramilitary groups. The aim is to minimize casualties on *all* sides. This involves, first of all, a different type of soldiery with new skills, such as languages, mediation, confidence-building skills, greater individual responsibility and different motivation.[8] This requires specialized training. Secondly, it involves a different composition of forces. Infantry are much more important than air or naval forces; there are greater logistical and engineering requirements than anticipated in the main European theatre. SDE 1993 emphasizes the need for 'endurance' and 'sustainability'. Finally, it requires different types and characteristics of equipment. Mobility and accuracy continue to be important, but not destructiveness. Reliability and efficiency (efficient use of fuel, spares and so on) are much more important. It is doubtful how useful the 'big' systems are in the new conflicts. In Yugoslavia, the British forces could have used *Warrior* and *Scimitar* armoured vehicles, but not *Challenger* tanks. Even the *Warrior* has proved 'somewhat heavy and unwieldy and difficult to control on ice and snow', even though it provides good protection.[9] Likewise, the role of sophisticated long-range combat aircraft is limited, but reconnaissance, close air support and, especially, helicopters are important.

THE SCALE OF THE BRITISH DEFENCE EFFORT

The Defence Budget

Britain spends around £24 billion per annum on defence. This represents 4 percent of GDP, 16 percent of total expenditure by local and central government (excluding transfer payments) and just under 30 percent of central government consumption. As a share of GDP, this is higher than any other NATO country except the United States and Greece. The United States spends 5.4 percent of GDP on defence and Greece spends 5.5 percent. France and West Germany spend 3.4 percent and 2.2 percent respectively.[10]

UK defence spending rose rather dramatically in the early 1950s, reaching over 8 percent of GDP in 1955. Thereafter, the rate fell and remained more or less constant throughout the 1960s. There was a significant rise in defence spending in the early 1980s, but, since 1984, it has declined slightly in real terms, falling as a share of GNP from 5.2 percent in 1984 to 4 percent in 1992.

It is worth noting that the decline in defence spending does not seem to have released much by way of a 'peace dividend'. It seems to have been one element of a general constraint on public expenditure under the Thatcher government. Or, to put it another way, in so far as there was a peace dividend, it did not take the form of social spending or investment in manufacturing. During this period, there was a significant rise in personal consumption and also in investment in services. In so far as the rise in personal consumption was a consequence of tax cuts or of lowered interest rates, owing to the reduction in public borrowing, the peace dividend could be said to have taken the form of private consumption.

Since the significant part of the British armed forces is stationed abroad, defence has always constituted a drain on the balance of payments. Although defence exports are considerably higher than defence imports, the surplus in goods has never been sufficient to cover the invisible deficit resulting from the deployment of troops abroad.

Defence Employment

The defence sector employs around one million people in Britain, or roughly 4 percent of the total workforce. A report from the main defence trades unions estimates that a further 500 000 people are dependent on the spending of defence workers, making a total of nearly 6 percent of the workforce.[11] Of those employed by the defence sector, around 30 percent are members of the armed forces, 16 percent are Ministry of Defence civilian staff and 44 percent work for the defence industry in making defence equipment both for the British armed forces and for export. Around 150 000 people are employed by the export sector, that is, about a quarter of total defence industry employment.

Defence employment has declined steadily, the decline being especially steep during the 1980s. Over 330 000 jobs have been lost, exclusively in the domestic defence sector. Some 60 000 jobs in the defence industry alone were lost between June 1990 and December 1991.[12] According to trades union estimates, over 100 000 jobs were lost in the three years following the announcement of 'Options for Change'.[13]

The decline in defence spending reflects a long-term rise in the capital intensity of defence spending. Expenditure per person employed in the defence sector almost doubled in real terms during the 1980s. This reflected both an increase in the capital intensity of warfare, that is, the amount of equipment per soldier, and the growth of output per person in the defence industry. During the 1980s, nearly 200 000 jobs were lost in the defence industry and yet defence production increased in real terms.

Defence Equipment

Both procurement expenditure, including research development production and imports of equipment, and R&D expenditure take an extremely high share of defence expenditure in Britain, in comparison with other countries and in comparison with other sectors. Spending on equipment represents a form of investment. In the economy as a whole, investment accounts for 16 percent of GDP while procurement expenditure accounts for 45 percent of the defence budget. Likewise total (military and civil) R&D expenditure accounts for just over 2 percent of GDP as a whole, while military R&D expenditure as a share of the total defence budget is 11 percent. Britain's spending on military R&D as a share of GDP (0.42) in 1988 is considerably higher than that of any of its main competitors except France and the USA. In fact, these figures underestimate the true size of defence R&D in Britain. A survey of the industry undertaken for the first time in 1989 revealed that it funded 26 percent of the defence R&D in Britain. This would suggest that the percentage share of R&D in GDP is as high as 0.57.[14]

The high levels of procurement and R&D reflect the rising cost of equipment, which in turn reflects the increase in embodied technology. The cost of four *Trident* nuclear weapons systems, for example, is £10,676 million. The development cost alone of the European fighter aircraft is estimated at £3,463 million.[15] It is usually estimated that the costs of individual weapons systems rise by 6 percent a year in real terms although, for some types of systems, such as aircraft, the rise is probably higher. The steady rise in unit costs has been paralleled by declining numbers both of weapon systems and of types of weapon systems, and this has been accentuated by the post-cold war cuts.

During the 1970s and 1980s technological advance consisted mainly of the application of electronics to weapons systems. As one recent report put it:

Increasingly, the requirements of systems integration, and therefore the

command of electronics and software skills, have been supplanting in importance the traditional skills of the builders of the major weapons platforms,
(ships, aircraft, tanks) leading to significant organisational changes.[16]

Developments in electronics, along with improvements in materials
and in the design of munitions, have greatly increased the accuracy and
destructiveness of all weapons systems. This has increased the vulnerability of weapons platforms, and therefore the cost of offensive
weapons. Given the potential effectiveness of electronic defences, offensive equipment has become much more expensive because of the need
for more effective protection and more complex electronics systems
which can help evade detection (stealth technology) and jam enemy
guidance systems. The rise in the cost of weaponry is thus linked with
the choice of offensive roles.

The Regional Impact of Defence Expenditure

The most striking feature of the regional breakdown of employment in
the defence industry is the concentration of defence employment
in England (85 percent) and in the south (58 percent). Defence industry
employment as a share of total manufacturing is particularly high in
the north, the south east and south west. To some extent this is due
to the decline in manufacturing in these regions. If one takes the sector,
metal goods, engineering and vehicles, which accounts for over 90
percent of defence equipment spending (SIC 3), some 53 percent of
jobs in the north are defence-dependent.[17] In the south east, defence
industry employment accounts for around 15 percent of manufacturing;
if one adds in employment generated by exports, the figure is likely to
be between 20 percent and 30 percent. (It is possible that the figures
are inflated because contracts are signed with head offices in London.)
One interesting implication is that the shift toward aerospace and electronics, away from shipbuilding and engineering and the defence boom
of the early 1980s, was probably a major factor in the boom in the south
east of England. By the same token, the decline in defence spending
may well be significant in explaining the current recession in the south
east, bringing it more into line with the north: defence industry employment in the south east declined by nearly half from 84 000 in 1985–6 to
44 000 in 1992–3.

In addition to particular regions, certain towns are often heavily
dependent on a particular weapons project or military base. Towns
dependent on weapons projects include Preston and Edinburgh (the
European fighter aircraft), Barrow-in-Furness (*Trident*), Yeovil

(helicopters), Bristol (military engines and aircraft), Stevenage (missiles), Brough, near Hull (*Hawk* aircraft) and Cheltenham (Smith Industries).[18] Because of the high skill base, the location of defence industries may be a significant factor in generating a cluster of high-tech firms in a region. This, for example, may well be the explanation for the prosperity of the M4 corridor or the so-called 'Silicon Glen' in Scotland. The chief economic development officer for Blackburn Borough Council has described the importance of the Royal Ordnance Factory, which makes fuses and timing devices for ammunition and missiles, in the following terms:

> For many years, Royal Ordnance has been at the forefront of skills training in the area and, through mobility in the labour force, the company has undoubtedly helped to raise the skill base of the economy as a whole. This in turn has helped to foster a wide range of new small companies, particularly in engineering and electronics. Also the presence of a large employer like Royal Ordnance is a persuasive argument in convincing incoming industries of the skill base of the area and this has been used to good effect.[19]

Similarly, military bases may dominate towns or rural areas where there is little developed manufacturing industry. Examples of such regions include the Fishguard area in West Wales (RNAD Milford Haven and RNAD Trecwn), Fife (Rosyth Naval Base and RAF Leuchars), Plymouth and Devonport (Devonport Dockyard, Plymouth Naval Base and RAF Mount Batten) and the cluster of army camps and training areas in Wiltshire and around Salisbury. Although bases do not have the same high-tech clustering effect, they do stimulate the local construction industry, as well as local services. A study undertaken of the Dyfed area around Fishguard showed that RNAD Trecwn was the biggest employer in the area after agriculture, although agricultural employment was declining. The two other employers are Sealink/Stena (a ferry company) and a clothing manufacturer, Slimna (which accounts for only around 150 jobs). In 1991, the area had unemployment amounting to 15.5 percent of the active population.[20]

John Lovering has argued that the geographical pattern of British defence manufacturing was established during the 1940s and 1950s and remained more or less static during the cold war period – he talks about the 'cold war spatial fix'.[21] During the 1920s and 1930s, new industries such as aircraft, vehicles and electrical engineering developed in the south of England and the Midlands and these were to become the backbone of a restructured defence industry. (The traditional 19th-century defence industry based on shipbuilding and engineering was largely located in Scotland and the north.) However, during World War Two, industries were relocated to 'safe areas' in the north and west to evade aerial attack. This pattern was reinforced by the cold war rearmament of the 1950s and was sustained up to the 1980s. Lovering argues that, in the post-cold war era, this spatial fix is dissolving. This is because of the growing importance of R&D, the division between production and R&D, and the growing importance of international networks as a result of which enterprises become detached from their local surroundings.

From the 1950s to the 1980s, the defence-dependent local economies of South Manchester, Preston, Derby, the Bristol subregion and North London/South Herefordshire could be regarded as manifestations of the cold war corporatist phase in the history of the British defence industry. By contrast, in the 1990s, the cluster of high-technology defence industries in the semi-rural south east and south west may be seen as expressing a new internationalized, deindustrialized UK defence industry.[22]

The interaction of the defence sector with the British economy as a whole cannot, however, be assessed in purely numerical terms. Even though it is clear that the defence sector represents a very important part of the British economy, especially in industrial and regional terms, the consequences of defence cuts can only be judged in the context of an analysis of how the defence sector functions and how it is changing.

THE FUNCTIONING OF THE DEFENCE SECTOR

If, in Eastern Europe, the defence sector represented the epitome and heart of the command system, in Britain, the defence sector operated rather differently from the rest of the economy. Indeed, in many respects, the defence sector during the cold war period worked rather like a command economy within a capitalist or mixed economy and this had far-reaching consequences for the economy as a whole.

The structure of the British defence sector was more or less established during World War Two. As we have seen, the military roles, the associated organization of the armed forces, and the location of bases and industries were all, to a large extent, the outcome of World War Two. Political choices about military roles have tended to reflect the desire to reinforce the perception of Britain's national and Atlanticist identity that was created in the 1940s; hence the conservatism about choice of roles. The organization of the armed forces cannot be disentangled from the roles the military are expected to perform. Moreover, armed forces everywhere tend to conservatism. The tendency to 'fight the last war' is a consequence both of the rational tendency to base planning and training on actual experience and of the bureaucratic tendency to inertia which is the result of an interest in institutional survival.

The defence industry was less conservative, however, because of the way it is organized. The industry was characterized, broadly speaking, by four types of company. First, there were, until recently, state-owned enterprises that were the oldest part of the defence industry: the Royal Ordnance Factories (ROF), the Royal Dockyards (RD) and the Research Establishments (RE). (The ROFs and Royal Dockyards have now been privatized.) The government was responsible for maintaining capacity in these enterprises for mobilization in case of war. These were not unlike state enterprises in centrally planned economies.

Secondly, there were the large private contractors which consolidated and became fewer in number over the last 40 years. By the end of the 1980s the British defence industry was dominated by one or, at most two, contractors in each major area of equipment. These included British Aerospace (fixed wing aircraft), Westland Group PLC (helicopters), VSEL Consortium Ltd (ships and engineering), General Electric Co. PLC (electronics) and Vickers PLC (tanks). By and large, these companies depended primarily on defence for their existence or, at least, they had large divisions, separate from the rest of the company, that were dependent on defence. They view defence as their 'core business'.

Thirdly, there were large numbers of middle-sized subcontractors whose defence dependence varied widely. Finally, there were a large number of small subcontractors, generally totally dependent on a prime contractor; often they were owner-managed firms set up by an ex-employee of a prime contractor to supply a specialized component or service on a commercial basis.

The composition of the dominant prime contractors has remained fairly stable although the number of prime contractors has been reduced through merger. There were, however, considerable changes in the composition of subcontractors, and a number of new medium-sized subcontractors have entered the market, specializing in new technologies. The defence industry was thus largely in private hands. Nevertheless, defence enterprises did not behave like typical capitalist firms; this is because of their dependence on a single state market. Even though many companies had and still have substantial exports, they are dependent on the domestic market to develop products, to achieve sufficient economies of scale to be able to sell at a relatively competitive price, and to reassure customers of the utility of the equipment.

The defence market can be described as a combination of monopsony and oligopoly. This leads to a situation not unlike that described by the theoreticians of the shortage economies that used to characterize Eastern Europe. In theory, defence spending is determined by political priorities at the centre, the companies compete for their share of the defence budget, and the choice of a particular contractor is supposed to be based on a considered judgement by the government as to the cost-effectiveness of that contractor in developing and producing equipment to fulfil a particular role. In practice, however, the government has to take into account the need to maintain a capacity to develop and produce a particular piece of equipment and, through a network of contacts and meetings (which, in the defence world, are what count as market research), the companies themselves contribute to the specification of equipment and, hence, the make-up of the budget. This process can be compared to the process of 'building up' and 'breaking down' the plan described by the Hungarian economist Tamas Bauer.[23] Also, because the largest prime contractors tend to be the most powerful or the most experienced at 'market research' there is a tendency to reproduce the composition of the prime contractors via this process. This is, in essence, similar to the 'input–output conservatism' which Alec Nove describes in relation to the Soviet economy.[24]

In the former centrally planned economies, a tendency to shortage arose from the fact that investment projects always cost more than anticipated. This was because enterprises tended to 'hook on' to the plan by underestimating costs or because, in the absence of competition and a hard budget constraint, enterprises solve unforeseen problems by spending more. This is similar to the cost overrun and delay problem in the defence industry which is notorious and shows little sign of abating despite numerous reforms. Even with fixed price contracts, once a company has obtained a contract, it is very difficult for the government to resist additional payment for unforeseen technical change, for example, because there are so few alternatives and, especially in the case of large projects, the consequences of cancellation would be disastrous.[25]

Where the British defence sector differed from a command system, however, was in the pace of technical change. If enterprises are state-owned and the government is responsible for maintaining capacity, there tends to be a resistance to technical change because this disrupts the normal routines and the established supply chains. Private enterprises, however, have to finance their own capacity and this requires continuous contracts. In order to obtain new contracts, companies have to be able to offer improvements on existing products. This gives rise to constant pressure for technical change which takes the form of product improvement, and hence the rising unit costs of equipment. In a market with a single dominant buyer and a few suppliers, it makes no sense to offer process improvement, which might reduce the cost of the product and, hence, the size of the overall market.

Thus technical change, in the form of product improvement, is a way of maintaining the stability of the prime contractors although it does involve considerable change in the composition of subcontractors. Particularly important in recent years has been the growth of electronics subcontractors as the traditional weapons platform becomes a platform for electronics systems. The attempt to improve products to fulfil traditional offensive roles has thus involved an escalation of cost. And this, in turn, puts perpetual pressure on the defence budget.

How did this sector interface with the rest of the economy? What were the consequences of the existence of a mini-command system within a capitalist economy? Britain's poor economic performance as compared with, for example, Germany or Japan has been widely noted. In particular, during the 1970s and 1980s, Britain experienced a dramatic decline in international competitiveness; a deficit in manufacturing trade emerged for the first time in 1981 and has widened subsequently. The connection between the existence of a large defence sector and poor economic performance has been explained in various ways, generally in terms of the opportunity cost of defence spending, particularly R&D spending. The analysis of the defence sector as a mini-command sector, however, suggests a specific explanation. On the one hand, the defence sector sustains certain sectors, such as aerospace, electronics, shipbuilding or nuclear energy, that might otherwise have run down. The regional clustering of industries described above is one way in which this is achieved. In this sense, a kind of 'imprinting' takes place similar to that which can be observed in Eastern Europe. On the other hand, the continued existence of these sectors may inhibit the emergence of other sectors, such as alternative energy sources, by absorbing scarce technological resources and, perhaps more importantly, by transferring habits, methods and design approaches of the defence sector to other sectors and distorting their development. Many commentators refer to the 'culture' of defence companies – the preoccupation with technical requirements rather than cost, the lack of marketing know-how, the preference for perfection above utility. As military technology has increasingly diverged from civil technology because of perpetual product improvements, these barriers to technical change in the civil sector have increased.

This argument is particularly relevant in the field of electronics. Until the early 1970s, Britain was at the forefront of electronics development because of the dominance of the defence sector. As developments in civilian technology began to move along a separate trajectory, however, the dominance of the defence sector became a handicap rather than an advantage, absorbing scarce skills, influencing design habits, and so on. Ferranti, for example, was responsible for the first European microprocessor but it was too complex and expensive for civilian application. In the last 20 years, electronics have become a key factor of production influencing every industrial sector. Thus the failure to keep up with civilian electronics may well have had pervasive effects on the economy.[26]

Whatever the explanation, Britain's poor economic performance constrained the growth of the defence budget even before the end of the cold war. The budgetary pressure caused by the rising cost of equipment due to technical change and cost overruns, combined with budgetary constraints, generated a series of responses, from both government and industry, which brought about significant changes in the defence sector, especially during the 1980s. These responses resemble reform efforts in Eastern Europe prior to 1989; each response generated new difficulties. Some analysts in Eastern Europe argue that continuous reform is a necessary attribute of command systems; this may also be true of the defence sector 'reforms', some of which we consider here.

Cuts and Defence Reviews

Advanced technological equipment does not only cost more to develop and produce, it also costs more to operate, service and maintain. As equipment grows in technological sophistication, it tends to require more parts, to use systems closer to their limits and to involve more complex interaction between parts and systems. This reduces reliability and durability and increases servicing requirements. Likewise, technologically sophisticated equipment tends to be more difficult to operate, increasing the requirements for training and practice, imposing more strain on the operator and increasing the requirements for highly skilled personnel; to be a *Tornado* pilot, it is said that you have to be the air equivalent of a concert pianist. Successive governments have been extremely concerned about the declining 'teeth-to-tail' ratio (that is the ratio between those who are likely to participate in actual fighting and those who support their activities), yet this may well be the consequence of the growing logistical and servicing requirements of technologically sophisticated equipment.

In a desperate effort to contain growing defence costs, successive governments have introduced a series of defence reviews (1957–8, 1966–8, 1974–5, 1981) and have been forced to introduce periodic cuts. These cuts and reviews have included cancellation of major projects

(TSR-2, the E-3 Airborne Electronic Warfare plane and so on), reductions in numbers of weapons systems and procurement stretch-outs (that is taking longer to produce equipment so as to economize on inputs), and savings on ammunition, spare parts, training and so on. Hence the tendency to shortage in the defence sector.

Procurement Reform: Competition, Contractorization and Privatization

From time to time, governments attempt to introduce reforms in the procurement system in order to overcome the problems of escalating cost and shortage. These include reshuffling departments, introducing procedures which approximate competition and so on. During the 1980s, special efforts were made by the Thatcher government. As in Eastern Europe, there were attempts to make a non-market system appear to be more like a market; they resembled the introduction of financial indicators to replace administrative directives which were carried out in several East European countries. These reforms have affected the administration of defence and the armed forces as well as industry. As elsewhere in British society, the government has introduced the notion of budgetary planning under its New Management Strategy (NMS). But the reforms in the relationship with industry were particularly important. The 1984 White Paper announced: 'Central to our strategy is the need to promote more extensive and effective competition in the supply of defence equipment. Competition is vital for the achievement of the best value for money, the most efficient use of industrial resources and the stimulation of innovation and new ideas.'[27]

In 1985, Peter Levene was recruited from United Scientific Holdings to become chief of defence procurement. Levene introduced a number of reforms.

Increased competition and fixed price contracts

The government attempted to increase the number of contracts issued by competitive tender, and to replace, where possible, cost plus contracts with fixed price contracts: that is to say, instead of prices based on actual costs plus a percentage fee, fixed prices are negotiated at the outset. The term used by the Ministry of Defence is 'taut contract'.

'The emphasis is on providing incentives to deliver on time and to cost, with preference being for "firm" price contracts where the contract price is what the supplier is paid. However, "fixed price" contracts which make an allowance for inflation and target cost or other incentive arrangement within an overall "maximum price" are also paid.'[28]

Following the appointment of Levene, contracts 'priced by competition' increased from 38 percent to 45 percent of the total value of contracts, and from 12 percent to 14 percent of the total number of contracts. However, total fixed price contracts declined from 9 to 4 percent of the total value of contracts and from 5 to 2 percent of the total number.

Defence contractors claim that these reforms have led to greater budgetary control and no doubt they provide a justification for restructuring and redundancies, along with the decline in the defence market. Nevertheless, it is impossible to introduce competition on the major projects such as *Trident* or the European fighter aircraft and it is always possible to find ways round fixed price contracts through amendments, that is technical additions. Now the government is once again limiting the number of companies invited to submit bids in order to simplify procedures.[29]

Again, to draw a parallel with Eastern Europe, it is impossible to introduce market conditions given the underlying relationship between the government and the companies and, in particular, the monopsonistic position of the government.

Contractorization

Another element of the 'Levene reforms' was to increase competition at the level of subcontractors and to encourage new small enterprises to enter the defence business as subcontractors. Both companies and military bases have been encouraged to contract out as much work as possible. Military bases are, for example, contracting out catering, cleaning and repair work instead of maintaining in-house chefs, cleaners or plumbers. Prime contractors will encourage employees to set up companies to supply parts or services previously undertaken in-house. For both bases and prime contractors, this is a way of shedding labour and cutting costs. As one contractor has put it, it is a way 'to shove the pain down the system'.[30] For prime contractors, it is also a way to increase their flexibility in defence markets. Technical change can be achieved much more easily through changing the composition of subcontractors than through internal restructuring.

Privatization

In 1987, the government decided to privatize the Royal Ordnance Factories and the Royal Dockyards. ROF Leeds was purchased by Vickers for £15 million. The remaining ROFs were purchased by British Aerospace (BAe) for £90 million. BAe then embarked on an asset-stripping exercise. A report from Warburg Securities concluded that property sales from the ROFs and the Rover group, also purchased by BAe, would recoup more than the £340 million paid for their purchase. A considerable number of jobs have been lost in the ROFs. The Royal Small Arms Factory at Enfield has been closed, together with the R&D centre at Waltham Abbey. There were also plans to close ROF Patricroft near Manchester and ROF Bishopton in Scotland. The latter has been saved as a result of a union campaign, but numbers will fall from 1100 to 700.

There have been similar job losses at the Royal Dockyards which have been placed under commercial management. Devonport Management Limited announced job losses of 5000 at Royal Dockyard Devonport (nearly half the total workforce), despite the fact that assurances were given to the High Court that job losses would be only 2300 when the unions challenged the legality of privatization.

The research establishments have also been reorganized as an independent trading company, the Defence Research Agency.

Internationalization: Exports, Collaboration and Transnational Mergers

A third approach to the problem of rising defence costs is internationalization: finding new foreign markets, or reducing costs through collaborative production. In addition, a new aspect of internationalization in the late 1980s and early 1990s is transnational merger.

Arms exports

Britain is now the second largest arms exporter in the world, after the United States. Considerable efforts were made to increase arms sales under the Thatcher government. The Defence Sales Organisation, set up in 1966, was renamed the Defence Export Services Organisation in 1985. The DESO, which has a staff of 400, provides marketing information to British companies and assists customers in raising finance.

Defence sales increased in the late 1980s, at a time when they were declining in other countries, but showed a substantial fall in 1990–92. The main reason for the increase was major contracts for *Tornado* aircraft and other equipment with Saudi Arabia and Malaysia. The share of the Middle East and North Africa in total arms sales increased from 35 percent to 61 percent between 1985 and 1990; Saudi Arabia alone is said to account for 20 percent of total arms sales. The share of the Far East and Asia has increased from 9 percent to 13 percent of the total. The market in other third world regions has declined owing to the debt crisis; this is particularly striking in Africa where the former

British colonies had always provided a relatively reliable market for British armaments. The market among other industrialized countries is stable or declining because of defence cuts.

Since the Gulf War, some doubt has hung over the future of British arms sales to the Middle East. This is because of supposed restraints on the delivery of arms to the region imposed by the major powers, the fact that, owing to promises made during the Gulf War, the USA is expected to displace West European countries as the dominant supplier to the region, the decline in oil revenues and the scandal surrounding secret deals with Iraq during the 1980s. The Memoranda of Understanding signed with Saudi Arabia in 1985 and 1988 – the so-called 'Al Yamanah agreements' – did not result in as many orders as expected. According to these contracts, Saudi Arabia agreed to ship 400 000 barrels of oil a day to Shell and British Petroleum. The proceeds of the sale of oil are then paid to the defence contractors, first and foremost British Aerospace. However, owing to the fall in the price of oil, the revenue from the sale of *Tornadoes* and *Hawk* trainers has been much less than expected. Nevertheless, in January 1993, the government announced an additional order for *Tornadoes* under the Al Yamanah agreements and orders for the new *Challenger 2* tank from the Sultan of Oman.

International collaboration
Successive governments have attempted to reduce defence costs by international collaboration in the development and production of defence equipment. The most important example of international collaboration is the *Tornado*, developed and produced jointly with Italy and Germany. A successor project, the European fighter aircraft, is currently under development, also involving Spain, although it has been scaled down as the result of pressure from Germany. SDE 1993 lists 22 international collaborative projects in production or in service as of 1 April 1993 and 23 projects in development or in early study phase at this time.

The experience of collaborative projects has been disappointing. Contracts have been issued according to the principle of *juste retour*, which means that each country's share of the work is proportionate to its financial contribution; this principle has overriden the principle of efficiency. In many cases, each country has its own assembly line, thereby reducing the possible economies of scale that might have been reaped from such projects. (This is not always the case: the series of Anglo-French helicopters was organized differently.) Each national defence ministry has its own competing requirements and compromises between these requirements often have to be built into the technology. Language difficulties, travel costs and so on add to the administrative overheads. For these reasons all the problems that have been experienced in national projects are multiplied in the case of collaborative projects. It is widely estimated that collaborative projects increase costs by 30–50 percent compared with purely national projects though, if the costs are shared, this will still result in some savings.

Although the idea of collaboration was enthusiastically embraced by governments from the 1960s onwards, collaborative projects still only account for 15 percent of total defence procurement. According to the National Audit Office, the 'lack of common requirements and time scale were significant factors preventing collaboration between 1984 and 1988'.[31]

Transnational mergers

As markets decline both because of defence cuts and as rationalization of the defence industry via national mergers and privatization reaches its limits, an obvious next step is rationalization across national borders. Until the 1980s, defence markets tended to be rather autarkic and defence companies epitomized the 'national champion' concept of the 1950s and 1960s. A new development during the 1990s, however, has been a rash of transnational mergers, especially in Europe.

The Stockholm International Peace Research Institute (SIPRI) lists 18 international takeovers in the arms-producing sector and three mergers in 1988–9, 20 takeovers and 11 mergers in 1990–91, and seven takeovers and 12 mergers in 1992. All the mergers except one involving the USA and Israel were trans-European. American and Canadian companies were initially involved in takeovers, although their role was almost negligible in 1990 and 1993.[32]

The most celebrated takeover was the joint GEC–Siemens bid for Plessey in 1989. This set the stage for a number of significant mergers in 1990–91. These include the merger of the helicopter divisions of MBB and Aérospatiale to create Eurocopter. (MBB has itself been taken over by Daimler-Benz, making it the largest defence company in Europe.) British Aerospace and Thomson CSF have merged their missile divisions into a single company, known as Eurodynamics. Thomson CSF has taken over the Philips (Netherlands) defence business and Ferranti's naval electronics division. Matra (France) and MBB have combined to form a joint company manufacturing dromes (pilotless planes), known as Eurodrome. Many commentators expect the European market to be dominated by four or five 'European' companies: Daimler Benz-MBB, British Aerospace, GEC, Aérospatiale/Dassault and Thomson CSF.

What these mergers do effectively is to break up national defence markets. At the same time, they mark the beginnings of a Europe-wide division of labour in the defence sector. On the one hand, they could constitute a future European military–industrial complex, powerful interests which could pressure a future European defence agency – 'pork-barrel monsters' as Callum McDonald has described them.[33] On the other hand, the merger process allows for a considerable reduction of the European defence industry and, moreover, national governments need no longer take responsibility for maintaining a national capacity to develop and produce particular types of military equipment.

The developments of the 1980s could thus be said to amount to an erosion of the defence sector as a command system. The attempt to introduce a market, through privatization and competition policy, and the increasing internationalization of the defence sector through trans-national mergers have led to considerable rationalization, the shedding of jobs, the changing composition of subcontractors and regional con-centration. This trend can be expected to accelerate with further defence cuts and further integration of the European defence industry. Whether this is, however, a prelude to a new generation of military technology and/or to the conversion of industrial structures and economies away from defence production depends on political choices.

DEFENCE CUTS AND CONVERSION

The Size of the 'Peace Dividend'

Although there have been substantial cuts in manpower, and in numbers of weapons systems, these are offset by the rising cost of equipment and growing expenditure per employee. The government held down the level of defence expenditure, which was expected to fall slightly to £23 billion, in 1993–94. The government anticipated a 12 percent reduction in defence expenditure in real terms by 1995–96 and it estimated that, as a share of GNP, defence spending would fall from the current 3.9 percent to 3.2 percent over the same period.

If, however, Britain were to make far-reaching changes in defence assumptions and to abandon the readiness for high-intensity conflict, much more substantial cuts could be made. In other words, Britain might abandon role two as well as the nuclear component of role one and focus on the security and integrity of the UK and dependent territories and on the British contribution to international peace and security. This would not mean entirely abandoning the NATO concept. Peace-keeping could be based on regional multinational formations maintained on different national territories. Combined with arms control inspections, joint exercises and other confidence-building measures, this would help to minimize the dangers of renationalization of defence in the European continent. But it would mean even bigger reductions in scale and a force restructuring away from World War Two-style rapid offensive roles with their very costly technological requirements.

It is possible to calculate in rough terms on the basis of the government's own figures what this would mean in terms of costs. On the assumption that forces earmarked for reinforcement in dependent territories and for intervention in regional conflicts should be included, this would mean a defence budget of £15 800 million, a reduction of around one-third in the current defence budget as shown in Table 4.1:[34]

Table 4.1   Breakdown of UK defence budget by objectives, 1993–4

	Gross costs (£ millions)
Security & integrity of UK, peacetime	1500
Northern Ireland	1600
Dependent territories: peacetime deployment	700
Regional security: peacetime activities & deployment (includes former Yugoslavia)	3700
Regional security: intervention capability	8300
Total	15 800

However, what either the present 'peace dividend' or more substantial cuts could mean for the British economy depends on the type of measures taken at macro- and microeconomic levels.

Macroeconomic Consequences

At a macroeconomic level, the effects of defence cuts will depend on whether the cuts lead to an increase in non-defence public expenditure, to reductions in taxation, or to reduced deficits or increased surpluses. These effects in turn are the subject of controversy. Thus would a reduced deficit encourage investment via lower interest rates or lower wage rates, or, assuming that wages are sticky downwards, would the increase in investment resulting from lower interest be much less than an increase in investment which would result from the multiplier effect of increased public expenditure? Even if it is assumed that defence cuts are compensated by public expenditure, the consequences will vary according to the type of public expenditure. Thus increases in social consumption (health and education) are likely to have direct employ-ment-creating effects but may not utilize the same skills as are released from the defence sector. Increases in capital expenditure could have larger growth effects because of the crowding in effect of public investment.

Barker, Dunne and Smith[35] have simulated the effects of a 50 percent cut in UK defence spending by the year 2000 using the Cambridge Multi-sectoral Dynamic Model. The model's assumptions about the relations of aggregate demand are Keynesian. They make two alterna-tive assumptions. In one case defence cuts are balanced by proportionate increases in different categories of public expenditure so as to leave total public expenditure unchanged. On this assumption, GDP is increased over and above the expected growth throughout a 10-year period by 2 percent and unemployment is reduced by half a million. Assuming the exchange rate remains unchanged, there is some deterioration in the balance of payments. According to the second assumption, there is no reallocation of public expenditure; that is, the overall total is reduced by the same amount as the defence cuts. On this assumption, GDP falls by 3.5 percent over the 10-year period and unemployment increases by half a million.

What kind of adjustment can we expect for the different options? In the case of the current government policy, we can expect a negligible adjustment to defence cuts; if anything, reductions in taxation are more likely than increases in public expenditure. In this case defence cuts can be expected to reinforce the recession and to increase unemployment, as has been the case up to now.

In the case of the more substantial cuts there is no a priori reason to assume any particular form of adjustment. However, an increased emphasis on Britain's contribution to international peace and security would imply a broader concept of security which would require increased economic assistance to Eastern Europe and the third world. A broader concept of security also might entail the need to confront economic, social and environmental sources of insecurity and hence would result in increases in public expenditure. Therefore defence cuts are likely to be compensated by increased public expenditure but a substantial part, for example one-third, would consist of foreign assistance which would only stimulate growth and reduce employment if it led to increased exports. Supposing increases in economic assistance amounted to an additional one percent of GDP, this would be roughly equivalent to the current external deficit. This would represent a doubling of the foreign exchange cost of security expenditure compared to the current cost of deploying troops abroad. Adjustment policies would have to take this foreign exchange cost into account. On the other hand, if one assumes that this stance takes place in a changed international context, and such a change is unlikely except on this assumption, then the increase in aid from other countries could help to stimulate British exports as well: this could be one element in a programme of global reflation.

A serious objection that has been raised against the Cambridge study is that the expected aggregate effects conceal the microeconomic consequences for particular regions, industries and skills. A major bankruptcy, for example, could have substantial repercussions at a macroeconomic level. Moreover, severe localized dislocations could constitute a political obstacle to further defence cuts.

Microeconomic Consequences: Conversion of Bases and Industries

The conversion debate in Britain has a long history. During the 1970s, workers at Lucas Aerospace and at Vickers developed alternative plans for socially useful production instead of defence production. These plans arose because of the commitment of the 1974 Labour government to cutting defence. (Actually, these commitments were never implemented.) As one of the Lucas Aerospace shop stewards put it recently, 'There is an assumption that our diversification strategy was peace-led. That was not actually the case. The beginning of the strategy was about job security: how can we develop a new strategy that will save our members' jobs?'

These plans were proposals for new technologies and product areas that could utilize the skills of the existing workforce. They included environmental products, such as alternative energy sources (waves, wind and so on) and recycling equipment; medical equipment, such as kidney machines; new forms of transport, and so on. Although the unions never succeeded in putting their proposals into practice and faced considerable resistance from management, the ideas caught the imagination of unions both in Britain and elsewhere and some of the products were developed in Germany and Sweden. Moreover, in the early 1980s, at least two local councils, the Greater London Council and Sheffield, initiated conversion plans. Conversion was included in the GLC Industrial Strategy and a London Conversion Council was established, although, of course, this was dismantled along with the GLC. Sheffield City Council established a Centre for Product Development Services which was inspired by the Lucas Aerospace plan. The task of the centre is to support and promote initiatives which are designed to maintain and create employment through the development of socially useful products, processes and series.[36] The policies of Sheffield local authority have undoubtedly contributed to the economic expansion of Sheffield during the 1980s.

During the 1980s, interest in conversion waned along with the defence boom. The term 'diversification' began to be used instead of 'conversion', because the latter term tended to be associated with job losses. Both the Labour and the Liberal Democrat parties are committed to the establishment of a Defence Diversification Agency. Labour would create such an agency in the Ministry of Defence. But the Conservative government has up to now been rather resistant to the idea, in line with its general laissez-faire attitude towards the economy. It has recently produced a publication, 'Changing Tack', to assist diversification and the new Defence Research Agency established in April 1993 is helping to fund a civil aerospace R&D programme as well as a series of seminars called 'Pathfinder'.

A series of reports in the mid-1980s suggested that high levels of military R&D were a significant factor in explaining the relative decline in Britain's technological performance.[37] Even the 1987 White Paper admitted that military R&D 'may crowd out valuable investment in the civil sector'.[38] One consequence was the establishment of a private company within the Ministry of Defence, Defence Technology Enterprises, whose role was to find and sell civil applications of technologies developed in the REs. The company was not, however, very successful and was closed down in 1990.

More interesting than the role of the government has been the role of local authorities, often working in partnership with trade unions, management and community groups, and the role of the European Union. There has been a spate of reports commissioned by local authorities describing the defence dependency of their area, the expected job losses, especially highly skilled jobs, and the prospects for conversion. These reports constitute valuable research material about the economic effects of military bases and defence companies. There are some general conclusions that emerge out of these surveys. First, as far as bases are concerned, the problem of closure is not markedly different from other sorts of job losses. Bases tend to make use of services, especially catering, cleaning and construction. The most significant job losses resulting from a base closure are probably in the construction industry. However, these are jobs that can easily be deployed elsewhere. Serious problems, of course, arise in remote areas where bases may be the only or the largest employer, as in Dyfed in West Wales. One report noted that bases often contain historic buildings that are extremely expensive to maintain and that cannot be opened to the public for security reasons. Base closure could make possible much more productive use of such buildings.[39]

As regards defence manufacturing, there is first of all general concern about the high levels of skill and the difficulties of preserving those skills and developing appropriate technological alternatives. Secondly, a number of reports comment on the great difficulty faced by large prime contractors in changing 'company culture'. Particular problems are marketing, design standards and costing. At ROF Blackburn, for example, 'Production costing ... is geared very much as one would expect towards the defence sector, either because of the need for quality control or due to the way in which the plant's large overheads are spread across the factory. When unit costs are of prime importance ... Royal Ordnance would find it hard to meet the financial criteria.'[40] The smaller subcontractors tend to be much more flexible than the prime contractors, although there are grave difficulties for highly specialized companies, which may be 90–100 percent dependent on the defence market.

The European Community supported projects of defence-dependent areas through the PERIFRA programme, which is a pilot project designed to assist areas adversely affected by the end of the cold war, and through the Konver initiative. The latter was a new initiative of the European Union, promoted by the European Parliament to provide 130 million ECUs in assistance for diversification to defence-dependent regions within the EU. Particular emphasis is given to encouraging small and medium-sized businesses and to environmental objectives.

So far, therefore, there has been very little *actual* conversion either of bases or of industries. (One celebrated example is Racal's diversification into the mobile telephone market.) The main effect of defence cuts so far has been unemployment. Indeed, the scale of redundancies suggests that the end of the cold war has been viewed by companies as an excuse for rationalization. In December 1990, British Aerospace announced 5000 lay-offs, including the closure of its Kingston and Preston plants. A further 2200 lay-offs were announced in March 1991 in Bristol, Lostock and Stevenage. Likewise VSEL announced 3500 lay-offs in November 1990, and a further 5500 in Barrow in March 1991. One Ferranti worker described the situation in his company as follows:

> At a recent meeting of trades unions with management on the Ferranti crisis, we were given the plan, not the possibility of diversification for the company. They indicated that if they get away with reducing the work force as they like and end up with a fitter, hungrier company, then they will go into the commercial market and play a role within there.[41]

The most noteworthy examples of actual conversion are Barrow-in-Furness and Lancashire. In both cases grants were received from the European Community's PERIFRA programme. In the case of Barrow, a one-company town that manufactures *Trident* submarines, government funds were also received. The funds were used for the provision of industrial premises by English Industrial Estates, road projects, training projects and a series of proposed projects including land reclamation, tourism development and the creation of a Diversification Zone.[42] Barrow was one of the areas where a conversion plan was produced by workers during the 1970s. On and off, throughout the 1980s, the unions continued to push for conversion together with peace activists.[43] The Cumbrian Technology Transfer Initiative was set up jointly by VSEL and Barrow-in-Furness Borough Council in 1981 with the aim of assisting the diversification of the industrial base of the town of Barrow.

In the case of Lancashire, Lancashire Enterprises, an economic development agency for the north west, set up two programmes. One is an agency, operated on behalf of BAe, for finding jobs, retaining schemes or self-employment options for former BAe employees. The programme, called 'New Start', involves an intensive process of counselling, planning, placement and follow-up. The other programme is the PERIFRA-funded Preston New Technology Park. The aim was the establishment of a regional centre for technology transfer and new product development. The Park aims to provide business start-up units (workshops for light engineering or offices for services such as software development), a training unit, a technology transfer unit (including technology transfer networks) and an enterprise innovation support unit, as well as other facilities such as meeting rooms and dining rooms. Also in Lancashire, Blackburn Borough Council has been working with a local R&D company to produce civil electronic and electrical products at ROF Blackburn.

One other development that should be mentioned is the establishment of a Joint Diversification Committee in Royal Ordnance, in which management and trades unions will join efforts in developing diversification strategies, and in particular drawing up project proposals to be submitted to Konver. This is something for which defence trade unions have campaigned for several years.

Regional plans do offer the best prospects for conversion. The problem with company-based conversion or diversification plans is that they are still caught in the 'spin-off' approach that characterized Defence Technology Enterprises and also alternative plans. Companies are organized around defence technology and the number of viable commercial applications are, in fact, rather limited, precisely because of the 'culture' of the companies and the specific development of military technology. A report undertaken for the government on this question concluded that fewer than 20 percent of defence technologies were likely to generate civil spin-offs.[44] Even with government assistance of the kind proposed by the Labour and Liberal Democrat parties, the risk is that diversification could turn out to be a mechanism for propping up defence companies, encouraging spin-off sectors which resemble the defence sectors and thus preserving a mini-command system.

It may be that slimming down and even closing defence companies is a more efficient method of restructuring, provided those skills that have potential value can be redeployed before they are lost. It is people rather than companies that have the versatility to respond to new markets or needs. Hence what is required is market- or need-led plans in localities where skills are concentrated. Retraining schemes and science parks provide a basis for redeploying defence skills that may be more appropriate than company-based diversification. However, in a recession, it is extremely difficult to envisage how the new enterprises so created can break into existing high-tech markets, which are dominated by firms who have accumulated considerable experience. To the extent that they do succeed, the main effect in the current climate could be labour displacement. It is already possible to observe that displaced defence workers take jobs in low-technology sectors, especially services, thereby displacing less qualified workers. Without new markets, there is a risk that these imaginative regional schemes will fail, compounding the current disillusion.

Environmental projects, transport projects and communications projects are particularly appropriate because they do utilize similar skills and, unlike consumer markets, they are not yet saturated. At present, Britain's spending on environmental R&D, for example, is a fraction of what is spent on military R&D and low compared with other countries. There are companies in Britain which are at the forefront of new environmental technologies, such as building controls for regulating and conserving energy or small energy-efficient power plants; however, these have difficulty in achieving sufficient economies of scale because of small domestic markets. An increase in expenditure on alternative energy provision or building controls for hospitals, schools and other public buildings could be one way of building up a comparative advantage in these areas and utilizing valuable skills in the defence sector.

What this suggests is that microeconomic adjustment cannot be treated separately from macroeconomic adjustment. Reductions in defence expenditure need to be accompanied by increases in other forms of public expenditure, especially expenditure on environment, transport, health or education, if regionally based conversion efforts are to succeed. Moreover, public expenditure needs to be geographically redistributed.

CONCLUSION

The main conclusion of this case-study is that any security policy has to take into account economic realities. The unimaginative approach to security policy of the current British government is untenable in the long run. The escalating costs of high technology, the restructuring of the defence industry and the economic burden of military spending mean that it is no longer feasible to maintain a comprehensive national capability for high-intensity warfare. A recent report from the House of Commons Defence Committee warns against further cuts in defence spending. In the case of the Royal Navy, for example, it argues that 'in the event of war, [it] would be incapable of defending our sea routes on which we depend both for trade and the movement of our armed forces'.[45] Yet even if there were an identifiable threat to Britain's sea routes, it is almost impossible to suppose that Britain could or would have to defend its sea routes single-handedly in the traditional manner. Small countries like Denmark or the Netherlands have always recognized their limitations and have sought alternative mechanisms to ensure their security. In the current context, a continued emphasis on a future high-intensity war of the World War Two type is actually a handicap, absorbing resources that might contribute more constructively to immediate security concerns in the post-cold war world, such as peace-keeping or economic assistance.

On the other hand, an alternative, more internationalist, security policy in which defence was a less important component and was more oriented towards peace-keeping and peace-enforcing could only be introduced in the context of appropriate economic adjustments. Otherwise, defence cuts would merely contribute to recession. There would have to be increases in civil public expenditure, especially in areas such as environment and infrastructure and, further to this, constructive regionally based conversion initiatives. One of the most positive findings of this study was the grass-roots development of local and regional diversification plans, often supported by the European Community and offering the prospect of breaking out of the defence dependence of the British economy.

Unlike the countries of Eastern Europe, the British policy-making elite has not yet absorbed the full implications of the end of the cold war. The main public criticisms of the government have been directed against the consequences of defence cuts. Yet a much more radical adjustment of the scale and orientation of Britain's defence posture will have to take place sooner or later. The current anachronistic posture is likely to lead to both economic pain and political confusion over the new few years – a 'sour and sunken island' adrift in the new post-cold war world.

NOTES

1. Speech to the Royal Institute of International Affairs, June 1990, reproduced 1990 *London Review of Books* as 'The Year Peace Broke Out'.
2. Ibid.
3. Richard Ware, *Background Paper No. 276, UK Defence Policy: Options for Change*, House of Commons Library, 4 October 1992.
4. SDE 1991, para. 306.
5. NATO, *Press Communiqué* S-1 (91) 85, 7 November 1991.
6. The decision to acquire nuclear weapons was taken by a small subcommittee of the cabinet in 1947, consisting of Stafford Cripps, Hugh Dalton, Clement Attlee and Ernest Bevin. Cripps and Dalton were against acquiring the bomb on cost grounds. Bevin arrived late after a lunch with the US Secretary of State, Byrnes. Bevin said: 'We've got to have this ... I don't mind for myself but I don't want any other Foreign Secretary of this country to be talked *at* or by a Secretary of State in the United States as I have just had in my discussion with Mr Byrnes. We have got to have this thing over here whatever it costs. ... We've got to have the bloody Union Jack flying on top of it.'
7. Speech to the Royal United Services Institute, 2 October 1969, quoted in Mary Kaldor and Albert Booth (1978), 'Alternative Employment for Naval Shipbuilding Workers: A Case Study of Resources devoted to the Production of the ASW Cruiser', in M. Kaldor, D. Smith and S. Vines (eds), *Democratic Socialism and the Cost of Defence*, London: Croom Helm, p. 395.
8. The House of Commons Defence Committee reported: 'As we observed in Cyprus and Bosnia, platoon commanders and NCOs are more than likely to be required to make swift and complex decisions, taking into account political, legal and ethical considerations outside most conventional military training. ... Exceptional adaptability is also required on the part of professional soldiers required to act against military logic – such as using open communications, tolerating high levels of provocation, wearing distinctive clothing rather than camouflage (all white for EC

monitors in the former Yugoslavia) and flying missions at a pre-ordained altitude and on a fixed route known to potentially hostile forces' (Defence Committee, 9 June 1993), *UK Peacekeeping and Intervention Forces*, Fourth Report, Session 1992–93, 188369, para. 73).

9. Ibid.
10. Stockholm International Peace Research Institute (SIPRI) (1993), 'World Armaments and Disarmament', *SIPRI Yearbook 1993*, Oxford: Oxford University Press.
11. IPMS (The Institution of Professionals, Managers and Specialists), MSF (Manufacturing, Science, Finance) and TGWU (Transport and General Workers Union) (1991), *The New Industrial Challenge – The Need for Defence Diversification*, London.
12. IPMS, MSF and TGWU, *Defence Employment Briefing*, No. 2, January 1992.
13. TGWU Press Release, 9 June 1993.
14. Report by Controller and Auditor General (5 December 1991), 'Classification of Defence Research and Development Expenditure', London: HMSO.
15. SDE 1993.
16. (1993) *Future Relations between Defence and Civil Science and Technology*, prepared by the DRC/SPSG Defence Science and Technology Policy Team for the Parliamentary Office of Science and Technology, SPSG Review, Paper No. 2.
17. IPMS, MSF and TGWU, *Defence Employment Briefing*, No. 2, January 1992.
18. Ibid.
19. Steve Hoyle, Chief of Economic Development, Blackburn Borough Council Royal Ordnance (1991), *Blackburn – A Framework for Cooperation: The Role of Local Authorities in Enabling Conversion Strategies*.
20. *The Future of RNAD Trecwn*, a report by the local authorities and joint trade unions steering group, September 1991.
21. See John Lovering, 'The Creation of a Spatial Fix' (forthcoming).
22. John Lovering (1991), 'The Changing Geography of Military Industry in Britain', *Regional Studies*, **25**, (4).
23. Tamas Bauer, 'Investment Cycles in Planned Economies', *Acta Oecomonica*, **21**, (3), 1978.
24. Alec Nove (1977), *The Soviet Economic System*, London: Allen & Unwin.
25. For recent cost overruns and time delays, see Committee on Public Accounts (1991), *The 1989 Statement on Major Defence Projects*, London: HMSO.
26. See M. Kaldor and W. Walker (1988), 'Technologie Militaire et Dynamisme économique', *La Recherche*, October.
27. SDE 1984.
28. SPSG review paper, *Future Relations*.
29. SDE 983, para. 504.
30. *The Impact of Reduced Military Expenditure on the Economy of South West England: A Report*, Research Unit in Economics, Bristol Polytechnic on behalf of Avon and Bristol City Councils, and Cornwall, Devon, Dorset, Gloucestershire, Somerset and Wiltshire County Councils, May 1991.
31. National Audit Office (1991), *Ministry of Defence Collaborative Projects*, London: HMSO.
32. *SIPRI Yearbook 1990, 1991*, and SIPRI (1993), 'World Armaments and Disarmament', Oxford: Oxford University Press.
32. See Callum Macdonald (1991), 'A New Model Army: Towards a a European Defence Community', *Fabian Discussion Paper No. 10*, London.
34. Calculated from SDE 1993.
35. Terry Barker, Paul Dunne and Ron Smith (1991), 'Measuring the Peace Divided in the United Kingdom', *Journal of Peace Research*, **28**, (4), November.
36. Nuclear Free Local Authorities (December 1990), *A National Steering Committee Briefing*.
37. Sir I. Maddock (1983), *Civil Exploitation of Defence Technology: Report to the Electronics EDC*, London: NEDO; House of Lords, First Report of the Select

Committee on Science and Technology, session 1986–7, *Civil Research and Development*, HC20–11.
38. SDE 1987.
39. Bristol Polytechnic report.
40. Steve Hoyle, *Blackburn* (1991).
41. Lothian Trades Union and Community Resource Centre (November 1989), *A Conference on Alternative Strategies for Defence Dependent Communities*, abridged report.
42. Barrow has been surprisingly successful in attracting visitors to a remote industrial town. In 1992, receipts from tourism amounted to £100 million. See 'Barrow Tourism Booms with help from Mr Toad', *The Guardian*, 18 September 1993.
43. Barrow Alternative Employment Committee (1987), *Oceans of Work, the case for non-military research development and production at VSEL Barrow*, Barrow.
44. Advisory Council on Science and Technology (ACOST) (May 1989), *Defence R&D: A National Resource*, London: HMSO.
45. See *Jane's Defence Weekly*, 30 October 1993.

5. France

Geneviève Schméder

INTRODUCTION

In order to understand the situation of the French military sector following the end of the cold war, one must be aware of some long-standing characteristics of the French security approach, based on the concepts of 'national independence' and 'military autonomy', and of the French industrial policy, based on dirigisme and voluntarism.

French strategy was sometimes called 'national–nuclear–neutralist': national, because of the very strong commitment to the concept of national independence and the emphasis on autonomy of decision ever since de Gaulle's critique of the superpower-dominated bipolar system led to France's withdrawal from NATO's integrated command structure in 1966; nuclear, because of the reliance on nuclear armament which was considered to be the most secure, painless and costless defence, as well as a ticket to the club of the 'great powers'; neutralist, because France's claimed 'non-alignment' and promotion of peoples' self-determination.

The hard core of French security policy since the 1960s was minimum nuclear deterrence, based on the assumption that any attack which threatened the country's 'basic interests', especially its territorial integrity, would provoke immediate nuclear retaliation involving the use of strategic nuclear weapons. This excluded by definition the concept of flexible response, the participation in a 'limited' war and the use of nuclear weapons in support of a war-fighting option.

In the industrial field, the search for national 'grandeur' and military autonomy implied technological prowess and advanced armaments capabilities. Independence in the production of military goods and technologies *vis-à-vis* foreign suppliers, especially the United States, required the development of a powerful arms industry and a high level of public resources committed to military R&D. This drive led to the subordination of economic objectives to strategic considerations and to the development, under the guidance of the state, of a powerful arms industry including nuclear, space, aeronautics and electronics.

These choices of all Fifth Republic governments, from the Gaullists to the Socialists, have profoundly shaped the structure of both French institutions and French industry, especially in high-tech sectors. The obsession with strategic independence led to the selective concentration of state interventionism on high-tech firms and sectors, to the detriment of traditional sectors and, more generally, the global economic environment. For many years, the 'French model' was considered very successful in terms of technological achievements and industrial vitality. Only in recent years has the centrality of the arms business in French industrial structures and public life begun to be criticized, less for the perverse effects of the French policy of arms sales *tous azimuts* on global security than for the dual industrial structure fostered by the permanent bias of industrial policy in favour of military-oriented industries and technologies.

In spite of its apparent simplicity, logic and coherence, France's strategic doctrine was never free from internal contradictions. These contradictions were exacerbated by the recent transformations in the European security environment. In particular, it appeared more and more problematic to develop an openly European political project to reassert the belonging of France to the Atlantic Alliance and to maintain a purely national based security strategy. When Mitterrand proposed in January 1992 that the French *force de frappe* should now be considered in a broader European framework and raised the question of the 'conceivability' of a European nuclear doctrine, he officially broached a taboo subject which had been untouched for more than 30 years.

While France has to make a difficult strategic move, since any reorientation of its long-term security policy implies a deep intellectual mutation, with the abandonment of purely national concepts, the traditional conservatism of French elites has until recently prevented any real public debate on French defence concepts and policies taking place in the political arena.

The first section of this chapter is about France's security policy and its evolution. The second is on the resources devoted to military efforts and capabilities. The third section is a description of the defence sector and section four considers the issues of disarmament and conversion.

FRANCE'S MILITARY DOCTRINE AND SECURITY POLICY

Security Concepts

Since World War Two, there has been in France an exceptionally strong political consensus on security issues, which appeared as a direct consequence of the trauma of the 1940s defeat and the occupation of French territory by German troops. There was, indeed, a deep conviction that nuclear weapons would better protect the 'national sanctuary' than conventional techniques, but the consensus was more profoundly about France's decay and the need to reassert both French sovereignty and a French sense of identity. After the impotence experienced in 1940, the nuclear deterrence option fulfilled the important political function of overcoming the experience of the defeat and restoring French confidence and political identity.[1]

When de Gaulle came back to power in 1958, one of his first claims was that France should be allowed to participate in the direction of Western nuclear affairs. In September 1958, he sent a memorandum to the United States and the United Kingdom asking for the creation of a tripartite organization in charge of defining Western strategic policy and deciding the use of nuclear weapons. The reaction of the United States, which was in the middle of the 'missile gap' crisis, was to propose that her allies widen their participation in the Western nuclear strategy by either buying or building nuclear weapons under licence, provided these weapons would remain under American control (August 1959). Britain and Belgium found the proposition too expensive; France rejected the control stipulation.

De Gaulle felt free hereafter to develop a new defence policy based on an independent nuclear deterrent, although still formally set within the Atlantic Alliance's framework. In de Gaulle's eyes, only countries which were members of the 'nuclear club' could pretend to possess real sovereignty: not having nuclear armaments meant strategic dependence, which itself implied political dependence. Conversely, to be a nuclear power ensured both military security and political independence. As a result of this policy, France tested its first atomic bomb in 1960 in the Sahara and its first thermonuclear bomb in 1968 in the Pacific atoll of Mururoa.

These weapons were in fact the results of long-lasting efforts that had been initiated under the Fourth Republic. After the launching of a *Plan quinquennal de l'Energie atomique* (five-year atomic energy plan) in 1952, the decision was taken in 1953 to undertake military nuclear research, and in 1956 to produce nuclear weapons. Curiously enough, these decisions were not supported at that time by any specific, consistent strategic thinking, since the best 'brains' in the army were mobilized by the wars of independence in Indochina and Algeria. It was only after de Gaulle's return to power in 1958 that theoretical rationalizations and a coherent political strategy were elaborated.

De Gaulle had already been the unsuccessful champion of the modernization of the French army in the 1930s, when he had – in vain – advocated the development of motorized troops of tanks capable of rapid and unexpected moves and tactics to meet the German threat.[3] In the late 1950s, his renewed concern for France's national *grandeur* led him to promote nuclear deterrence and to advocate autonomy of decision *vis-à-vis* what he called the 'American protectorate'. In a speech delivered in November 1959, he insisted that

> France's defence must be French. . . . Of course, French defence could eventually be joined with that of other countries. . . . But it must remain ours, France must defend by itself, for itself and in its own way. If it would not be the case, if one would admit for a long time that French defence would stop being integrated into a national framework and confused, or joined, with something else, it would not be possible to maintain a home state. . . . We must provide ourselves a *force de frappe* which can be deployed anytime and anywhere. It goes without saying that the basis of this force would be nuclear armament.

Besides de Gaulle, the most influential thinkers of the so-called 'French strategic school' were General Gallois, Raymond Aron and General Beauffre. Gallois shared with McNamara the idea that the concepts of 'nuclear deterrence' and 'alliance' were fundamentally incompatible. He developed the axioms of the equalizing power of the atom ('in the field of deterrence, there can no longer be "strong" and "weak" nations') and of 'proportionate deterrence' ('a small country can prevent a big country from attacking with limited means of deterrence, i.e. proportional to the value of the stake that the small country represents'). On the contrary, Raymond Aron was quite sceptical about the efficiency of the 'weak to the strong' (*faible au fort*) deterrence (he denounced the 'logical delirium' and 'dogmatism' of Gallois) and criticized the French attitude towards the Atlantic Alliance. Both Gallois and Aron were discussing what was in fact the core of the French debate: how to reconcile both the autonomy of decision and the necessary contribution to allied security.

General Beauffre was the founder of the *Institut Français d'Etudes Stratégiques* and of its review, *Stratégie*. He developed the concept of 'total strategy' which took into account political, economic, diplomatic and military dimensions as well as nuclear and classical levels of force intervention. He pushed ahead the concept of 'limited war' and advocated the use of conventional and nuclear tactical weapons (said to be 'pre-strategic') in order to discourage military aggressions and concentrations in the heart of Europe. According to his views, nuclear tactical weapons were needed to have a deterrent function in 'non-sanctuarized' spaces and reinforce the credibility of the strategic threat.

The permanent ambiguity of French strategy was indeed its relation to NATO and the contribution of France to the defence of Europe. It was never made clear how the approach in terms of 'national sanctuary' and 'armed neutrality' would be reconciled with the proclaimed commitment to France's allies in case of a war in Europe. The official doctrine claimed that nuclear weapons were intended to 'sanctuarize' France and protect its 'vital interests', but what these were exactly was never made explicit, nor was what would be the scope of France's contribution to the security of its allies. Even though the argument was that 'uncertainty' was the most crucial element of deterrence, in fact, more pragmatically, the coexistence inside each French political party of both nationalist and Atlanticist interpretations always made this issue an absolute political taboo.

The same ambiguity characterized the apparently unique historical consensus around the French nuclear doctrine. When, everywhere else in the West, public opinions, political parties and even experts were deeply divided on security issues, France appeared as a counter-model. Not only did French people seem to be massively proud and satisfied with their defence policy based on nuclear arms (in a 1981 poll, 72 percent of French people considered French nuclear deterrent forces 'indispensable'), but they were massively in favour of the deployment of Pershings in Europe (with the unique exception of the French Communist Party). Thus, when masses of people were demonstrating in other European democracies against Pershings and cruise missiles, French people supported their president, who advocated their deployment in the Bundestag.

The reasons for this unique historical consensus were certainly deeply rooted in French experience: five 'hot' wars in four generations (three of them on French territory, most of them actually lost) made war a very concrete and proximate notion for French people, who always felt more inclined to rely for their protection on technology than on the military capabilities of their generals. Moreover, nuclear weapons are supposed to be less demanding than conventional defence in terms of staff and monetary requirements. The French like the idea of being defended but were not always known for their determination to resist when confronted by an enemy. It was precisely on this point that limits to the French consensus appeared.

In a poll conducted in 1980, 72 percent of French people declared that they were opposed to any use of nuclear weapons by the President of the Republic; 65 percent were even against the 'threat to use them'. In 1983, in response to the question: 'Imagine that a big power is on the verge of entering French territory. What do you think should be the reaction of the president?', the answers were: (1) 'He should threaten to use nuclear weapons' (11 percent – two months later, 6 percent); (2) 'He should not threaten to use nuclear weapons but oppose the big power by any other means' (14 percent); (3) 'He should undertake immediate negotiations with the big power' (68 percent); (4) 'Without any opinion' (7 percent). In addition, 90 percent of the people questioned considered themselves to be underinformed or not informed at all on security issues.

This makes the famous French consensus seem more like a French version of 'better red than dead' than a strong military–political commitment. Though any use of French strategic weapons would have meant suicide for France, this apocalyptic perspective seemed to make nuclear weapons so completely irrelevant that the ordinary citizen felt perfectly happy with them. In people's minds, they came to be purely abstract symbols of national status rather than real instruments of destruction. In other words, for French public opinion, nuclear is more a 'non-war' magic totem than an instrument of rational 'defence'. One understands in these circumstances why French political circles have always been so reluctant to open a public debate on security issues.

French Defence Policy

French military doctrine and defence policy traditionally have two aspects. One is a stationary aspect, whose aim is to guard the national territory against a Soviet-type threat and whose means is nuclear deterrence. The other is a 'fluid' or mobile aspect, whose aim is to deal with sudden threats to French interests and with peace-keeping duties in major flashpoints of the world, and which implies external action. Until the disappearance of the Warsaw Pact and the break-up of the former Soviet Union, the first was clearly more important than the second. With the end of the cold war, however, priorities have been reversed.

Nuclear deterrence: the *Force Nucléaire Stratégique*
Traditional pillars of French defence policy are strategic nuclear forces, which include three different components (the so-called 'Triad'):

- a 'sea' component, the *Force Océanique Stratégique* (FOST) equipped with five missile launch submarines (SNLE) and 80 ballistic missiles;
- an 'air' component, the *Forces Aériennes Stratégiques*, essentially equipped with 18 (quite old) *Mirage 4* fighters;
- a 'land' component equipped with 18 (also quite old) S3 surface-to-air ballistic intercontinental missiles deployed in silos and to be launched from the Plateau d'Albion in Provence.

In spite of the official statement that nuclear weapons would never be used in support of a war-fighting option, strategic forces were complemented after 1974 by nuclear battlefield forces (said to be 'pre-strategic'), which also included three components: a land component equipped with nuclear artillery (32 *Pluton* short-range missiles and 20 *Hades* missiles), a sea component with fighter planes and 40 *Super-Etendard* aircraft (with an additional 24 in reserve) and an air component with helicopters and *Jaguar*, *Mirage 3* and *2000N* planes. These short-range tactical weapons were intended to reinforce conventional armament to fight a classical war in Central Europe in the framework of NATO.

Other missions
NATO membership as well as French post-colonial responsibilities as an ex-imperial power led France to maintain conventional capabilities. After 1983, the army developed a military capability of intervention 'out of area': the Rapid Action Force (FAR), including five divisions of mechanized tanks, among them one air-mobile with 240 helicopters. This force was supposed to be used in Europe to counter Soviet divisions when allied troops had already been defeated. Part of it was located in Germany, where more than 50 000 French soldiers were permanently stationed. The FAR was also used in military interventions in other parts of the world, in particular in Africa (Zaire and Chad), where relatively 'light' units were engaged, in Iraq, where the Daguet Division was deployed, and in several UNO protection missions all around the world.

Besides the FAR, the land army was traditionally organized in two other corps in charge of defence operations in Europe. They included 10 divisions (of which six were tank divisions) equipped with helicopters, missiles and tanks (in particular, 30-year-old AMX-30 tanks and their modernized AMX-30 B2 version, to be replaced by a new generation of *Leclerc* tanks). Mention must also be made of the Franco-German Brigade, which was created in 1987, and of the troops which are permanently deployed overseas: 20 000 soldiers are stationed in Chad, Djibouti, the Republic of Central Africa, Gabon, Ivory Coast and Senegal, while France has permanent garrisons in its overseas possessions (DOM-TOM: Antilles-Guyanne, Mayotte, La Réunion, New Caledonia and Polynesia).

Air forces were traditionally organized in three *Commandements*: the CAFDA (*Commandement de défense aérienne*), the COTAM (*Commandement du transport aérien*) and the CEAA (*Commandement d'entraînement*). They were equipped with 100 interceptors, 84 transport planes, 200 helicopters and 270 fighter planes.

Navy forces included four regional *Commandements*, corresponding to the Atlantic, Mediterranean, Indian Ocean and Pacific squadrons (*Escadres de l'Atlantique, de la Méditerranée, de l'Océan Indien et du Pacifique*). Altogether, they had at their disposal 115 ships, including two aircraft carriers (equipped with 80 planes) and 13 attack submarines.

The *Gendarmerie* military forces, in charge of domestic security, are distributed between 'departmental' (locally affected) and 'mobile' gendarmes.

In June 1989, an initial plan for the reorganization of the armed forces was launched. Its objectives were to reduce effective forces, to build up a specific mix of forces for each type of crisis and to reinforce internal cooperation. This *Armées 2000 Plan* entailed:

- reducing France's three army corps to two: the FAR and a *Corps Blindé Mécanisé* (Tank Mechanized Corps) for defence operations in Europe;
- regrouping the six previous French 'military regions' into three major zones covering the north and north east, the Mediterranean and the Atlantic (corresponding respectively to threats in Central Europe, Southern Europe and to supply routes and nuclear submarine patrol lanes in the Atlantic);
- reducing the maritime zones to two: the Atlantic and the Mediterranean;
- creating two inter-service operational commands.

Recent Developments

Although recent developments in Europe and elsewhere have seriously damaged France's strategic doctrine, the transformation of the security environment has so far been only reluctantly integrated into French thinking. The end of the cold war, which indeed gave France a privileged position in Europe, was not welcomed by French rulers who were hardly prepared to admit any change in European relations. Hence the extremely conservative attitude of French presidential diplomacy after the fall of the Berlin Wall, trying to slow down the German reunification process and welcoming the coup in Moscow.

Officially, nuclear forces remain the 'essential cornerstone' of France's security. They are presented as a protection against the dangers of nuclear proliferation and as an element of stability in Europe, all the more necessary since the bipolar system has disappeared. Deterrence is said not to be linked to any particular threat but opposed to all: even though the threat might decrease or change its nature, the necessity of deterrence itself remains.[3]

However, France can no more pretend to replace the USA in the protection of its Continental allies than it can retire to its nuclear castle, since this would break up the European dynamics. These uncertainties have been reflected in the hesitations and ambiguities of French diplomacy. Having advocated at the end of 1990 the creation of a European 'Confederation', François Mitterrand explained in April 1991 that 'defence of Western Europe can only, for the time being and for years to come, be conceived in relation to the Atlantic Alliance. There is no reason to create a European Defence Organisation which would replace the NATO one.' He then suggested, in January 1992, that the French *force de frappe* should be considered in a broader European framework and integrated into a European nuclear doctrine.

The Gulf crisis brought on the same kind of passive, reluctant and confused reaction. French political leaders, who were pulled between France's traditional 'Arab policy' and their loyalty to their Western allies, were all the more embarrassed that France was one of the main suppliers of arms to Iraq.[4] Having tried to treat both sides tactfully, the French government eventually decided to participate in the war (with less than 3 percent of the forces engaged) in order to preserve its permanent seat in the UNO Security Council.

The Gulf War made the French military establishment realize the weakness of France's military means in the event of a conventional war. The army was not prepared for this type of conflict as far as men or equipment were concerned.[5] The (undisputed) decision not to send conscripts created serious problems and delays since, conventional weaponry being traditionally allocated to the conscript regiments, professionals had to be given emergency training to be able to use it.[6] This difficult situation was reflected by the fact that, with an army of 280 000 (including 110 000 professionals), only 12 000 soldiers could be sent to the Gulf area, with the possibility of replacing them just once, whereas, with 160 000 professionals, the British army could send immediately a force of 35 000. After this experience, it was decided to reduce the length of service from 12 to 10 months and to completely professionalize the Rapid Action Force.

Since conscripts were already excluded from nuclear forces, some wondered whether, in view of the new situation, conscription should not be abandoned.[7] Conscription has been traditionally justified on the ground that it is the guarantee of a 'democratic' army, but it was never egalitarian and became progressively inequitable and unpopular.[8] Only one young man in two completes his military service and out of 10 million reservists, fewer than 100 000 would be mobilized in the event of a real conflict. Since the end of the 1980s, between 60 percent and 70 percent of the population declare that they are opposed to conscription.[9] In these conditions, the future of conscription appears problematic.

In accordance with the tradition of preparing for the last war, the main effect of the Gulf War was to push the French military–industrial establishment into giving a high priority to the reinforcement of conventional forces and to the development of high-tech defence technologies. But intelligence, space and communication research being very costly, especially for a medium-sized country like France in a context of economic recession and budgetary limitations, the new imperative appears hardly compatible (at least financially) with the previous doctrine. Hence two inevitable conclusions, which still have not been officially drawn up: (1) the growing gap between 'needs' – however defined – and resources will impose drastic conceptual and technological choices, and (2) France's strategic independence, defined as the possibility of dispensing with any cooperation, is definitely over.[10] Less than ever can strategy be separated from the economy.

Precisely because of the new strategic priority given to the technologies of 'intelligence', the discussion on the need to keep the Triad as it was became very hot after the Gulf War. It was especially serious because all three services were at that time in the process of developing very costly new systems: the air forces the new *Rafale* fighter plane, the army a new generation of *Albion* missiles and the *Hades* missile, the navy the new generation of nuclear submarines – with more silent characteristics and particularly sophisticated 'lure' equipment.

The first concession to the new situation was the reduction and re-organization of the nuclear element. Tests were suspended and the level of nuclear alert was reduced, as was the number of people who serviced nuclear weapons. The modernization of the Strategic Oceanic Force (FOST) was not questioned, but the decision was taken to reduce the number of nuclear submarines: it was decided to have by 1996 four instead of six strategic new generation missile launch submarines (SNLE), six instead of eight nuclear attack submarines, and one instead of two fleet, of *Super-Etendard* attack planes on board the navy aircraft carriers *Foch* and *Clemenceau* (to which would be added the new *de Gaulle* unit after 1998).[11]

The *Rafale* programme and the supply of six new nuclear *Mirage 2000* to the air forces were maintained, but it was decided to withdraw by 1996 all *Mirage IV* nuclear bombers and not to replace the interconti-nental missiles on the Plateau d'Albion when they become obsolete at the beginning of the next century. A progressive reduction of the French pre-strategic arsenal was also decided: regiments of *Pluton* nuclear missiles were reduced from five to one and the *Hades* programme was cancelled.[12]

These cuts suggested that, in spite of official declarations, nuclear deterrence was no longer considered as the spearhead of French military doctrine. When questioned on the apparent scaling down of nuclear defences, President Mitterrand conceded that France was 'diversifying its defence priorities'.

The French armed forces were also radically reorganized. Chevène-ment's successor, Joxe, presented in April 1992 an *Armée 1997* project with drastic measures affecting all three services. Besides spectacular manpower cuts, especially in the army (a 20 percent reduction by 1997), the plan forecast complete withdrawal of French troops from Germany, a reduction of tank divisions from six to three and of the FAR divisions from five to four.[13] It was decided to supply 750 *Leclerc* tanks instead of 1400 (a halving of the actual fleet) and to cut some equipment programmes (like the S45 ballistic missile or the *Brevel* pilotless aircraft). It was also decided to reorganize French military intelligence by giving it more people and financial support (all the ministry's military intelligence operations agencies were gathered in a new inter-service organization called *Direction du Renseignement Militaire*). The objective of the reorganization was to be able to 'project' 35 000 people immedi-ately and to mobilize ultimately 320 000 people, including selected 'reservists'.

As to the naval forces, it was decided to redeploy all warships to Toulon or Bret by 1996. The Mediterranean Squadron (*Escadre de la Méditerranée*), based in Toulon, was transformed into a *Force d'Action Navale* in charge of 'projecting' forces overseas,[14] while the Atlantic Squadron (*Escadre de l'Atlantique*), based in Brest, became a *Groupe d'Action Sous-Marine* (GASM) in charge of French nuclear missile launch submarines. A third *commandement*, the *Force de Guerre des Mines* (FGM), was also created in Brest.

In the air force, it was decided to reduce the number of *Mirage 200N* squadrons from five to three by 1996, and of planes from 450 to 390 in 1994; to bring all tactical aircraft under the single command of the *Force Aérienne Tactique* (FATAC), and all aircraft designed to carry nuclear weapons under the *Commandement des Forces Aériennes Stratégiques* (CoFAS).

A European Corps including the Franco-German Brigade (4500 personnel) and a French and a German division was created. This corps is in principle open to other countries and is intended to operate in close cooperation with NATO.

The reorganization and reduction of armed forces was not accompanied by any change in their role, even if the increased professionalization of the land forces reflects the emphasis now put on 'projection' rather than on static nuclear defence.

MILITARY EFFORTS AND CAPABILITIES

The Financial Effort

As Table 5.1 shows, in 1992, the French defeat budget amounted to FF195.2 billion (3.25 percent of the GDP) and in 1993, FF197.9 billion (3.15 percent of GDP). This 1.35 percent increase in current terms corresponded to a 1.5 percent decrease in real terms.

Table 5.1   Evolution of the defence budget, 1988–94 (FF billions)

	1988	1989	1990	1991	1992	1993	1994
Amount	174.2	182.3	189.4	194.5	195.2	197.9	193.82
Change (%)	+3.0	+4.6	+3.9	+2.7	+0.4	+1.4	+3.6

Source: Délégation Générale pour l'Armement.

In terms of share of GDP, France is behind the USSR, the USA and the UK and at the same level as Germany and Japan.[15] The long-term evolution has been a decrease from the late 1960s to the mid-1970s, a slow increase until the end of the 1980s and a further decrease since then (Table 5.2). In 1981, when the Socialist and Communist parties came to power, the share was more than four percent. It remained so until 1985.

Table 5.2 Military expenditures as a percentage of GDP, 1960–90

1960	1965	1970	1975	1980	1985	1990
6.2	4.8	3.9	3.4	4.0	3.8	3.5

Source: Délégation Générale pour l'Armement.

Between 1963 and 1990, military expenditures grew at an average rate of 2.13 percent per year, that is less than the 3.6 percent growth rate of the GNP (which increased by 3.6 times during the same period). Up to the end of the 1960s, defence was the most important item in the state budget.[16] It still represented 15.3 percent of this in 1991, the same proportion as employment and civil equipment. It was surpassed only by education.

Within the French military budget itself, there is a clear-cut division between the 'operational budget' and the 'equipment budget'. While the overall military budget which includes both is voted each year by Parliament, the equipment budget is, in addition, planned in advance on a five-yearly basis in an 'Orientation and Programming Act' (OPA), which determines the government's long-term orientations and aims to provide all actors with a comprehensive set of priorities. Although the system never worked out perfectly, because systematic delays obliged each OPA to be replaced by a new one, seven OPAs have been voted between 1960 and 1988, allowing military equipment expenditures to increase by 3 percent per year in real terms between 1965 and 1988. The non-issuing of a new OPA since the end of the cold war is further evidence of the hesitations of the government to take long-term decisions.

Functional Analysis of Defence Expenditures

In 1991, the defence budget was distributed in the following way:

22%   Nuclear forces
18%   Land forces
12%   Air forces
12%   Navy
 8%   *Gendarmerie*
 4%   General administration
 9%   Material and manpower support
 6%   Training
 6%   R&D and testing
 3%   Overseas

This functional distribution has changed over time. Under de Gaulle, the high priority placed on nuclear deterrence meant that between 30 percent and 50 percent of all military expenditure was devoted to nuclear research, development, production and operation. These items represented 40 percent of the global budget in 1970, 30 percent in 1980 and still 22.6 percent in 1990, while almost one-third of military investment (one-quarter in 1993) was devoted to the nuclear element. For the first time in 30 years, nuclear spending was reduced by 3.2 percent in 1992 (11.5 percent in 1993). Further reductions seem certain. In the 1994 budget there also appeared for the first time a specific endowment for the dismantling of obsolete nuclear weapons.

The allocation in the military budget of 'equipment' and 'operation' expenditures also changed over time. The share of equipment increased constantly relative to the operational budget between 1980 and 1990, as shown in Table 5.3, even though it decreased slightly after 1990, owing to a large increase in military wages.[17] Equipment credits amounted to FF103 billion in 1992 and 1993, and FF95 billion in 1994.[18]

Table 5.3   *Distribution between equipment and operational budgets (percent), 1980–93*

	1980	1983	1986	1989	1990	1991	1992	1993
Equip.	45	45.7	47.8	53.7	53.9	53.0	52.7	52.0
Operat.	55	54.3	52.2	46.3	46.1	47.0	47.3	48.0

Source: Parliamentary sources.

The increasing weight of the equipment budget reflects the growing importance of technological investment, which represents between 16 and 20 percent of total military expenditures.

Defence Equipment and Technology

Between 1974 and 1987, while the annual rate of growth of industrial productive investment was 5 percent, military equipment grew at an annual rate of 8 percent. This reflected the fact that, outside the United States, no country had ever made technological autonomy as central to its security posture as had France. The British have been far more disposed to rely on US technology for big submarine and aircraft orders. Even Israel, whose security dilemma was obviously more immediate than France's, was dissuaded from developing its own fighter aircraft. As a result, France used to produce about 90 percent of the weaponry it required.

Politicians did not hesitate to launch new programmes at regular intervals, since they knew that the final bill would be presented years later to their successors. The *Leclerc* tank, for example, which was part of a larger programme of development of entirely new high-tech weapons,[19] involved a cost of only FF200 million in 1991. However, the annual cost was expected to rise to FF4 billion in 1996, while the total cost (including research, development and industrialization) was estimated at FF63 billion (for a production of 800 units). As a result, programme reductions and cancellations have always been a feature of French defence procurements. They were regularly imposed by the rising costs of military equipment, reflecting both the increased cost of arms (which is estimated to be in France of an order of magnitude of 5 percent per annum)[20] and the exponentially growing incorporation of sophisticated technologies in weapons systems.[21] It had already become obvious before the end of the cold war that budgetary constraints would make it impossible for France to sustain the modernization of its strategic, pre-strategic and conventional weapons while simultaneously remaining self-sufficient technologically. Several programmes had already had to be postponed and the length of the series involved reduced.[22]

With the end of the cold war, however, programme reductions have changed in magnitude. Even though a painful re-examination leading to drastic choices has not yet been achieved,[23] some of the big programmes like the *Rafale*, the nuclear aircraft carrier and the *Leclerc* have been further slowed down. Military space programmes were in return increased by 17.5 percent in 1992, and by 20 percent in 1993, with priority given to the development of new communication satellites.[24]

Military R&D

Military R&D includes the so-called 'upstream studies' (including all operations from fundamental and applied research through development to the elaboration of prototypes) and the development of new weapons systems. In 1989, the first item was given FF8.9 billion (26.2 percent) and the second FF25.1 billion out of a total of FF34 billion. Its sharp increase since the second half of the 1980s, in a context of limited or reduced military budgets, was only possible because of cuts in other items, especially 'manpower' (whose share decreased from 38.7 percent of the global budget in 1978 to 32.5 percent in 1990)[25] and 'current expenditures' ('operational stocks' and 'training decreased from 14.9 to 10.6 percent of the budget during the same period). As shown in Table 5.4, military R&D increased both as a percentage of military expenditure and of military R&D.

Table 5.4   Importance of military R&D, 1975–90

	1975	1980	1985	1990
% of Military Expenditures	11.5	12.8	15.7	—
% of Govt R&D	28.3	35.7	31.5	35.2

Source: Parliamentary documents.

Table 5.5 shows how military R&D was distributed in 1991 amongst various fields of research.

Table 5.5   Distribution of R&D military budget, 1991

Nuclear	Electron.	Vehicles	Aerosp.	Ammun.	Shipbuilding	Tanks
20%	25%	15%	18%	12%	7%	3%

Source: Délégation Générale pour l'Armement.

In a joint communication made in February 1992, the French Ministers of Defence and Research stressed the need to give to defence a higher priority in the public research budget (which in 1991 devoted FF48 billion to civil research and FF34 billion to military research), deplored the gap between space military and commercial achievements and invited space specialists from the former USSR to come to work in France.

Defence Employment

In 1991 the French defence sector still employed more than one million people, roughly 5 percent of the total workforce. While 400 000 people worked for arms industries, 670 000 people were employed directly by French military forces: 300 000 professional soldiers, 242 000 conscripts and 128 000 civilian staff.

Table 5.6   Distribution of military employment, 1991

	Army	Air Force	Navy	Gendarmerie
Numbers	280 000	92 000	65 000	85 000
Career (%)	39	62	71	
Conscripts (%)	61	38	29	

Source: Délégation Générale pour l'Armement.

Nuclear forces employed 38 000 career servicemen, conscripts and civilians, among them 18 700 in strategic and 8450 in pre-strategic forces. When all the staff working in arsenals, research establishments and companies are included, the number of French people working in the nuclear military sector totals 60 000.

In the arms industries, around 254 000 people (between 5 and 7 percent of manufacturing manpower, 1 percent of the total labour force) were employed directly by prime contractors, the rest being employed by suppliers and subcontractors. In terms of field of activity, military–industrial employment was distributed as shown in Table 5.7.

Table 5.7   Sectoral distribution of the workforce in arms industries (prime contractors), 1991

DGA	GIAT	Nuclear	Aerospace	Electronics	Other
54 000	13 000	10 000	63 000	53 000	61 000

Source: Délégation Générale pour l'Armement, 1992.

In terms of institutional distribution, the picture was as shown in Table 5.8.

Table 5.8   Institutional distribution of the workforce in arms industries (prime contractors), 1991

DGA	GIAT	CEA	Public firms	Private firms
54 000	13 000	10 000	79 000	98 000

Source: Délégation Générale pour l'Armement, 1992.

When subcontractors are included, 120 000 people were employed in aeronautics and 75 000 in land warfare industries. The distribution in aeronautics is shown in Table 5.9.

Table 5.9   Manpower distribution in the aerospace industry, year end 1990

Aircraft missiles	Engines	Equipment	Total
57 500	27 100	35 400	120 000

Source: Aerospace industry.

In addition to the 6000 researchers who were employed by the *Direction des applications militaires* of the *Commissariat à l'Energie Atomique* (CEA) (which spends annually more than FF8.5 billion in R&D), almost 20 000 people worked for military research in about 20 labs, *centres d'essai* and *sous tutelle* facilities.

DESCRIPTION AND FUNCTIONING OF THE DEFENCE SECTOR

Given the industrial and technological leading role of the French arms sector, it is not enough to assess its economic impact through its quantitative performance. Its effects are also qualitative and of a structural character. The decisive importance of the French arms sector results less from its size than from its strategic position, which is the direct consequence of the privileged relationships it traditionally has with the state.[26]

The overlapping of industrial and bureaucratic interests linked to the military business has in France a long tradition since at least Colbert in the 17th century. After World War Two, the revival of the domestic arms industry was one of the Fifth republic's top priorities. With the Fourth Republic's obsession with strategic independence, however, the traditional imperative to manufacture arms was supplemented by the new imperative to sell them.

Institutional Aspects

In order to meet the requirements of its security policy, France built up an adequate infrastructure, comparable to the type of organization which successfully produced the TGV (high speed train) or nuclear energy. There are always three main ingredients in the structure: a wealthy administration, industrialists strongly dependent on the state and a human and cultural cohesion between the bureaucratic and industrial elites. This cohesion is an outcome of the way the French technical–industrial–political elite is selected and trained through the system of the *Grandes Ecoles*, amongst which the most famous is the military Ecole Polytechnique. It is reinforced by the fact that many high-ranking civil servants spend part of their career in administration and ministerial cabinets before working in national industries. A basic belief of this elite is that production and sale of arms both stimulate the civilian economy and strengthen France's competitive position in world markets.[27] As a result of the remarkable homogeneity and cohesion of this elite, no counter-elite has ever been in a position to challenge this equation of arms sales and economic vitality.

At the heart of the system is the Ministry of Defence (261 000 staff in 1989), within which bureaucratic power is concentrated in the DGA (*Délégation Générale pour l'Armement*). Dominated by the military engineers of the prestigious *Corps de l'armement*, the DGA is the central arbiter between military services, arms manufacturers and foreign arms purchasers. It is a very secretive administrative body, which employs more than 54 000 officials in a series of functional directorates, state-operated arsenals and worldwide sales and servicing bureaux, while running several high-tech engineering schools.

At once architect of the defence programmes, industrialist and seller, the DGA is a quintessential example of French administrative power and centralism. Its first mission is to anticipate future threats and to identify the needs of *Etats-majors*. But its directorates are more generally responsible for planning the modernization of the French military forces, operating arsenals and shipyards, inspecting materials before delivery to the military branches, administrating major R&D contracts, negotiating and servicing arms contracts abroad, and so on. Because of its overlapping missions, it is difficult to describe the complex network of relations between DGA and defence companies, which are all highly dependent on the state for such things as money, orders, exports, insurance and guarantees.

One of the most important roles of DGA is technological leadership. The close link established between technology and the notion of 'national independence' led it to privilege industrial and research objectives considered as important from this point of view and to devote huge financial, institutional and human resources to their fulfilment. These resources are traditionally put together in 'big programmes' largely centred around the military. The so-called '*Plan Calcul*', for instance, was launched in the early 1960s after the refusal of the United States to supply France with the big computers needed for the French nuclear programme.

Although the concept of the 'big programme' is by no means exclusive to France, it has become the archetypal instrument of French industrial policy. The state has an irrepressible tendency to use it – whatever the actual problem and the political orientation of the government – each time the 'national interest' is mentioned. It appears to be the 'natural' mode of action in a country where bureaucracy is very centralized, high-rank technocrats all come out of the same training mould (with a statist–military style) and the financial system is entirely dominated by the state. This marked preference for 'big projects' guided by public authorities resulted in the concentration of public funds in sectors like the military dominated by state procurements and in a very specific division of labour between the state and industry, with industry realizing the project and in charge of research and production tasks and the state providing orders, money and captive markets.

One consequence of the massive intervention of the state in industry under the guidance of military, diplomatic and prestige considerations has been the concentration in a small number of firms and industries (public and private) of a large share of scarce resources, in particular most of the national scientific, technological and industrial potential. The arms-producing sector, which realizes slightly more than 5 percent of manufacturing production, absorbs more than 40 percent of public subsidies to the manufacturing sector and benefits from 35 percent of public R&D expenditure which is military-oriented.

All the expressions used to describe this specific French industrial and technological model – 'Colbertist model' (P. Papon 1978), 'bureaucratic centralism' (P. Cohendet and A. Lebeau), 'strategy of the arsenal' (J.J. Salomon), 'arms model' (P. Dussauge) and 'high-tech Colbertism' (E. Cohen) – stress both the economic importance of the arms complex and its role as a policy tool.[28] A constant drive of French industrial policy has been the willingness to keep the most advanced technology under national control and to have it produced by a French firm.

Successes and failures of this 'Colbertist approach' are well-known. Careful examination of areas where French performance has been successful shows some common characteristics with weapons production: 'heavy' collective equipment which is extremely costly to develop, produce and buy; industrial sectors (aeronautics, space, telecommunications, professional electronics, nuclear plants, transport, energy) with either captive or very strongly protected markets; firms and industries servicing government contracts. Failures are not less characteristic. They have been almost systematic in goods which address large civilian consumption markets and which must adapt to a demand arising from numerous potential clients in the context of competitive supply.

This model has come to be more and more sharply criticized. It is accused of giving too much power to the state, the 'enlightened despotism' of which has progressively become a timorous conservatism. It is also accused of having become counterproductive in terms of global industrial performance, because of the bias in favour of 'big projects' of a statist and military inspiration.

The French Arms Industry

The French arms industry contributed in 1991 to about 7 percent of domestic industrial activity. The evolution of its sales between 1982 and 1992 is given in Table 5.10.

Table 5.10 Evolution of arms industry sales (billions current FF, before tax)

1982	1984	1986	1988	1990	1992
75.5	98.3	108.4	119.2	124.5	113.1

Source: Délégation Générale pour l'Armement.

However, it is difficult to give reliable statistical estimates of the arms industry, since there is no such industry in French National Accounts: the industry called 'aeronautics, shipbuilding and arms' excludes military electronics and telecommunications and transport material.[29] See Table 5.11.

Table 5.11 *Percentage share of 'aeronautics, shipbuilding and arms' (as a proxy of the arms industry) in total manufacturing industry*

	1973	1988
Production	3.92	5.30
Manpower	4.06	4.67
Value-added	3.77	4.10
Investment	2.39	1.36
Exports FOB	5.51	8.60
Imports CAF	3.56	4.10

Source: Délégation Générale pour l'Armement.

Compared to the global manufacturing industry, the sector appears to be highly dependent on exports and shows bad productivity performance (share of manpower compared to share of value-added) as well as a low level of investment.[30]

The other factor which makes it difficult to give reliable statistical data is that civilian and military activities overlap in many industries (see Table 5.12).

Table 5.12 *Share of military activities in selected industries*

	Percentage of military sales in the industry	Percentage of the industry in global military sales
Nuclear	25	5
Aerospace	52	32
Electronics	12	33
Metalworking	1	15
Others (chem. etc)	—	15
Total	100	100

Source: Délégation Générale pour l'Armement.

The main characteristic of the sector is its high level of concentration: 13 contractors perform 90 percent of the programmes,[31] 10 producers are responsible for 85 percent of the global output of the sector and 60 percent of French forces procurement (the similar proportion in the

USA is only one-third). In 1988, the 'aeronautics, shipbuilding and arms' industry represented only 0.5 percent of French facilities (1697 out of 3 422 858), but 7 percent of those employing more than 2000 people (16 out of 237).

The arms production complex includes an elaborate network of approximately 5000 private firms, nationalized enterprises and state-operated arsenals. Part of it was nationalized after 1981, when the practices of the left came to power, but came back to the private sector during the 'cohabitation' of a socialist president and a Gaullist prime minister between 1986 and 1988.[32]

In spite of this strong concentration, the size of the arms firms is relatively small (see Table 5.13): in 1987, in terms of sales, the biggest arms firm (Thomson-CSF) was 5.5 times smaller than the first industrial firm (Renault) and the fifth arms firm (Matra) 18 times smaller than the fifth industrial firm (Peugeot). The sector is dominated by three main firms: Thomson-CSF (electronics, missiles), Aérospatiale (missiles, spacecraft, helicopters) and Dassault-Aviation (aircraft), but the ranking of the firms according to their size has changed over time. While the development of some of them was based on internal resources (AMD-BA, Turbomeca), others emphasized external growth through purchases and sales (Thomson, Matra). New firms have also appeared, such as Sextant Avionique, which gathered electronics activities of Thomson CSF and Aérospatiale.

As indicated above, French defence firms are characterized by a strong overlapping of military and civilian activities. In the aerospace industry, for instance, Aérospatiale produces military plane and helicopters (*Gazelle, Puma, Superfrelon*) as well as rockets and missiles (*Exocet, AS 30*), but it also produces *Airbus* and spacecraft. The same is true of Dassault, which produces the *Falcon* civilian plane as well as heads for anti-air missiles, the *Mirage, Alpha-Jet* and the *Rafale*. In the power plant branch, Snecma makes high-power civil and military turbojets, Turbomeca small and medium-power turbines, Microturbo low-power jets for light aircrafts and missiles, SEP booster rockets for missiles, satellites and space vehicles, etc.

Aerospace is clearly an industry whose military component is crucial, but the situation is similar in other sectors. In electronics, Thomson produces military systems and missiles but also chips, computers, white goods, televisions and telephones. Matra has activities in space, telecommunications, computers and cars as well as in transport (underground) systems.

Table 5.13   Ranking of the first nine French arms firms, by military sales (FF billions)

1977	1987
1. Aérospatiale (6.2)	1. Thomson-CSF (21)
2. AMD-BA (5.2)	2. Aérospatiale (16.1)
3. Thomson-CSF (2.85)	3. AMD-BA (10.3)
4. Snecma (1.8)	4. Matra (4.9)
5. Matra (1.0)	5. Snecma (3.6)
6. SNPE (0.65)	6. ESD (2.8)
7. ESD (0.62)	7. SNPE (1.7)
8. Turbomeca (0.44)	8. Turbomeca (1.4)
9. SAGEM (0.36)	9. SAGEM (1.4)

Source: J.P. Hébert (1991), *Stratégie française et industrie d'armement*, Paris: FEDN, p. 235. (Non-consolidated data.)

As for industries, it is difficult to determine the share of military activities for each firm. Not only is this share unstable over time, owing to attempts at diversification, changing company strategies and restructuring processes, but it might differ in some firms depending on whether one considers sales of the parent company or sales of the consolidated group. This leads to important discrepancies in data, as shown in Table 5.14.

A third characteristic of military firms and industries is their high technological level. While defence industries contribute only 2 percent to GDP, their contribution to domestic R&D is 18 percent. This is the result of a policy which has always identified military activities and technological excellence: even though the arms sector represents less than 10 percent of manufacturing production and 20 percent of exports, it receives more than 90 percent of public subsidies to industrial research. As a consequence, most French technological leaders are firms which have military activities (see Table 5.15).

Table 5.14 Main French arms producers: share of military activities (percent)

	1977	1987	1988
Thomson-CSF	47	77	94
DCN[1]	100	100	100
Aérospatiale	65	65	49
AMD-BA[2]	91	66	86
CEA[3]	—	—	30
GIAT[4]	100	100	100
Matra	50 (in 1979)	—	33
SNECMA[5]	79	38	20
ESD[6]	86	76	80
SAGEM[7]	40	66	30
SNPE[8]	61	25	69
Turbomeca	47	64	—

Notes:
1. DCN: Direction des Constructions Navales.
2. AMD-BA: Avions Marcel Dassault – Bréguet Aviation.
3. CEA: Commissariat à l'Energie Atomique.
4. GIAT: Groupement Industriel des Armements Terrestres.
5. SNECMA: Sociëté Nationale d'Etudes et de Construction de Moteurs.
6. ESD: Electronique Serge Dassault.
7. SAGEM:
8. SNPE: Société Nationale de Propulsion.

Sources: For 1977 and 1987, parliamentary data; for 1988, *Le Monde*, 10 June 1989. (Non-consolidated data.)

The fourth striking feature of the arms sector is the strong division of labour between firms and industries. The prime contractor realizes generally less than 30 percent of the value-added of a large programme and the rest is distributed among numerous suppliers and subcontractors. In the *Mirage 2000* programme, the two prime contractors are Dassault (AMD-BA) for the airframe and SNIAS for the engine, but Thomson-CSF (radar equipment), Matra (missiles), GIAT (guns) and more than one hundred other companies are also participating. This interdependence has of course a negative multiplier effect in the event of restrictions of activity. According to some estimates, any single job

Table 5.15   The top 25 French R&D performers, 1986 (FF millions)

Rank	Firm	Activity	R&D expenditures
1	*Thomson*	Electronics	7800
2	*Aérospatiale*	Aeronautics	7300
3	CGE	Energy-Communic.	5500
4	*Snecma*	Aeronautics	3555
5	Renault	Automotives	3550
6	Rhône-Poulenc	Chemicals	2950
7	PSA	Automotives	2700
7	Elf Aquitaine	Energy	2700
9	Michelin	Tyres	2330
10	Bull	Computers	1840
11	Philips	Electronics	1530
12	*Matra*	Electr.-Transp.	1500
13	Roussel-Uclaf	Pharm.	1180
14	Sanofi	Pharm.	1100
15	Saint Gobain	Chemicals	995
15	L'Oréal	Chemicals	995
17	SAT	Telecomm.	800
18	Usinor-Sacilor	Steel	730
19	Péchiney	Metal	720
20	Total	Energy	670
21	*Dassault-Electronique*	Electronics	640
22	L'Air Liquide	Chemicals	620
23	Valéo	Autom. Equip.	470
24	CFD Chimie	Chemicals	370
25	Charbonnages de France	Energy	330

Note: Military firms are in italics.

Source: Le Monde, 17 November 1987.

lost by a prime contractor is accompanied by the suppression of two jobs in equipment manufacturers and subcontractors.

The last important characteristic of the arms sector is the weight of exports, which represent between 35 percent and 40 percent of the sales. In aeronautics, the proportion is even higher (about 60 percent): fighter aircraft produced by Dassault, *Mirages, Alpha Jets,* helicopters and missiles produced by Aérospatiale are to be found all over the third world.

The French Trade in Arms

French arms industry is heavily dependent on arms exports, which are also a major component of the French foreign trade balance. In the early 1990s, they represented about 15 percent of capital goods exports and 5 percent of all French exports, while approximately 50 000 people (20 percent of military–industrial employment) were directly dependent on export orders.

Under de Gaulle, when the nuclear burden left reduced domestic resources to support conventional weapons systems, arms sales 'tous azimuts' were seen as a solution. In the 1970s, France became the third largest exporter of weapons (the first on a per capita basis), with a share in total arms exports to the third world which reached 10 percent in the early 1980s. The rate of growth was 13 percent per year in the 1970s, 8 percent in the first half of the 1980s. By the mid-1980s, France was exporting considerably more major weapons than any other West European country with a comparable arms industry, 90 percent of exports going to third world countries. This growth was fuelled both by the wish of recipient countries for independence from superpower domination and the increase in income for some of them, especially the oil-rich Middle East countries. In spite of the election campaign announcements of the Socialist and Communist Parties, military exports remained unaffected by the 1981 elections.

French arms exports have always been strongly promoted, supported and controlled by successive governments, which have to grant licences for the export of everything classified as 'war material'. Final responsibility lies with the prime minister, who is advised by an ad hoc committee which includes representatives from the defence, foreign, economic and budget ministries, in close cooperation with the DGA and its International Affairs Directorate (DAI) from the first stage of contacts until final delivery.

While French manufacturers may negotiate on their own, there are a number of ways in which the DAI and other state organizations support arms exports, from the arms *attachés* in French embassies abroad to the coordination of all information and its transmission to the arms producers. The state also backs up export risks through the state-owned Foreign Trade Insurance Company (COFACE), while companies can apply for financial support to the government's Foreign Trade Bank (BFCE). There are also a number of specialized marketing companies which are fully or partly state-owned (OGA and OFEMA for aerospace products, SOFEMA for ground material, SOFREXAN for naval material).[33] The DGA helps firms to get loans, either from commercial banks backed up by COFACE or directly from the government. The BFCE and COFACE also renegotiate foreign military debts, as they did with Iraq.[34]

An important element of French sales strategy is the combination of arms deliveries with the training of personnel, either in France or by French military personnel or arms contractors in the recipient country. To this must be added the delivery of spare parts and repairs by specialized state-run companies (OGEMA and OGA in the case of aircraft). The French arms marketing system has been changed and expanded several times. More emphasis was put on coordinating sales between the armed forces and arms-producing companies when Giscard d'Estaing came to power in 1973. After 1981, the Mitterrand government strengthened the training and after-sales elements.

Recipient patterns also have changed over time. In the early 1960s, Israel was the most important customer for French weapons. After the embargo on arms exports to Israel in 1967, arms exporters turned to Arab countries.[35] Libya, Iraq, Algeria and, later, Saudi Arabia and Syria became the most important customers of the French arms industry (from 1971 to 1975, Libya was the second largest customer with 16 percent of French arms exports; from 1981 to 1985, Iraq was the first, with 21 percent of the total sales).

Another important early customer was South Africa. After the 1963 UN arms embargo, France became South Africa's main supplier and, between 1971 and 1975, South Africa was France's main customer with a quarter of French exports, until it eventually succumbed to the mandatory embargo in 1977. France also became a major supplier to Latin America after the USA tried to limit arms exports to the continent in the late 1960s. The first jet fighters delivered to South America were French *Mirages* sold in 1969–70.

France's position as an arms supplier was strengthened by the ups and downs of the arms exports policies of the superpowers, as well as the performance of French weapons in wars (such as the sinking of British warships in the Falklands War by French *Exocet* missiles). Although the Gulf War was a relatively negative shop window for French military technologies, Taiwan, the United Arab Emirates and Saudi Arabia are now becoming major customers. However, French arms exports began to decline even before the Gulf War, as shown in Tables 5.16 and 5.17. The decrease after 1986 reflected both the loss of purchasing power of France's traditional customers and the growing international competition: the world arms market is no longer flourishing as it was in the 1970s, owing to the growing indebtedness of the third world, the entry of new dynamic competitors on international markets and the end of the cold war.

The deterioration of the arms trade balance (see Table 5.18) is not just due to the fall of exports, but also to the sharp rise of imports, which represented FF1 billion per year in the 1970s, 5 billion in the early 1980s, 9.2 billion in 1988 and 13.5 billion in 1989. This increase reflects not only the fact that more weapons are bought abroad (like AWACS and US C130 aeroplanes, Spanish CASA aeroplanes and so on), but also the increasing dependence of French weapons upon foreign intermediate components. According to some estimates, induced imports of intermediate goods represent in the case of military goods 31.5 percent of the value of exports, while they represent 27.1 percent in the case of civil goods.[36] The consequence is not just economic but also political, in the view of the alleged French policy of 'national independence'.

Table 5.16   Arms exports as a percentage of arms sales

1986	1988	1990	1992
40	33	31	25

Source: DGA.

Table 5.17   Defence exports as a share of total exports (percent)

1978	1980	1982	1984	1986	1988
5.01	4.78	4.57	4.93	5.08	3.83

Source: DGA.

Table 5.18   Balance of French arms trade (FF billions)

	1980	1982	1984	1986	1988	1990
Current	16.3	20.1	31.7	34.1	24.5	27.3
Constant	31.8	36.4	39.2	37.1	25.2	27.3

Note: (FF constant 1993)
Source: DGA.

The economic significance of the balance itself has been questioned, since it does not take into account the whole range of expenditures which have been necessary in order to make the arms sales possible. Besides induced imports of intermediate goods, two other factors are likely to modify the economic impact of arms exports. One has to do with the 'compensations' granted to the client country in order to induce it to buy;[37] the other is linked to public subsidies either to the buyer or to the seller. It has been argued that, if all these factors were taken into account, the macroeconomic benefits would appear much smaller.

DISARMAMENT AND CONVERSION ISSUES

National and Macroeconomic Aspects

France's military expenditure have not been immediately reduced in the same proportion as in the United States, Germany or the United Kingdom. Reductions have taken place essentially in real terms: maintaining the 1993 equipment budget at the 1992 level (FF103 billion) meant in real terms a reduction of 3 percent. According to DGA estimates, an increase of 2–2.5 percent per year would be necessary to maintain full employment in French arms industries.

As far as employment is concerned, the most immediate consequence of the new situation was a drastic reduction in military forces, the most important since the post-Algerian War period, when 290 000 soldiers were returned to civilian life over two years (between 1963 and 1965).[38] After 1976, the decrease was 5700 per year.[39] The objective put forward in the 1989 *Armées 2000* plan was to remove 35 000 people from the army in five years, but this long-term trend was drastically accelerated. The official objective is now to reduce the army from 280 000 in 1992 to 225 000 people by 1997 (72 000 professionals, 38 000 volunteers and 115 000 conscripts, to which must be added 30 500 *civilian* employees). During the same period, the air force and the navy will lose between 5 percent and 10 percent of their personnel.

In addition to the reduction of people working *in* the army, the number of those working directly and indirectly *for* the army will be reduced, since French military industries are suffering from huge excess capacity. According to DGA estimates, between 100 000 and 150 000 jobs will be directly affected in the next few years. Estimates of the *Commissariat au Plan* are for between 58 000 and 132 000 in five years. Just to compare, the automotive industry, which drastically reduced its workforce in the 1980s, lost 'only' 86 000 jobs in 10 years.

It is difficult to assess the final impact of these cuts on global employment and welfare. At the macro level, the main economic and social problem of the 1990s is the high level of unemployment (more than three million people in France in 1993 – 10 percent of the total workforce) and its apparent insensitiveness to any type of macro measures. Although military unemployment is only part of this global problem, it has particularly important macro-qualitative aspects, since it implies the social loss of intellectual and scientific competencies which are incorporated in the high-level skilled scientists, engineers and technicians working for the military. This loss, however, is not considered by governments as a political priority (perhaps because engineers do not demonstrate violently in the street like farmers or lorry drivers).

In public, officials are very optimistic and claim that it will be possible to reduce employment progressively thanks to increased arms exports and retirement schemes. Conversely, French producers explain that the reduction of national orders has a 'dissuasive effect' on foreign markets.[40] They prefer lobbying very strongly in order to increase domestic orders to undertaking conversion efforts. This attitude is shared by most unions,[41] whose reactions have been exceptionally moderate. The green parties are the only political parties which officially deplore arms sales, especially to undemocratic countries.

Local and Microeconomic Aspects

Cuts in military forces have been accompanied by a far-reaching process of restructuring. Dissolution of regiments, closures and transfers of bases and defence premises, concentration in fewer locations of troops and materials are expected to affect directly 29 000 people (24 000 soldiers, including 16 000 conscripts, and 5 000 civilians employed by the army) and 97 cities, among which four in Germany.[42] In 1992 alone, 75 bases and 93 defence premises were closed down or merged throughout France. Another one hundred military sites are involved. Several regiments have been or will be dissolved in Germany and in the north and east of France, and several bases closed in the east, south and west of the country. Planes and ships are also concentrated in fewer locations. The most affected areas are Picardy, Alsace, Provence, Brittany and Corsica. In the city of Altkirch in Alsace, for instance, 20 percent of the population is directly employed by the army. No elected representatives have been associated with the decisions, which were locally very unpopular.

The regional impact of defence industries must also be underlined. Of the 254 000 people employed in 1991 by prime contractors, 92 000 worked in the Paris region, 162 000 in the rest of the country. Although the arms industries are located all over the country, except in those areas near the northern and eastern borders which were historically the most threatened, their higher concentration in some specific regions make particular areas highly dependent on them. In four French regions – Aquitaine, Ile de France, Provence–Côte d'Azur and Brittany – direct employment linked to military industrial activities exceeds 10 percent of industrial employment. It even exceeds 20 percent in four *départements* (Var, Cher, Hautes Pyrénées and Finistère) where more than one industrial job in two depends on the arms industry.

A particularly localized industry is the aerospace industry, which employs very highly skilled people in its ultra-modern plants of the Paris region and the south-west of France. Vélizy near Paris, a high-tech military pole, used to experience an exceptionally low rate of unemployment which is now expected to increase tremendously. In the Aquitaine area, almost 30 000 people are employed by Aérospatiale, SEP, SNPE, Dassault, Thomson, Sextant Avionique, CEA and so on. If aerospace is principally located in the south-west of France, electronics is concentrated in the Paris region and shipbuilding in Normandy, Brittany and on the Riviera.

Local employment problems are made worse when military industries are located in backward industrial areas: the difficulties of arms industries add to already existing industrial difficulties. This localization in poor areas is often the experience of producers of traditional Fordist-type military goods (tanks, ammunitions, ships and so on). GIAT Industries, for instance (tanks, turrets and ammunition), is mainly located in the Massif Central or the Pyrenean region; naval dockyards are settled in Cherbourg, Brest, Lorient and Toulon.

In the city of Roanne, where the rate of unemployment is already more than 10 percent (because of the bankruptcy of many textiles and metalworking firms), the arsenal belonging to GIAT Industries produced 458 tanks and employed 3500 people in 1978, but only produced 120 tanks and employed 2450 people in 1991. This arsenal, whose production is 100 percent military, represents 10 percent of the city's direct industrial employment – 20 percent if one adds employment in mechanics, electricity or electronics. It has been estimated that 100 *Leclerc* tanks would have to be produced annually to maintain the current level of employment in the factory. The French army ordered 16 in 1989, 10 in 1990, 12 in 1991, 30 in 1992 and, in spite of sales of *Leclerc* tanks to Abu Dhabi and prospects of sales to Saudi Arabia, Qatar and Sweden, the plant is expected to lose half of its employees in five years. The same situation is found in the other GIAT locations in Saint Etienne, Tarbes, Tulle, Bourges and Toulouse

In spite of this disastrous situation, very few local initiatives have been taken. In November 1992, the Aquitaine local authorities organized a regional conference on conversion in Bordeaux and brought together industrialists, unionists, representatives, academics and researchers. If the *Conseil Régional d'Aquitaine* decided to devote funds to help 'changes in the defence industry of aeronautics and space' this was a rather isolated initiative.

Conversion Policies

The concept of 'conversion policy' is quite ambiguous since, under the Fifth Republic, military production has been considered an activity for which France has 'peculiar powers bestowed by nature' – to use Ricardo's terms – given the country's industrial habits, structures and traditions. This privileged situation was justified on behalf of three alleged specificities of defence industries: their strategic role, their specific technological and financial needs and their positive economic impact. As one French minister put it, 'armaments programmes are the true locomotive of French economic development'.[43] It seems, however, that even in France the period of unconditional state support for military industries is definitely over: not only must the country adapt to the rules of future European cooperation, but economic requirements call for more competition. While the most severe economic recession since World War Two slows the level of armed mobilization, strategic 'new realities' involve a restructuring and a recomposition of the military sector.

At the national level, the only concrete measures which have until now been taken aimed at facilitating the individual 'conversion' of military personnel and people working in the arsenals.[44] Financially, the reduction of the size of the armed forces will probably not provide any immediate 'peace dividends', because of the obsolescence of actual materials, the increase in the cost of equipment imposed by the technological mutation, the financial estate and property needs created by geographic restructuring and the necessity to revalorize wages in the forces.

The military–industrial conversion problem has until now been treated essentially as any other industrial redeployment problem. In a macroeconomic context where more than 100 000 jobs are eliminated every year, while there is a drastic increase in the number of areas which are faced with serious employment difficulties, priority has been given to the already existing institutional framework. This includes public services like the DATAR (*Délégation à l'Aménagement du Territoire et à l'Action Régionale*) in charge of local development. Indeed, the term 'conversion' has been used for a long time without any particular military connotation.[45] The main problem, nevertheless, is a lack of quantitative and qualitative means, even though, in 1992, a venture capital fund of FF700 million was created in order to help firms to restructure and diversify.

There are two important differences between military industries and traditional industries like textiles, steel, coal or shipbuilding, which have confronted excess capacity and loss of markets in the past to the benefit of more competitive or innovative competitors. The first is public interventionism, which must be excluded since its main effect was precisely to keep firms alive artificially. The second is technological sophistication, which creates serious problems of dead loss in terms of technical skills and intellectual investment. This risk of dead loss is probably the most decisive argument in favour of conversion policies, since actively promoting radical qualitative changes linked to disarmament is certainly more effective in minimizing the loss than passively allowing the sector to proceed to a reluctant adaptation. Only the development of new goods and services will allow skills which have become redundant to be 'reinjected' into the economy. A way of doing this would be the development of big civilian projects. Some possibilities exist in the fields of energy, environment, telecommunications or transport, where potential demand is still important. Another promising field is linked to the widening of the notion of 'security', which could include non-military 'threats' such as accidents or pollution. One can imagine much more 'voluntarist' policies in this field.

Even though France has been much more successful in terms of economic and social achievements than the ex-socialist countries from Eastern Europe, it has many similarities with them. One may find it rather strange, after all, that in a Western country like France, when a MP writes (in 1993) that in the French economy 'the military sector conditions the existence of the civilian one',[46] he does not consider the situation as unfortunate. Quite the contrary: he blames the UK, Germany and the USA for having reduced their military programmes.

Independent of public action, there are also private companies specializing in industrial conversion (through re-employment and reindustrialization).[47] They are often professional subsidiary companies or branches of big firms.[48] As far as individual or local attempts at conversion are concerned, there may be wide variations from one firm to another and from one region to another, but one can nevertheless present some general features. At the firm level, two different types of reaction are observed. On the one hand, big contractors typically focus on the best way to preserve their technological edge while waiting for an eventual new boom in military activity. Their preoccupations are more than ever productivity, exports, alliances and diversification. On the other hand, their suppliers wonder how they will survive, since they are woefully lacking in the financial resources necessary to support R&D and diversify. Altogether, there is no real conversion process, even if some try to diversify and to increase their civil goods production. SNPE, for instance, became the world leader in fingernail enamel. Other firms try to restructure and specialize even more, with the aim of improving their position in the international division of labour. The main obsession of all firms is to survive until a recovery of export markets owing to the cyclical renewal of some armaments.

CONCLUSIONS

After the cold war it became difficult for France to keep simultaneously a national arms industry, strategic and pre-strategic nuclear weapons, a navy organized around nuclear aircraft carriers, 350 fighter planes with a range of 1000 km, a professional 'Rapid Intervention Force', a corps of 800 modern tanks, general conscription and 45 000 soldiers maintained permanently abroad while developing the new flexible and sophisticated weapons which French officials believe are necessary in the new situation.

Although a new strategic doctrine has not yet been elaborated, the reduction of the risk of a major East–West confrontation and the increased possibility of new types of conflicts has until now led French authorities to promote an adaptation rather than a reduction of military-linked activities. The initial consequences of the new situation have been major cuts in manpower and equipment in the French armed forces which have closed many military bases and sites, and a major restructuring process in French military industries. The objectives of this restructuring are manifold: reducing the format of the industry in order to fit the new dimension of the market; reorienting the 'technical–military style' in order to adapt to the new strategic situation; increasing specialization in the perspective of the new European division of labour; fostering greater industrial cooperation with foreign suppliers; and maintaining a technological edge. In this context, 'civilianization' of the activities of military firms appears more a way for military firms to 'catch up' with the new technology and become more efficient in military production than a real change of orientation.

Job losses are a direct consequence of financial constraints affecting all activities associated with the military (armed forces, military bases and arsenals, industrial and research facilities linked to defence, and so on), but they are also the price to be paid for modernization and rationalization in a sector where state support has delayed necessary adjustments for too long and which has become largely obsolescent with the end of the East–West confrontation. Many French defence analysts believe that France could and should go much further in manpower and procurements cuts, even though this would increase unemployment, which is already a major social and political problem.

NOTES

1. The domestic political importance of nuclear weapons is associated with an exaggerated perception of France's influence: when 72 percent of French people who were questioned in a poll in February 1991 considered France a 'great power', 62 percent of US, 70 percent of British and 55 percent of German people thought the reverse to be true.
2. Charles de Gaulle (1935), *Vers l'armée de métier.*
3. 'There is no question of shutting down the French deterrent because dangers still exist objectively, even if they may seem politically implausible,' said then French Minister of Defence, Joxe. 'There is a gigantic nuclear arsenal sitting quite close to us in the former Soviet Union – Ukraine alone currently possesses more nuclear weapons than France and Britain combined – while political instability in Eastern Europe could hold dangers for the West.'
4. French Defence Minister Chevènement, who resigned just before the military operations began, was the chairman of the Franco–Iraqi Friendship Association.
5. AMX 30 tanks were one generation older than US *Abrams* or UK *Challenger* tanks. *Jaguar* planes could not fly at night and their power was much less than other planes. Mirage 2000s had too short a range and were designed for low-altitude attacks (when the planes had to fly above 10,000 feet in order to avoid the Iraqi air defence). The only thing which turned out to be really useful was the *Orchidée* heliported radar, whose project had just been officially cancelled. Its sole prototype had to be sent hastily to the Gulf area.
6. Conscripts have been excluded from military overseas interventions since the end of the Algerian War.
7. A serious obstacle is that ending conscription would release 156 000 young people onto the employment market.
8. Originally created by the right (in 1798), conscription became only tardily an idea of the left. It was given up during most of the 19th century, re-established in 1872, and generalized only after 1905. In his book, *Vers l'armée de métier* (1935), de Gaulle advocated its abandonment, but he maintained it after he came to power.
9. On the other hand, in May 1992, while 72 percent of people were 'in favour of a professional army', 60 percent declared that 'France could not correctly secure its security without conscription' (Poll SOFRES-BVA, quoted by SIRPA)!
10. In fact, France had already engaged in bilateral or multilateral cooperation, especially in 'European' projects: the Franco–German *Tiger* helicopter, the NH90 transport helicopter with Germany, the Netherlands and Italy, the *Cobra* radar and anti-tank missiles with Germany and the UK, the *Helios* observation satellite with Spain and Italy. The *Leclerc* tank was initially a Franco–German joint project and

the *Rafale* a Franco-British project before, respectively, Germany and Britain pulled out.

11. It became politically impossible to cancel this last aircraft carrier after its name was purposely changed.

12. Germany was always strongly opposed to the development of these 480 km range missiles with a possible neutronic charge. The Hades project originally included 60 launchers and 120 missile units. It was officially and definitively interrupted in June 1992 after 11 billion francs had been spent on it. In fact, French officials admitted that the programme had gone on secretly.

13. As well as their strengthening with heavy armour in anticipation of a Gulf conflict-style scenario.

14. The gathering of all French 'projection' resources in Toulon appears to reflect the conviction that the major threats to French interests would come from North Africa or the Middle East.

15. In 1963, just after the Algerian War, France devoted 6 percent of its GDP to defence.

16. It represented more than 50 percent of public expenditures before 1914.

17. The budget devoted to wages increased by 4.82 percent in 1993, which means, if one takes job cuts into account, a real increase of 5.52 percent since 1992. The French army, which is still based on conscription, is nevertheless not as expensive as professional armies (20 percent less expensive than the British army, whose personnel are half as numerous).

18. It is difficult to compare successive budgets, since equipment credits may be different from equipment expenditures. In 1993, for instance, equipment expenditures (available credits) only amounted to FF97.5 billion.

19. Including the *Tiger* helicopter, an anti-tank missile of the third generation and so on whose aim is to transform in depth the operation and organization of the land forces through the use of huge networks of telecommunications.

20. Jean-Paul Hébert (1991), *Stratégie française et industrie d'armement*, Paris: Fondation pour les Etudes de la Défense Nationale, La Documentation Française, pp. 113–42.

21. Electronics represents, for instance, 60 percent of the cost of the *Leclerc* tank.

22. The inertia of the so-called 'big programmes' is such that their total cancellation is almost inconceivable. See François Chesnais and Claude Serfati (1992), *L'armement en France, genèse, ampleur et coût d'une industrie*, Paris: Nathan.

23. The French minister of defence manages simultaneously more than one hundred different programmes in the nuclear, ballistic, space and classical fields.

24. The telecommunications satellite, *Syracuse*, is an example. *Helios* (optical observation), *Osiris* (radar) and *Zenon* (receiver) programmes must also be mentioned. 25. The most drastic manpower cuts had taken place in land forces: French regiments had become the equivalents of batallions in other countries; divisions were just slightly reinforced brigades.

26. See E.A. Kolo-dziej (1987), *Making and Marketing Arms: The French Experience and its Implications for the International System*, Princeton: Princeton V.P.

27. As late as 1985, a poll showed that two-thirds of French students had a favourable opinion of arms sales.

28. Pierre Papon (1978), *Le pouvoir et la science en France*, Paris: Le Centurion; Patrick Cohendet and André Lebeau (1987), *Choix stratégiques et grands programmes civils*, Paris: Economica; Jean-Jacques Salomon (1985), *Le Gaulois, le Cow-Boy et le Samouraï*, Paris: Economica; Pierre Dussauge (1985), *L'industrie française de l'armement*, Paris: Economica; Elie Cohen (1989), *L'Etat brancardier*, Paris: Calmann-Lévy.

29. One generally estimates that, while in the 'real' arms sector aerospace represents 34 percent, electronics 29 percent and ship or land transport 28 percent of total production, in the so-called 'aeronautics, shipbuilding and arms' industry, aeronautics accounts for 75 percent, shipbuilding for 15 percent and weapons for 10 percent of total production. These sectoral data are nevertheless very useful for comparisons

over time, especially for those 'classical' arms products which are most threatened by actual cuts.

30. Other characteristics are the high level of financial overheads, twice as high as in the rest of manufacturing industry (7.3 percent of sales and 16.8 percent of value-added against 3.5 percent and 9.8 percent) and of indebtedness. The 'results' indicators are also below average.

31. The list includes Aérospatiale, Alcatel, CEA, Dassault Aviation, Dassault Electronique, DCN (*Direction des Constructions navales*), Eurocopter, GIAT Industries, Matra défense espace, Sagem, Sextant Avionique, SNECMA and Thomson CSF.

32. See Jean Paul Hébert (1991), *Stratégie française*, pp. 213–55.

33. In some cases, the different organizations specialize in different countries; for example, on the Indian subcontinent, OGA covers Pakistan and Bangladesh while OFREMA is responsible for India.

34. Iraq's debt to France was FF25 billion (excluding interest) just before the Gulf War, FF14 billion of which was due to military supplies.

35. Relations between France and Israel cooled after the war of 1967, but the embargo was respected after French weapons delivered for defensive purposes were used in an attack on Beirut.

36. J. Aben (1984), 'Les socialistes français face au problème des exportations d'armes', in *Social-démocratie et défense en Europe*, IPIE, Paris X, Nanterre.

37. In the case of the sale of *Leclerc* tanks to the Emirates, for instance, 60 percent of the money has to be invested in local 'development projects' aimed at transferring military technology.

38. In 1962, the French army had 721 000 men. It was reorganized after the Algerian War: an army with large battalions was turned into a smaller, more mechanized force, better able to fight in Europe under a nuclear threat.

39. Both professionals and conscripts, 80 percent of which from the land forces.

40. Successive French governments were very sensitive to this argument.

41. While the traditionally anti-communist FO (Force Ouvrière) and the communist CGT are strongly opposed to any change, the social-democratic CFDT (Confédération Française du Travail) and the managerial CGC (Confédération Générale des Cadres) are more prepared to accept a restructuring process and a diversification based on high-level skills.

42. Besides the more distant impact, like that of Mururoa.

43. Minister of Defence Giraud in a speech to the Parliament in 1987, quoted in François Chesnais (1990), *Compétitivité internationale et dépenses militaires*, Paris: Economica.

44. State workers employed in the arsenals have a privileged status compared with workers in 'normal' defence industrial firms like, for instance, Matra, Thomson or Sextant Avionique. It gives them the right to be re-employed by local administrations. As a result, a double labour market is developing in sensitive areas. The most disadvantaged workers are those who are employed by subcontractors, since the first measure in the event of cuts is the reintegration by the prime contractor of activities which it had previously subcontracted: these workers have no future in defence and no priority for re-employment.

45. DATAR vocabulary includes terms like 'conversion sites' or conversion poles' which have an absolutely general meaning.

46. René Galy-Dejean, 'La crise des industries de défense', Rapport d'information, Assemblée nationale, 5 October 1993.

47. The Ministry of Industry gives direct subsidies to investment, but the main structure is the DATAR (Délégation à l'Aménagement du Territoire et à l'Action Régionale), which specializes in both regional interventions and collective actions.

48. Charbonnages de France (coal) and Saint Gobain (glass and chemicals), for instance, have their own conversion companies. Another one exists in steel (*Société de Redéploiement Sidérurgique*). Elf Aquitaine (oil) created a conversion company when Pyrenean gas came to exhaustion. Altogether, there are a dozen of them including one belonging to Thomson.

6. Germany

Ulrich Albrecht and Petra Opitz

The great upheavals of 1989–90 which marked the end of the cold war and the opening of a new era in European politics benefited Germans in particular. The main accomplishment for them remains unification into one German state – a situation which, since the Middle Ages, they had enjoyed for a mere 75 years, a period marked by two world wars and the crimes of National Socialism. Thus Europeans are faced with the question, which course will the new Germany take? This question is crucial to understanding the post-cold war period.

Germans have also profited greatly from the new European security situation. Before the fall of the Berlin Wall, the two military blocs massed their troops and armour on the soil of the two Germanys, pitted against each other, armed to the teeth with nuclear and chemical weapons. The two German states enjoyed the dubious distinction of being the most heavily militarized regions on earth, on any count. The 'Western Group of Soviet Forces' in the former GDR fielded eight tank divisions and eight motorized rifle divisions against the West, supported by nine fighter regiments and eight air regiments for ground attack, armed with nuclear missiles including modern SS-23 weapons. The American counterweight was no less formidable, provided by the V and VII Corps of the US Army, which with reference to its enormous nuclear arsenal was called 'hell on wheels', supported by two air divisions of the US Air Force. The British Army of the Rhine and the French forces, both of which were equipped with nuclear weapons, together with Belgium, Canadian and Dutch forces, combined with the 500 000 Bundeswehr troops to stem a potential attack from the East. And the Germans knew that World War Three would be fought on their soil, very likely with nuclear exchanges. Exercises for American field officers ended in the (theoretical) firing of dozens of atomic warheads.[1] By now this awesome threat has evaporated. Germany today is, according to the minister of defence, surrounded by countries with which it is either allied or friendly. The former great antagonist, Russia, is desperately seeking German support for the gargantuan task of reconstructing a society of some 200 million people. There is virtually no

117

external threat to the country, a situation perfectly new and beyond all historical experience.

There is apparently no institutionalized way to find a new defence doctrine and to redirect the military establishment accordingly. The minister of defence made a basic proposal in early 1992 which did not find much support. Thus the Federal armed forces were in the position of defining for themselves their future role. The *Heeresstruktur 5* (Army structure 5) which evolved ends the nuclear role of the German army. The air force will retain three *Tornado* squadrons for nuclear missions and expects the introduction of the new W89 warhead. In general, the Bundeswehr is going to be divided into a relatively small permanent force using advanced equipment, and a main contingent of reserve forces, taking advantage of greatly extended warning times in an emergency. This reflects the basic NATO categories of highly mobile Reaction Forces, Main Defence Forces and Augmentation Forces.

The Bundeswehr is eager to participate in future UN combat missions 'on an equal footing' and expects the removal of the constitutional barriers which stand against deployment 'out of area' of the North Atlantic Treaty. The inspector general of the Bundeswehr, the highest-ranking German soldier, describes as main tasks 'peace-keeping' (*Friedensabsicherung*) with a view to instabilities in the former USSR, 'peace implementation' (*Friedensdurchsetzung*) with regard to Eastern Europe and 'peace enforcement' (*Friedenserzwingung*) in the third world.[2] In particular, the Bundesmarine has high hopes of developing into a blue-water navy according to these new concepts and the Luft-waffe is envisaging the requirement for long-range airlift capabilities – hitherto the Bundeswehr was restricted to the role of a home defence force with very limited possibilities of projecting power into other regions of the world.

The role of politics in this debate is currently restricted to sanctioning military planning. The position of the generals, that the German military would be an obvious choice when looking for forces to quell disturbances in Eastern Europe or in the third world, is questioned by the main parties. Political quarters in Bonn are preoccupied, in a situation of deep recession, by the economic consequences of the end of the East–West conflict. One is aware that the new Germany is being closely observed from the outside, and the fear of making mistakes adds to the indecisiveness and the tendency to muddle through which is so characteristic of the Kohl government. The Social Democrats, as the main opposition party, are internally split on whether they should support an expanded role for the Bundeswehr or stick to their traditional pacifist ideals.

Historically, there is nothing new in Germany in the reorientation from rearmament to demobilization, from a war-oriented economy to a predominantly civilian market and vice versa; marked shifts in the respective emphasis on military and non-military priorities in society are a customary part of German experience. Nevertheless, the present situation is in many ways unique; there is little in the accumulated historical experience of this country of relevance to the tasks Germany is now facing.

The international accords related to the unification of Germany entail the biggest reductions in armed forces on a given territory within a brief period ever agreed, opening up vast opportunities for conversion. The agreed reductions in manpower signal also a decrease in arms industry activities, conventionally seen as the core of the conversion issue. Before the 'change' (*die Wende*), the democratic revolution in East Germany, around 1.3 million men under arms were positioned in confrontation on the territory of the two German states. Altogether, almost one million troops from eight nations were to withdraw from Germany or be disbanded by the end of 1994, thereafter leaving 370 000 Bundeswehr soldiers plus an undisclosed number of (remaining) American troops. The details of this crude calculation are as follows. The 2+4 agreement regulating the international aspects of unification called for the withdrawal of the 338 000 troops of the so-called 'Western Group of Soviet Forces' by the end of 1994. Accordingly, the governments of France (52 700), the United Kingdom (67 200), Canada (7100), the Netherlands (5700) and Belgium (24 900) announced the withdrawal of their armed forces from German soil. The National People's Army of the defunct GDR disappeared, and some 45 000 of their strength of 193 000 were incorporated into the Bundeswehr. The level of cuts in the 242 000 US troops in Germany (mainly the V and VII Corps of the US Army and some 30 000 US Air Force personnel) remains somewhat open. It is generally assumed that the size of the US military presence will be around 100 000 troops in the future.

The reduction in troop numbers translates directly into deep cuts in the Bundeswehr arsenal. The Vienna Treaty requires that end-1990 stocks of the united Germany be reduced by 41 percent for main battle tanks (from 7075 to 4166), by 42 percent for artillery pieces (from 4639 down to 2705) and by a sensational 61 percent for armed personnel carriers (APCs) (from 8950 to 3446). The Luftwaffe is less affected: the number of combat aircraft, according to the treaty, is to be reduced by 14 percent (from 1050 to 900).[3] These figures certainly do not reflect general disarmament: after implementation, Germany still possesses the highest number of main battle tanks within NATO, and remains number two in amount of artillery (behind Turkey), and number three in the case of APCs (behind the USA and France). Yet, for the German arms industry, these figures signal that the Bundeswehr will not be in a position to acquire any armoured fighting vehicles for years to come, and that the aerospace sector also will face reductions. Thus a general slump in military contracts, and a harsh incentive towards conversion, might be expected.

In 1993, Defence Minister Rühe froze all new procurement until revised plans for a smaller Bundeswehr were elaborated. He had already announced in December 1992 that the procurement budget would be cut by $15.3 billion between 1994 and 2006. The cuts were necessary as this sector's contribution to reducing the growing public deficit arising from reunification.

The actual record of adaptation to these new conditions in Germany is very different in the 'old' FRG, the former Western half of the country, and in the new provinces in the East, the former GDR. Hence the following assessment follows the former division. Ulrich Albrecht treats conversion in the capitalist system of the FRG and Petra Opitz looks at transition in formerly state-socialist Eastern Germany.

THE CASE OF WEST GERMANY

Responses by Military Contractors

German arms markers report cuts in industrial activity that directly reflect reductions in the procurement budget. Krauss-Maffei, the leading producer of tanks, submitted the following data: in 1985, during the 'new cold war', military orders accounted for the employment of 33 percent of personnel. This share was expected to shrink to 20 percent by the end of 1993. In terms of turnover, Krauss-Maffei's military business will shrink from a peak of 77 percent in 1985 to a mere 33 percent in 1993.[4] Deutsche Aerospace, a firm owned by Daimler which has a monopoly in German military aviation, reported a loss in contract value of 43 percent in 1990, mainly caused by the slump in military business. In 1993, Deutsche Aerospace announced dramatic cuts. Out of a total of 80 000 workers in the German aviation industry 10 300 were to be made redundant, and six production locations scattered across the country closed down.

Moreover, industry is badly equipped to deal with these reductions at this juncture since the large procurement programmes of the last decade (*Leopard II* and *Tornado* serial production) are now coming to an end. Thus the German arms industry is currently wandering, according to a popular phrase, through a 'valley of tears'. German firms do not look for bold business strategies as they adjust to the decline in procurement orders. There is a general consensus that the size of the (by international comparison, relatively small) arms industry ought to be reduced. Out of the present 180 000 jobs in the hard core of the German armaments industry, it was estimated that 85 000 would be lost during the next decade.[5]

The first response by German armaments firms is reducing size mainly by making part of the workforce redundant. These moves are commonly shrouded in programmes aimed at improving efficiency, such as total quality management (TQM) and other improvement concepts. The companies' goal is to get more productivity out of a smaller workforce. The intention is to position the company to compete in more highly competitive markets after the introduction of the single European market. Thus Deutsche Aerospace announced that the cancellation of the European fighter aircraft order would mean a reduction of half of the workforce at the Messerschmitt plants in Augsburg and Manching of wartime fame.

A second key element in business strategies to address the slump in military contracts is concentration. The formation of one single aerospace company, Deutsche Aerospace (DASA), established a monopoly in German aeronautical production. Traditional firms such as Dornier were amalgamated with their arch rivals, MBB, under one of the top German companies, Daimler-Benz. In tank making, another mainstay of German military–industrial activities, less potent competitors sold out to companies keener to remain in the field (the traditional Krupp-MAD shop in Kiel, the last remaining tank-producing element in the Krupp conglomerate of the once world-famous arms-making firm, was traded to Rheinmetall, now the principal gunmakers for German tanks, and leaders in APC production in the country).

A third trend, international amalgamation of branches of hitherto national firms, reflects in part the first two approaches – reduction and concentration. There are initial indications of international mergers of the traditionally national tank makers: Daimler-Benz had contracted to develop light tanks in collaboration with the French firm of Panhard.[6] Peugeot, which owns both Panhard and the competitor Levassor, formed a new firm, Euro LAV, with a competitor, Rheinmetall, in order to produce light armoured vehicles. The creation of Eurocopter, the combination of all French and German helicopter activities in one firm, exceeds by far the customary moves of the past to build joint-sales firms (such as the notorious *Euromissile*, which contributed greatly to the

Middle East military build-up) or to farm out production, as with the Airbus consortium. That the economic impact of Eurocopter will be qualitatively different from such moves is a conviction held with particular firmness in Munich, also headquarters of MBB, the leading German helicopter firm.[7] The Munich city council is afraid of losing all helicopter work to France. The city, made the blossoming centre of German high-tech weaponry by Franz-Josef Strauss, is now facing the prospect of deindustrialization if the hoped-for orders for the European fighter aircraft (EFA) fail to materialize, helicopter business is moved to Toulouse, and tank making by Krauss-Maffei (to name only the general contractors) comes to an abrupt end.[8]

The employment effect of all of these three moves is generally a reduction in the number of jobs – the definition of becoming more competitive through collaboration or amalgamation is closely tied to cutting the new work units down to a 'manageable' or 'useful' size. It is difficult to obtain precise data in support of this argument. However, a rough comparison of the employment figures cited above with the overall jobs quoted for the newly-created firms gives an indication of general employment losses.

Because of redundancies and the general political problem spurred by higher levels of reduction, top managers are now publicly calling on the government to come in and assist them. DASA threatened 'mass redundancies', including closing down production sites, 'if the Federal Government fails to acknowledge its commitment to the European space programmes *Ariane 5*, *Columbus* and *Hermes*'.[9] DASA asked the Federal Government to increase spending on space activities by 12 percent per year until 2000, and thereafter to engage in manned space programmes.[10] Bonn's assistance is seen as vital if a decision is taken not to go ahead with the European fighter aircraft.

The big German aerospace employer, DASA, has some 46 percent of the workforce in military business, with 25 000 jobs. In the philosophy of the firm, job reductions in defence contracts are primarily achieved by natural wastage (this resulted in cutting 4000 jobs over two years). The time required to reorient the bulk of the workforce in new directions has been estimated at between five and 10 years. The company rejects the notion of conversion (an 'overloaded term') and prefers to speak about 'product substitution'. Thus the chief executive of DASA refers to the 'replacement of decreasing sales in defence technology by future-oriented civilian activities'.[11] Substitution actually means that former defence employees are not re-employed in alternative jobs. Rather, entirely new plants are erected, and a new workforce is hired, in order to expand into new businesses.[12]

Observers generally note that German industry is wary of the concept of conversion. 'Not a single board member turned for help to one of the many working groups on conversion that were especially created in university towns. Will these now disband?' asks a leading German periodical wryly.[13] Journalists noted that chief executives of Deutsche Aerospace persistently avoided the term 'conversion' despite pertinent questions during the main annual press conference of the company in 1991.[14]

The actual conversion substitution experience of German aerospace firms remains rather mixed. An effort to systematize experiments in medical technology was cancelled by Deutsche Aerospace after the loss of several hundred million Deutschmarks (resulting, as is internally conceded, from managerial mistakes: a revolutionary kidney stone-dispersing device developed by the venerable firm of Dornier has been badly marketed, and so on). The primary approach now is to build entirely new plants for alternative products, such as new plants for the *Airbus* range of transport planes. The firm thus profits from regional programmes to establish advanced industries (according to Deutsche Aerospace, altogether 1.8 billion Deutschmarks have been invested in company-owned funds to get the programme off the ground). After the failure of the programme in medical technology, Deutsche Aerospace is now investing DM350 million in a microelectronics subsidiary, which it hopes will lead to the creation of 4000 jobs with an annual turnover of DM2 billion. Employees of DASA, the firm suggests, are eligible for employment in the subsidiary, if they quality for these jobs. If not, they will be fired.

The new company remains remarkable on a number of counts, which all reflect novel managerial strategies to convert the heritage of military production to future civilian business. Along with DASA, Daimler-Benz has used another acquisition, the well-known AEG (among other things, one of the main producers of military radar sets), to 'father' the new company. Thus an initial corporate strategy is to use various former military facilities in order to develop promising civilian follow-up projects (instead of converting individual military production units, merely converting output). The AEG addition to the DASA investment adds up to a capital of DM600 million for the new firm.

Secondly, in order to get the new amalgamated firm running in 1993, Daimler-Benz was committed to purchasing 20 percent of its output (mainly electronic equipment for cars), thus feather-bedding the launch experiment. Besides such equipment, the new firm is divided into divisions for semiconductors, microsystems and 'special technology'; in Germany, this latter term has been a euphemism for military hardware since the days of the National Socialists. The target figures for actual sales reflect the conversion goal. 'Special technology' was earmarked to account for a mere 10 percent of turnover. The thrust items are semiconductors (one-quarter of sales) and electronic equipment for cars, the intimate Daimler-Benz interest. Thirdly, the European dimension of recent corporate strategies becomes apparent in the fact that AEG planned to use its shares in the French firm Matra MHS, Nantes, to increase the capital stocks of the new company.

There is a general tendency in the German industrial system to realign the principal makers of weapons platforms (combat aircraft are to be made by Deutsche Aerospace, while main battle tanks are Kraus-Maffei business, and warship making has also been left to one key contractor) with the biggest corporations in the national economy. Thus Daimler-Benz took over what is now Deutsche Aerospace and Siemens became a prime source of industrial activity in military electronics. German capital is eager to prepare for the big contest in the single European market, and the sluggish business in the armaments sector is not seen as creating a major obstacle in this strategy.

In the German arms sector, the reason for seeking alliances with the biggest firms in German industry was the need for capital. The challenges perceived as arising from the creation of the single European market and adjustment to decreased Bundeswehr orders, were understood to require, above all, capital. Yet absorption of former prime military contractors by the biggest German companies is not an easy operation. Participants in the process complain about the difficulty in assimilating a different corporate culture. The actual record of the swallowing of smaller traditional military producers by Daimler-Benz indicates many of the difficulties experienced in the transition of such firms to civilian markets. Daimler encountered problems in managing two 'systems' – one for its mainstay, common 'civilian' products such as cars and heavy-duty vehicles, and one for its aerospace divisions MBB and Dornier) with their traditional disregard for costs. The claim of the latter, that the transfer to commercial businesses of expertise gained under government contracts would contribute to diversification strategies and the business mix of the parent company, has yet to be borne out by experience.

One might think that the major companies in military production would have looked at ways they could use their skills to enter other markets, that is, conversion. But that was not the case. With a few notable exceptions, most officials and managers assumed that cuts in procurement would not affect their segment of activity significantly. Rather, they believed that the procurement sectors they did not serve would be affected most. Thus the aerospace company believes in the future of the European fighter aircraft, while shipbuilders envisage a need for a German blue-water navy for operations 'out of area'. The tank industry considered both aspirations as altogether illusory, at least as compared with the need for tanks.

The few exceptional companies maintain that they have identified commercial markets where their technologies have applications. They attempt to take advantage of this state of affairs by designing state-of-the-art products based on military ones. The prime objective, however, is normally labelled a 'side strategy'; learning from a commercial customer how to become more competitive. Generally, opportunities for diversification are evaluated on a case-by-case basis, as they are identified, and not in a systematic, concentrated manner. The government is still seen as a prime source of contracts, if not in the military field, then in civilian R&D and other categories of public spending.

In conclusion, very few companies in Germany have managed diversification strategies, let alone conversion. The real emphasis has been on reducing size, by a multitude of strategies, while maintaining levels of profitability. Compared with commercially oriented companies that are forced to react quickly to changing market conditions, German military prime contractors are sluggish in adapting and move at a very slow pace. They remain oriented towards serving one customer, the German federal government, now opting for non-military contracts offered by this source. This prevents them from easily moving into commercial work. Cleaning up the environment emerges as a top alternative to the military contracts of the past. Thus a former main military contractor is now developing bacteriological means to purify soil polluted by oil and diesel fuel, as found in fuelling stations in barracks and training grounds.

Yet these government markets remain based on the principle beloved by military contractors whereby the customer issues a specification describing the goods desired, as opposed to the supplier defining a product through market research, putting up his own money, and developing and selling the item on the free market.

Trade Unions

Trade unions also, especially the powerful metalworkers' union IG Metall, were not looking seriously towards commercial markets when they called for German conversion strategies. They mainly envisaged alternative public contracts to keep the workforce in military industries employed. Thus the argument about future conversion strategies should focus upon this question: whether viable ways out of the arms-making priorities of the past remain married to public contracts, or whether there is a truly free-market alternative. All participants in German debates appeared to have opted for the statist path as a means of finding a way out of the dilemma via the public purse. One account finds: 'If the state, so the argument runs, as monopolistic purchaser in the military sector does not intervene in a planned manner in the process of restructuring, then large unemployment and structural crises will occur in many regions of the FRG.'[15]

The German trade unions turned to the conversion question belatedly, but intensively. The symbol of all trade union commitment to conversion, the well-known case of Lucas Aerospace, received much attention in Germany, and Mike Cooley, the German-speaking chairman of the shop stewards' committee of the firm, was a frequent and sought-after speaker in green circles and social democratic gatherings. During the government of Helmut Schmidt (until 1982), trade union representatives in the arms industry discovered that they were more successful at mobilizing support within the federal government for reducing restrictions on arms exports (the contentious issue was then the export of *Leopard* tanks to Saudi Arabia) than were the representatives of the boards of their companies. Before Chancellor Helmut Schmidt travelled to Saudi Arabia, representatives of the trade unions paid him a visit and handed over a memorandum suggesting how he should handle this politically most sensitive affair, including Saudi offset orders. The IG Metall leadership was extremely alarmed by the episode and decided to take active steps in order to counter the moves of a tiny fraction of their constituency which challenged the traditional anti-militaristic stance of the trade union movement in Germany. Membership instruction courses and other ways of forming membership opinion were regeared towards the conversion issue, shop-based initiatives for conversion (*Arbeitskreise*) were encouraged to start work, and the rhetoric of the trade union was adapted to the new priority. As a consequence, a significant number of shop-based study groups were launched at MBB, Krupp MaK, Daimler-Benz and a number of shipyards.

Despite impressive beginnings, the efforts of the trade unions were frustrated during the 1980s. Management was unwilling to concede any codetermination (*Mitbistimmung*) to the shop floor in product strategy. Such concessions inside the arms industry were considered to be potential break-throughs for the (long-standing) demands of the unions for democratization of industry (which originated in the famous debate about *Wirtschaftsdemokratie* during the Weimar Republic). Statements about 'political learning' on the part of the workforce or about 'democratic concepts of conversion as a means of political emancipation' nourished far-reaching fears within management that the old ambitions of the unions were still alive.[16]

It also became apparent, especially in the demand that conversion strategies should not be geared to producing just anything but solely 'socially useful products', that the conversion issue far surpassed the erstwhile horizon of union strategies. In a phrase of escalating ecological awareness and principled debates about the future of consumerist production strategies, more fundamental questions were to be addressed than the unions wanted to answer.

Regional economic slumps caused by reductions caused local trade union representatives, such as those in Flensburg, to call for the preservation of military facilities in their district. Under pressure, the formerly moderate representatives of shop stewards in the German aerospace industry, who hitherto had steered a middle course, openly supported the argument of management that the European fighter aircraft must be built because of employment needs.

New Actors

The attempts by both management and the unions to bring in the state as an additional actor in the conversion issue have so far failed. Officially, the federal government, formed by a conservative–liberal coalition, was following the course announced in the 1985 White Paper on Defence: 'the federal government is unable and unwilling to take over entrepreneurial responsibility from the arms-producing industry'.[17]

The government, especially the foreign ministry, submitted a few ideas about how to facilitate conversion (Junior Minister Adam-Schwätzer proposed at the UN conversion conference in August 1990 the formation of a 'study group on conversion research' and the foundation of a 'clearing house for cooperation between enterprises', and repeated Genscher's proposal to establish a research institute).[18] However, the magnitude of the problem brought in a number of new actors, such as business consultants, who in the past would never have given a thought to the odd issue of conversion. A number of ideas and proposals submitted reflect general problems of high-tech countries. In Germany, they focus on environmental issues, and the destruction of high-tech military equipment by, as they say, 'methods beyond hand-work' that is with machines and not by hand (as observed in comparable activities in the USA and the former USSR).

In Rhineland–Palatine, formerly one of the mainstays of the US Army in Germany, the regional government called in the well-known

Swiss Prognos Institute for help.[19] Their recipe for the huge Mainzer Industrie-und Panzerwerk (with 5750 employees before 'the change', this was the biggest repair facility of the US Army in Western Europe) deserves special attention. As usual, the first recommendation by Prognos was to reduce the workforce. In 1996, the figure is expected to have decreased to 1300 workers. This workforce, about one-fourth of that formerly employed in the tank repair shop, is advised to turn to alternative production, with emphasis on novel environmental activities.

Along with conventional recommendations (to develop civilian engines and transmission gears, special containers and general environmental technology), one of the five recommendations made by Prognos for future civilian businesses remains unique: one thousand sedan limousines were to be dismantled according to strict environmental standards by mid-1992. Over three to four years, Prognos recommends a capacity to recycle 75 000 cars and to upgrade 1500 lorries. The strategy envisaged by Prognos involves the use of public finance to cover the costs involved in the process of learning how to destroy heavy-duty equipment in a way that is both economically feasible and environmentally acceptable. It is based on the assumption that public finance will be available to cover the costs if, following cuts imposed by the Vienna treaty, military vehicles are prototype items in this endeavour. Little wonder that the largest German carmaker and leading producer of lorries, Daimler-Benz, purchased the idea and invested in the Mainzer Industrie-und Panzerwerk. Thus steps towards disarmament (the destruction of armour) help the private economy to socialize the learning costs of coping with future standards of environmentally acceptable industrial activities (recycling of large equipment such as lorries).

THE CASE OF EAST GERMANY

The issue of conversion poses rather different problems in the new territory of the Federal Republic of Germany, the former GDR, from those it presents in the old. Both the historical context and the dimensions of the problem are strikingly different in the former GDR.

On 3 October 1990 this state ceased to exist as a separate entity at the same time as its social and economic system – elements which would normally provide the framework for the conversion process – were dissolved and replaced by completely new conditions. Thus, in the new Federal *Länder*, conversion is not only taking place in conditions of a severe social and economic crisis, but also in conditions of systemic transformation.

The Dimension of the Problem

The GDR was not among the leading arms producers in the Warsaw Treaty Organization, nor was the GDR named in the international lists of the world's major arms exporters. Nevertheless, in comparison with the country's size, the GDR's arms production was considerable. According to official budget data, the GDR's military expenditure (defence expenditure plus expenditure on securing national borders) amounted to 16 billion GDR Marks in 1989, following a 10 percent cut in the defence budget from 16.2 billion to 14.8 billion GDR Marks or US$7.048 million[20] (the remaining 1.2 billion being accounted for by expenditure on the border troops). This is the equivalent of 4.5 percent of GNP. To assess the significance of these figures, it must be borne in mind that certain categories of military-related expenditure are not included, among them the following: subsidies for investments in military production; payments made to conscripts' dependants; and expenditure on conscription offices.

Hidden costs must also be taken into consideration. As a result of the former planning and budgetary mechanisms, such costs were contained in other budgetary items. They represented an additional source of financing for the acquisition of military technology. Among them may be counted the financial adjustment between actual import prices and low fixed prices paid by the GDR army for final products, a difference borne by the national budget, and income from services performed by the National People's Army (NPA) for the civilian sector and which remained available to the NPA.

Arms production in its narrow definition was comparatively limited in scope. In 1989, more than 41 000 employees worked in approximately 74 enterprises producing arms, of which 31 were dedicated mainly to arms production. They produced military goods and services of a total value of 3.7 billion GDR Marks, or 0.75 percent of total industrial production.[21] Of the arms produced, 40 percent were exported, mostly to member states of the Warsaw Treaty Organization (WTO). The arms enterprises of the GDR mainly produced weapons on the basis of Soviet licences. With the exception of certain special ships, big weapons were not produced; production was mainly of spare parts, integrated components, munitions and handguns.[22] Some 28 percent of arms industrial activity was accounted for by repair and maintenance services.

These armaments factories did not form a separate industrial complex comparable to that in the Soviet Union. Rather, they depended on the relevant ministries of the different branches of industry. With the exception of the former combined works 'Kombinat Spezialtechnik Dresden' consisting of 11 factories with a workforce of some 11 000 and almost exclusively devoted to arms production, the remaining factories were integrated into combined works largely dedicated to civilian production, where they accounted for 10–20 percent of total production. Following the dissolution of these combined works, the arms-producing factories are largely classifiable as medium-sized industries.

If we add to this arms production in its narrow definition those goods and services whose use is civilian and which were produced throughout the GDR for the so-called 'economic securing of defence tasks', the total sum reaches 10.99 billion GDR Marks (about US$5.21 billion) in 1989. Approximately 2300 factories participated to varying degrees in this production.

Areas used for military purposes by the NPA and the Western Group of the Soviet armed forces accounted for more than 4.5 percent of the entire territory of the new Federal *Länder*. (By comparison, military areas of the old Federal *Länder* account for 5.6 percent of the entire territory of the old FRG.) The greater part of these military areas is now being freed for potential civilian use, but before this potential can become reality, enormous problems of environmental rehabilitation (including the financial burdens this implies) must be addressed.

Target strength of the NPA was 168 000 and, according to official figures, state security employed at least 85 000; over one-quarter of a million persons were thus affected by the process both of disarmament and of dissolution of the GDR. (No more than 25 000 officers and junior officers of the former NPA have been accepted into the new German Federal Army, 19 000 of them for an initial trial period of two years.[23])

The entire military material of the NPA, the border troops, the state security and the fighting groups, present a fourth category where problems of conversion arise.

The First Stage of Conversion in the Last Year of the GDR

The GDR's arms production experienced its first substantial modification in connection with the unilateral disarmament which the GDR introduced at the beginning of 1989, as did most other WTO member states. Following this, the first conversion measures for approximately 30 arms-producing plants were introduced in February 1989. These measures, elaborated by the central planning department, were aimed at substituting imports of goods from the West, increasing exports to the USSR (the main foreign customer of GDR industrial goods) and increasing the output of consumer goods for GDR customers.

In the autumn of 1989, a process of disarmament and demilitarization was initiated that was unique in its radicalism. This process included the dismantling of the internal power apparatus of the state (dissolution of state security or *Stasi*, the 'fighting units of the working class' and other paramilitary organizations) and the demand for public control over such institutions. This disarmament process was thus more far-reaching than any previous steps towards disarmament. This was a societal disarmament process that also affected the entire material basis for military power, arms production and research, military infrastructure, areas in military use and existing military technology.

The Round Table[24] on military reform debated the total demilitarization of the then existing GDR. Civil rights movements were able to force through the dissolution of state security. The ruling Socialist Unity Party of Germany (SED) abolished the 'fighting units of the working class' (which included 300 000 men). Within the Round Table there was agreement on the need to direct and control the conversion process, rather than simply leaving it to chance. A draft law on conversion was drawn up to provide a general framework to ensure that the conversion process occurred in such a way as not to cause undue social hardship; conversion was also to be environmentally sound and economically effective. Among the main provisions of the new law were the following:[25]

- promoting the reintegration of military personnel into civilian life;
- commissioning former arms factories to dismantle and recycle military technology;
- financial compensation for the losses suffered by armaments enterprises as a result of unexpected and large-scale cancellations of orders;
- support for local authorities in their efforts to convert military areas for civilian use;
- ecological rehabilitation of areas under military use;
- creation of a conversion fund.

The state's responsibility for conversion became formally institutionalized: the Ministry of Defence was renamed the Ministry of Disarmament and Defence in March 1990 and its tasks were redefined. Within the ministry, a State Secretariat for Disarmament was created, one of its functions being to prepare for the retraining of military personnel. A Conversion Office was created within the Ministry of Economics to deal with the arms industry.

Economic union with the Federal Republic of Germany on 1 July 1990 put an end to the GDR's role within the autarchic economic system practised by the CMEA (Council for Mutual Economic Assistance) countries. Virtually overnight, the East German economy had to contend with world market competition. The latent economic crisis of the GDR became drastically apparent; the entire economy collapsed. Following the Caucuses summit meeting between FRG Chancellor Kohl and Gorbachev in July 1990, where it became clear that a second army would not continue to exist in the eastern part of Germany on 1 August 1990, the government of the GDR cancelled all the contracts with the arms industry. Only 35 percent of the commitments that had been entered into with foreign contracting partners were fulfilled by the time of German unification on 3 October 1990.[26] The subsequent integration of the former GDR territory into NATO and the extension of all FRG legislation to the new territory signified also the end of the previous GDR arms exports. The entire arms industry of the GDR was faced with extinction.

When German unification occurred on 3 October 1991, all the conversion institutions and the proposals of the draft conversion law became redundant. The issue of conversion is not treated anywhere in the Treaty of Unification between the FRG and the GDR, and the regulations that had come into effect in the last year of the GDR's existence as an independent state thus ceased to have any legal standing. Therefore conditions in which conversion was to take place worsened rapidly.

Although the hope of comprehensive demilitarization, supported first of all by the citizens' movements but also by many 'normal' citizens, proved to be an illusion, it remains the case that the solution of very real conversion problems is one of the most urgent tasks facing the new Federal *Länder* today. There exists a de facto pressure to carry out conversion measures; however, this relates mainly to so-called 'site conversion', the civilian use of areas that hitherto have been used for military purposes. At the regional level, however, the conversion of former arms industries plays an important role in employment, economic and technology policy.

Specific Features of the Conversion of Arms Production in the New Federal *Länder*

Although, compared with the rest of GDR industry, the arms industry was well-equipped with relatively modern technology thanks to the privileged status of so-called 'special production', the armament enterprises were unable, in the short time available, to convert to production of civilian items that would have been competitive in the conditions of the market economy. The unplanned cessation of production made it impossible to draw up and carry out conversion plans. The criteria applied in the approaches to conversion developed in 1989 ceased to make economic sense, for these approaches were postulated on the assumption of a development of the GDR economy with its specific conditions.

Trade union initiatives, comparable for example with the working groups on alternative production existing in the old FRG *Länder*, did not exist. Mass redundancies were at first postponed through regulations on part-time work (in some cases, these regulations kept people in employment up to the end of 1991).

Today arms conversion in the new *Länder* is only one aspect of the 'conversion' of the entire East German economy. There is virtually no enterprise in East Germany that can continue to exist with its former production line. For civilian production, too, demand has fallen radically: domestically, it has been supplanted by more productive competitors, about all from West Germany; externally, it suffers from the payment difficulties of the former CMEA trading partners and the abolition of export subsidies for trade with Western states.

Differences between the present situations of civilian and former military industry, arising on the one hand from the privileged position of the arms industry and on the other from its greater isolation from the market, are thus only a question of degree. The specifics of arms production in a centrally planned economy of distribution were merely the incarnation of mechanisms that, in principle, were valid throughout the economy.

Industrial production is falling at an alarming rate; in 1992, it amounted to about 30 percent of the 1989 level. This applies not only to branches typical of arms production (electronics and mechanical engineering) but to the entire industrial structure. Problems typical of conversion are the following:

- the development and production of new goods;
- survival without massive state subsidies;

- demonopolization, that is efficient production in the competitive conditions of the market;
- the creation of appropriate management and marketing structures;
- retraining; and
- devaluation of part of the capital stock.

These have become central elements of the survival strategy being pursued by all enterprises, whether civil or military. Thus the arms industry has largely ceased to reveal any specific characteristics in this process. This has been recognized by the directors of former arms-producing enterprises; in mid-1991, they dissolved the association of enterprises affected by conversion that they had formed only the previous year to represent their common interests (for example, as regards the debt question).

Problems of conversion of the arms industry of the former GDR currently centre on three main aspects: questions of property, winning new markets and the regional significance of conversion. Technical or technological questions are almost irrelevant, a fact that results from the structure of the arms-producing enterprises in the former GDR.

In order to avoid misunderstandings, it must be stated that speaking of conversion of arms industries in the ex-GDR does not mean conversion with the aim of altering production to new lines explicitly oriented to peaceful ends, but rather an adjustment the enterprises feel compelled to make if they are to continue to exist. The majority of the former arms industries are attempting to adapt to civilian production, which they see as their only hope of survival. Virtue is born of necessity, so to speak.

However, the former military plants face a difficult situation. On the one hand, their employees are highly-qualified and trained (under the conditions of a deficit economy) to improvise and, given the structure of former arms production, they can be employed in various fields. Moreover, the enterprises dispose of a well-developed infrastructure, often including their own railway connections, intact communications networks and large areas that can be put to industrial use. On the other hand, the enterprises possess no financial capital of their own. In accordance with the specific mechanisms of the centrally administered economy, investments and wages were paid from centrally administered funds, material was forcibly loaned and money was deprived of its original function as a general equivalent and means of payment within the sphere of production. Autonomous economic activity and strategies that went beyond the directives of the plan were thus limited for all enterprises; for the arms enterprises, they were unimaginable. After the transition, they went heavily into debt and these debts have not been written off; rather, they have been converted into Deutschmarks and had to be repaid to the Treuhandanstalt[27] in hard currency.

Questions of Property and the Role of the Treuhand

Because of this indebtedness, banks hesitated to provide fresh loans that would be necessary for conversion. This 'credit unworthiness' renders a new beginning more difficult or indeed impossible; above all, it hinders management buy-outs. Even where the factories concerned had developed their own strategies for reorganization, the Treuhand largely disregarded such efforts if it was able to find Western buyers; the sell-off of East German industry took priority. As long as they are not privatized, the enterprises remain subject to the administration and the unlimited decision-making powers of the Treuhandanstalt and its successor organizations. For this institution's privatization strategy, concerned to achieve immediate effects through sales, the aims and criteria of conversion were irrelevant.

The beginning of the adjustment process has generally been characterized by the unravelling of the enterprise structures existing hitherto. Certain spheres of enterprise activity have been separated out[28] and privatized on an individual basis or transferred to the property of the local administration (this is above all the case with social facilities such as health care institutions and kindergartens). The remaining cores have, as a rule, been taken over by Western concerns for two main reasons: the use of wage cost advantages; and provisions in the unification treaty that envisage a participation of East German enterprises in the process of exploiting the military technology and the munitions of the former National People's Army. A specific example is the decartelization of the famous Carl-Zeiss-Jena enterprise which had an important military component (30 percent). Some factories involved in military production were closed but a significant element, including special research in high-tech dual-use branches, was converted into the corporation 'Jenoptik' owned by the new province of Saxony. Given the danger of advancing deindustrialization of the eastern part of Germany, such efforts to rehabilitate and redevelop industrial facilities with the help of state (Treuhand) investments and credits are necessary. In some cases also a temporary mixed ownership of Federal institutions like the Treuhand or successor bodies, *Länder* governments and trade unions or other institutions seem to be useful.

In the meantime, since unification, only a few enterprises have become independently privatized through a management buy-out. Others have been assessed by the Treuhand as unsaleable to private buyers in their present state and uneconomical to rehabilitate; these have been liquidated. Some former military enterprises remain in state hands.

New Fields of Activity for Former Arms Industries

The first and not insignificant sphere is the disarmament economy. The need here is tremendous. In 1991, the costs (and thus the value of contacts to recycling businesses) of destroying the munitions of the former NPA were estimated at DM1.5 billion. Two to three billion DM was the estimated cost of dismantling and scrapping military technology.[29] Existing capacities, above all existing technologies, are not adequate for the task.

A number of former arms enterprises of the ex-GDR began the elimination of the munitions or military technology they themselves produced or maintained. This has been especially true of former munitions producers, such as the enterprises in Lübben and Königswartha, and military enterprises in the ex-GDR previously involved in repair and maintenance work which compete for these contracts. Granting contracts to these firms, which were usually the biggest employers and economic factors in their respective regions, would enable them to continue to offer employment to at least a part of their former workforce. In addition, this would help to win time in order to develop civilian production strategies for the period when these recycling contacts come to an end.

Buck-INPAR-Pinnow[30] provides a good example. A pilot plant for the recycling of various types of ammunition, said to fulfil high standards of environmental safety, was installed. It is intended in the long run to handle dangerous civilian waste as well. Although this might require additional adaptation of the technology, it would permit operations to continue after the military waste has been eliminated. Economically, the costs of dismantling and recycling ammunition and military equipment are very high and could not be covered by selling the final materials. Thus the central government of the FRG must share the financial responsibility for these tasks. To avoid this financial burden (the deferred costs of the armament race) and its responsibility, the Federal government is selling military technology of the former NPA on a large scale. Profitable exports take priority over dismantling and recycling.

What is at issue is not simply the dismantling and destruction of military technology and munitions, but also the ecological reconstruction of areas that have been used for military purposes. The state must bear responsibility for ecological damage caused by military activities (ground water pollution, soil contamination, destruction of forested areas, spoilation of the countryside and so on); thus means should be allocated within the Federal budget to cover the costs of repairing such damage. Although ecological rehabilitation is only a precondition of civilian use, it is also an activity that would create employment and new markets.

A further sphere is represented by those areas of economic activity that have until now been deficient, including environmental relief, public transport and suburban traffic, infrastructure, ecological energy technologies and communications technology. Former repair and maintenance plants have a chance of finding new markets in these spheres. The character of their work processes would in general remain unchanged; from the point of view of technological modifications, the necessary adaptations could be carried out in a relatively short period of time. Instead of military goods, they could now assemble, for example, wind generators, or modernize and repair trams, as in a former military plant in Mittenwalde.

Production profiles should be oriented directly to regional needs and thus depend directly on the demand of the regional public purse. Given the fact that the new Federal states are at present financially weak, the possibilities for extending these markets are limited. In principle, again only Western partners can help to compensate for deficiencies by contributing capital, technological know-how and marketing experience.

Regional Conversion

Even in those cases where production lines have been successfully converted, only some 30–40 percent of those hitherto employed in the arms industry found new employment straight away. In the context of the necessary macroeconomic structural changes and adjustments, it will not always make sense to create new jobs for employees at their former workplaces. Conversion must be planned, not at the factory, but at the regional level.

A considerable number of arms-producing enterprises were situated in regions with low levels of industrial activity, for example in small towns in Brandenburg and Mecklenburg-Vorpommern in the north of the GDR. After 1945, these regions were characterized by agricultural production. Although on the basis of size as measured in terms of employees (on average between 400 and 600) they may be counted only as medium-sized, the arms factories located in these predominantly agricultural areas were usually the most important source of employment in the immediate vicinity. With the entire economy, including the agricultural sector, in a state of collapse, they could in many cases be the last pillars of hope for the rebuilding of regional economic structures.

Conversion of military plants is only one task. Together with conversion of territories used by the military, former army personnel and civil plants into new market fields, it is part of the necessary restructuring of the whole economy of the region. Retraining, further qualifications and the creation of new fields of activity (including non-industrial activity) are called for, and this implies that the potential for conversion be integrated into regional development concepts.

Despite the obvious need for societal guidance of these processes, the beginnings of a conversion process in the former GDR were chaotic and largely unregulated. The social and political costs of this are high. In view of the desolate overall economic and social situation in the eastern part of Germany, virtually any opportunity for employment is exploited. The proposal to save some 150 jobs (out of 4500) in the military plant in Neubrandenburg by remodelling armoured personnel carriers of the NPA for military use within the Bundeswehr reflects this situation. Among others, factories that have been taken over by Western concerns have continued to produce or repair military goods.[31]

In sum, one of the most important lessons from the East German experience with conversion is that a meaningful, effective and ecologically acceptable use of the resources that become available calls for integration into a concept of regional development. Only in this way can all relevant aspects be adequately dealt with, including the social, economic and ecological dimensions. All those affected by the process should be included in the search for and formulation of solutions; the process must include relevant institutions, ministries and political and social groups. Only in this way will it be possible to observe democratic procedures in solving complex problems often involving conflicts of interests; only such a procedure will help to ensure the role of imagination and creativity in developing alternatives.

But although some *Länder* governments (Brandenburg, Saxony) in the former GDR are gradually developing a sense of responsibility, especially in connection with the possible civilian use of former military areas, the problems of conversion cannot be solved at the *Länder* level alone. The Federal government must recognize and assume its responsibility for the process of conversion. This responsibility entails, above all, the creation of the necessary political, legal and financial framework for conversion.

In contrast to other Eastern European countries, the conditions of transformation under which conversion has to take place in the former GDR have a special character because of the country's accession to the Federal Republic of Germany. In terms of political order and economic policy, the framework for this process of transformation is set by the extension of the political, economic and legal structures of the ex-FRG. In contrast to the situation elsewhere in Eastern Europe, what is happening in the former GDR is not the creation of a market economy from scratch. Rather, it is the integration of the East German economy – or what is left of it – and East German wage and salary earners in the existing market structures of the Federal Republic. This state of affairs has specific consequences.

The advantages consist in the existence of a functioning legal system and the possibility of building up a market-economy infrastructure in a very short space of time. Moreover, negative effects of the social and economic dislocations are cushioned by the social policy legislation of the Federal Republic and by financial transfers from the Federal budget (such transfers amounted to DM140 billion in 1991 alone). The disadvantages result from (1) the unexpected collapse of the East German internal market for East German products in all sectors of the economy; (2) the fact that the East German economy was unable to become competitive overnight;[32] (3) the already concluded sharing-out of the market in which East German enterprises must integrate themselves as best they can; and (4) the difficult economic conditions in which the enterprises must embark on this process.

An additional and considerable handicap is the desolate financial situation of the East German *Läder* and local authorities. As a result of economic decline in East Germany, these have a low tax income and until 1994 they remained excluded from the general redistribution of tax income within the framework of the financial equalization between the Federal *Länder* (the so-called *Länderfinanzausgleich*). This means that the local authorities in the new *Länder* have only very limited possibilities for using former military areas for civilian purposes. (The entire area formerly in military use, whether controlled by the NPA or Soviet troops, has or will become the property of the Federal government. This property is administered by a Federal institution, the Bundesvermögensanstalt, which markets these former military areas to the highest bidder. Thus local East German authorities wishing to put such territory to civil use must first buy it back from the Federal government; in most cases, they then have to spend considerable sums on ecological rehabilitation.) An additional problem in this initial phase is that the local administration has no experience of the FRG's legal system, or of the rights and obligations of local government. Thus the problem of conversion in practice is characterized by a muddling through, concentrating on the problems of site conversion.

COMMON FINDINGS

Perspectives

The unexpected end of the East–West confrontation brought two entirely new challenges to the German arms industry beyond the fulfilment of future military orders in both parts of the country. The first is the destruction of huge amounts of conventional weapons left over from the cold war. The second is adaptation to new threat scenarios which have suddenly emerged, and their translation into new products.

Industry has discovered that current methods of destroying military equipment largely reflect the pre-Fordist world. Tanks and other military goods are at present destroyed in fulfilment of the Vienna treaty by hand-held devices, by non-serialized techniques. Industry now finds itself called upon to develop methods of destroying equipment comparable in sophistication to the ways and means used to produce the equipment in the first place. Diehl, a leading maker of ammunition and tracks for armoured vehicles, was successful in getting large contracts for the depletion of the vast stocks of live ammunition left over from the cold war in Germany. Krupp, the pre-eminent firm in German arms manufacture, produces huge presses to convert combat aircraft into packs of metal, like the familiar shredders used in scrapping motor vehicles. The firm also achieved the ultimate goal of pressing complete tanks down to size, and put this heavy-duty equipment on the market.

The demilitarization of former equipment of the armed forces in the wake of the drastic reductions is seen by former military producers as a major opportunity to obtain large government contracts. Towards the end of its existence, the GDR's capacity to destroy tanks was a few dozen vehicles per month, a figure which needs to be compared with the inventory of several thousand combat vehicles awaiting destruction. The arms-manufacturing industry views itself as ideally suited to carry out the destruction of the sophisticated weapons it once manufactured.

These jobs are by no means a small business. The magnitude of orders remains especially impressive for East Germany. Owing to scepticism regarding the abilities of the supply system to actually deliver, the so-called 'First Strategic Echelon' of the former WTO relied heavily on previously accumulated piles of munitions. The leftovers of the former GDR NPA represented, inter alia, 300 000 tons of live ammunition, and Russia's 'Western Group of Forces' around one million tons of ammunition, which must either be transferred to the East (unlikely) or destroyed. Germany's industrial capacity for dismantling ammunition was assumed to amount to a few thousand tons per year. According to an estimate widely cited in 1991, the destruction of munitions inherited from the GDR will cost around half a billion Deutschmarks over a period of 30 to 40 years, based on new technology which is expected to become available.[33] It is estimated that the destruction of military equipment, such as tanks, will require a much shorter period. Of 10 000 armoured vehicles to be destroyed by Germany, 2000 were earmarked for export, leaving the remaining 8000 for destruction. The Federal government issued a tender for the least cost-intensive mode of destroying tanks. (The primitive technique of explosion has been discounted for environmental reasons.) As the data show, the business was obtained more or less exclusively by West German firms. Eastern companies who hoped to survive partly through destruction orders for weapons were generally unsuccessful in their bids and have since gone out of business.

As regards the second challenge, German defence contractors, almost all of which have headquarters in the West, are actively following the change in threat perceptions, from the heavily militarized East–West confrontations to the new 'post-materialist' threats posed by environmental hazards, large-scale migration from the East and the South to the affluent centres of Europe, due to economic decay and political fragmentation, and the prospects for conflict posed by the North–South confrontation. The firms are certainly not envisaging that uprisings be put down by conventional armed force, but they feel that states will adapt to the new threats and that they, as intimate partners of state procurement bodies, will have an advantage in selling equipment which is now needed. Hence they try to read the technology requirements for protection against the new threats and to persuade their state counterparts to furnish contracts for applied research and pilot projects.

Relatively close to past activities are projections to fill in the generally expected active participation of Germany in UN missions. Beyond peace-keeping, peace-enforcement is seen as a likely role for German military contingents. Implications at a technological level are in the fields of long-range air transport equipment, and army equipment suitable for any environment, even in deserts.

Most of the perceived new threats are seen as requiring vast extensions of capabilities in reconnaissance, surveillance, data processing and comparable monitoring technologies. The range of products in this area converges with the large demand envisaged for verification technology. German industry assumes that a number of European states will be eager to participate in verification processes of future arms limitation accords, such as a chemical weapons convention, either by national means or in multilateral arrangements, but that few of these states will be capable of producing the necessary equipment domestically.

The repressive technologies supposedly needed to answer the new threats are seen as closer to the requirements of policing than to those of high-tech combat forces: population control, quelling riots and giving technical tools to state authorities to contain all kinds of unrest. Generally, the arms industry does not give the impression of having properly understood the technological repercussions of new threat environments, but during the 1980s, the MBB in particular turned its attention to the technological implications of peace research proposals for non-offensive defence, discovering that these could also provide a market for high-tech products. The outcome appears somewhat intermediary, but this company appears to have been the first to respond to these new challenges to public policies, and may thus have an advantage compared to other competitors.

Conclusions

There are only limited recent experiences in actual conversion efforts in (West) Germany, but these merit generalization. Conversion is defined differently by participating actors and is differently understood in the process. Terminology varies, as is common in new endeavours. The term 'conversion' is used by politicians, political scientists and trade union representatives. However, economists and managers in Germany apparently do not care for the term and use surrogate expressions.

The actual conversion experience of arms industries in Germany firmly established that the reconversion experience of large plants after World War Two (when huge facilities undertook military production during the war and then returned to their original tasks) does not at all apply to recent conversion efforts. The present run-down of arms-manufacturing facilities and their reorientation to alternative production purposes entails much more than was originally envisaged. The conversion paradigm started with simple assumptions. The pressings for steel helmets, it was assumed, only needed to be modified to make them identical to those used for turning out cooking pots. This has always been an oversimplification. Yet debate about the real issues in

conversion, as this brief survey suggests, has since moved from technological questions to social (science) issues. The main problems now
are sluggish adaptation of conversion candidates to civilian market
standards, the incorporation of values of extreme high performance
with a disregard of costs in engineering objectives by former military
contractor staff and similar hurdles in reorientation.

In the course of debate, the focus of conversion strategies has also
changed. In the early years, trade unions preferred to discuss conversion
needs by focusing upon their respective constituencies – the employees
in given plants. The goals were to convert plants with neutral effects
on the workforce. This approach has been frustrated, as has been the
centralist concept of nationwide conversion plans. The Soviet 'national
plan' accounted by Gorbachev before the General Assembly of the UN
failed to materialize. In the meantime, the economic region became the
focus of conversion strategies, notably in Germany, and it is hoped that
this approach will prove to be viable.[34]

German industry is disenchanted with the conversion idea. Provided
public finance is forthcoming for conversion schemes, managers are
prepared to embark on them, but they do not believe in them. Replacement of former military production rather than conversion is the
preferred notion.

The trade unions, above all the IG Metall, remain stubborn. The
workforce hitherto engaged in military production is ill-prepared to
follow the bold moves of industry into alternative markets. Fitters or
specialists in aerodynamics are simply not able to make the necessary
adjustments. There are substantial fears in the workforce engaged in
military contract work that they will become personal victims of disarmament – that they, despite lukewarm applause for recent political
developments, will be obliged to leave their professions in order to
implement these developments. There is a diffuse, general fear of being
made redundant, of economic decay and technological degradation.
Human capital thus appears as the most complicated issue in the
German conversion experience.

NOTES

1. Ulrich Albrecht (1982), *Kündigt den Nachrüstungsbeschluß!* (Denounce the double
   track decision!), Frankfurt am Main: Fischer Taschenbuch, Chapter IV.
2. Speech by Inspector General Klaus Naumann in Berlin, 29 January 1992.
3. Figures cited from the German Ministry of Defence, Fü S III 4 ('Fü S' means 'Führungsstab
   Streitkräfte', the shadow replica of the prohibited General Staff). The author is indebted
   to Peter Barth for transmitting these figures.

The European rupture

4. Dr.-Ing. Bernhard Nill, Krauss-Maffei AG, in a special hearing called by the alarmed administration: Landeshauptstadt München, Referat für Arbeit und Wirtschaft, Produktkonversion. Kurzdokumentation einer Anhörung der Landeschauptstadt München (Country Capital Munich, Department for Labour and Economics: Product Conversion. Brief of a hearing by the country capital Munich), Munich, 1991, p. 11.
5. Oral communication by Dip.-Ing. Hans-Jürgen Wieland, Deutsche Aerospace, Munich.
6. *Die Tageszeitung*, 16 April 1992, p. 4.
7. See Peter Lock, 'Arms production in Southern Germany – The Munich area an aborted "Silicon Valley"?', unpublished paper, Berlin 1992. Lock (p. 2) interprets the Daimler-Benz/Mitsubishi collaboration as an effort 'to wind up global corporate alliances'.
8. See above.
9. 'Rüstung und Raumfahrt ziehen Sasa nach unten' (Armaments and Space Drag Down), *Die Tageszeitungm*, 24 May 1991.
10. See *Aviation Week & Space Technology*, 22 June 1992, p. 27.
11. 'Daimler rüstet für den Frieden' (Daimler arms for peace), *Frankfurter Rundschau*, 4 March 1992.
12. Oral statement by Dipl-Ing. Wieland of Deutsche Aerospace, and by Dr. Oetting of Treuhand AG, the agency in charge of reconstruction of the East German economy.
13. *Wehrtechnik*, no. 2/1992, p. 3.
14. Cf. *Frankfurter Rundschau*, 3 June 1992, p. 12.
15. Thomas Küchenmeister, 'Politisch–volkswirtschaftliche Aspekte der Konversion', *antimilitarismus information*, **21**, (5), May 1991, p. 5.
16. Cf. Christoph Butterwegge, 'Rüstungskonversion als Chance demokratischer Partizipation' (Conversion as the chance for democratic participation), *antimilitarismus information*, **21**, (5), May 1991, esp. pp. 15 and 18.
17. Der Bundesminister der Verteidigung, *Weißbuch 1985 Zur Lage und Entwicklung der Bundeswehr*, Bonn, 1985, p. 369.
18. 'Konversion: Ökonomische Anpassung im Zeitalter der Abrüstung. Rede von Staatsministerin Dr. Adam-Schwätzer in Moskau' (Conversion: economic adjustment in the era of disarmament), Presse- und Informationsamt der Bundesregierung (ed.) (1990), *Bulletin*, No. 100, 22 August, p. 850.
19. A publicly accessible summary of the Prognos paper can be found in *Forum Arbeit*, **1**, 1992, p. 8.
20. According to SIPRI *Yearbook*, 1990.
21. Cf. *Statistischer Bericht des Amtes für Statistik der DDR für das 1. Halbjahr 1990*, p. 4.
22. For more detailed information on the structure of arms production in the GDR, see P. Opitz (1991), 'Arms Production and Arms Export of the German Democratic Republic' (English version of Berghof-Arbeitspapier Nr. 45, Berlin).
23. Cf. *Berliner Zeitung*, 19 September 1991, p. 4.
24. The Round Table was the first democratic decision-making institution, spontaneously installed after the events of autumn 1989. All parties and citizen movements were represented on the basis of equal rights (one institution, one voice). Round Tables existed at several levels and for different areas: economic questions, military questions, preparation of elections and so on. The Round Table for military reform had agreed on the total demilitarization of the GDR. The Round Tables were liquidated by the new government elected in March 1990.
25. The text of the draft law ('Gesetz zur Ungestaltung des Militär-und Wehrwirtschaftsbereichs der DDR – Konversionsgesetz'), can be found, for example in *MEDIATUS*, Special Issue 1/9, pp. 50–51.
26. Statistisches Ant der neuen Bundesländer, Abschlußbericht zur speziellen Produktion 1990; cf. also Petra Opitz (1991), 'Rüstungsproduktion und Rüstungsexport der DDR', Working Papers of the Berghof-Stiftung für Konfliktforschung, Nr. 45, Berlin, p. 17.
27. This institution was set up to privatize the entire state-owned property of the former GDR.
28. Enterprises in the centrally administered economy, plagued by shortages, had a high degree of vertical integration of production. They did virtually everything themselves so as to minimize the disruptive effects of unstable economic relations outside the enterprise.

29. Cf. *Die Zeit*, 30 August 1991.
30. This is a former DGR military plant which produced anti-tank missiles and military containers and repaired radar systems, situated in Brandenburg. It is now a West German-owned facility.
31. One example is the facility in Ludwigsfelde, a small town near Berlin, now repairing engines for *Phantom* jets of the Bundeswehr and owned by MTU, a well-known West German military producer.
32. Other East European countries enjoy relative wage-cost advantages but the decision to convert GDR wages to the Deutschmark on the basis that one GDR Mark equals one Deutschmark deprived the East German economy of this potential advantage. Within a unified state, significant regional differences in wage levels cannot in any case be maintained in the longer term.
33. Werner Hänsel and Heinz Michael, 'Rüstungskonversion in den neuen Bundesländern' (Arms conversion in the new Federal countries), *antimilitarismus information*, **21**, (4), May 1991, p. 37. One German firm, the well-known tank turret specialists Wegmann in Kassel, wrote, together with their subsidiary (Frank Abels Consulting & Technology GmbH), a letter to all members of the Federal diet suggesting that the least dangerous way for the environment and the cheapest method to get rid of munitions was to fire them, for which they were originally designed (see *Wehrdienst*, no. 1256, 1991, p. 3).
34. Such regional schemes exist for the greater Munich area, Potsdam and the North German shipbuilding areas. For a general account of the German regional experience, see Chapter IV in Lutz Köllner and Burkhardt J. Huck (eds) (1990), *Abrüstung und Konversion. Politische Voraussetzungen und wirtschaftliche Folgen in der Bundesrepublik* (Disarmament and conversion. Political requirements and economic consequences in the FRG), Frankfurt: Campus, or (from an East German perspective) Karsten Fischer, Thomas Schulze and Holger Wetuschat, 'Konversion – Chance für regionale Entwicklungspolitik' (Conversion – a chance for regional development policies), *antimilitarismus information*, **21**, (5), May 1991, and Küchenmeister, 'Aspecte', ibid.; about the Bremen region, see Butterwegge, 'Rüstungskonversion' (1991). The role of regionalism in the conversion issue has been recently depicted by Christoph Butterwegge and Eva Senghaas-Knobloch (1992), *Von der Blockkonfrontation zur Rüstungskonversion?* (From bloc confrontation to conversion?), Munster: Lit. 2nd Impr. 1994.

7. The Former Czechoslovakia

Yudit Kiss

Unlike the other countries of the region, before World War Two Czecho-slovakia was a developed industrialized country, with fairly strong democratic traditions. Although decades of doctrinaire state socialism seemed to have smothered this heritage, when the 'Velvet Revolution' took place in 1989, the country woke up and found itself in a better situation than its fellow 'new democracies': it still had a relatively solid industrial base, with a well-trained workforce, a comparatively balanced macroeconomic structure and very small foreign debt. The 'Velvet Revolution' was a smooth, civilized walk away from a mistaken path of development, enjoying wide social support and the euphoria of fulfilled desires after the failure of radical reforms in the 1960s and the punish-ment of normalization in the 1970s. Moreover, Czechoslovakia's newly elected President, Vaclav Havel, was a very popular, charismatic leader, a man of principles, who seemed to be able to unite the different political and social forces that were to take part in the transformation.

Despite this relatively advantageous beginning, the problems stem-ming from the negative heritage of state socialism and the difficulties of the social–economic transformation quickly began to surface. Although the economy was relatively developed, there were only a few healthy, competitive sectors, the enterprises were rigid and managed with inertia, there was devastating ecological damage and an almost total lack of market institutions. The decades of state socialism had wiped away the functioning democratic institutions and civil society. When it began to create a new market economy and democratic society, Czechoslovakia had to start from scratch, which slowed down the pace of changes, and diverted a lot of energy from the solution of other pressing economic and social problems. At the same time, the country enjoyed the advantage of being a 'latecomer' to reforms, com-pared with Hungary and Poland, a factor which created significant dynamism in the structuring of the new system.

The most dangerous element of this legacy was the 'time bomb' of nationalism. National tensions had been present in the contradictory history of the country ever since the formation of the Czechoslovak state after the collapse of the Austro-Hungarian Empire; however, these tensions were reactivated by the disastrous social effects of the 'moderated economic shock therapy', which neglected the unexpectedly high social costs and the democratic requirements of the transformation. The absence of credible political and economic alternatives also paved the way for the re-emergence of nationalist politics. The problems of the defence industry and conversion played a crucial role in this process, which ended with the break-up of the country.

THE DEFENCE INDUSTRY IN THE FORMER CZECHOSLOVAKIA

Czechoslovakia was one of the most militarized countries of the Warsaw Pact. In 1987, when Czechoslovakia's military production reached record levels, almost 40 percent of output was produced in the Czech lands and more than 60 percent in Slovakia. This represented roughly 3 percent of the GDP and 10.5 percent of the total industrial production. A year later, when production had already fallen slightly, armament production still represented 24 percent of the total output in engineering and electrotechnics in Slovakia and 7 percent in the Czech lands.

In 1990, when the government launched its conversion programme, total military output had already dropped by nearly 50 percent. The aggregated value of production was almost equally distributed between the two republics. Arms exports suffered a similar decrease in the late 1980s. In 1987, weapons sales reached a value of Kcs 22.740 billion, but as early as 1990 sales had dropped to Kcs 7.907 billion. In 1987–8 there were 111 factories engaged in military production, 75 in the Czech lands and 36 in Slovakia. (The number of defence industry enterprises varies considerably, depending on whether only end-producers or major suppliers as well are taken into consideration.) According to Ministry of Defence figures, the sector used to employ directly 73 000 workers, with another 50–60 000 people indirectly involved in military production.[1] On the basis of these figures 1.5 percent of the workforce was employed by the military sector.

The changes in the concept of security, disarmament and the economic difficulties accompanying the country's radical transformation, have had a significant impact on the military budget since the political changes of 1989 (see Table 7.1). Military expenditures represented 3.4 percent of GDP in 1987. They reached a peak of 3.7 percent in 1989, before falling to 3.1 percent in 1990, the level roughly maintained since then. Even this reduced military expenditure absorbed 6.7 percent of

central government expenditures in 1990, in contrast with 1.8 percent
received by education and 0.4 percent by the health sector.

Table 7.1   Defence expenditure, nominal value (Kcs, billions)

	1987	1988	1989	1990	1991
Total	34.9	36.2	35.1	32.3	28.1
Development	12.6	13.3	12.2	10.0	3.3

Note: Development refers to weapons and other acquisitions.

Source: Ministry of Defence, 1992.

These figures give an indication of the importance of the military
sector in the Czechoslovak economy. They must, however, be viewed
with a certain caution because of systematic disinformation by the
state, both with regard to cold war adversaries and to the population,
particularly during the period of political détente. Despite the declared
openness since the glasnost period, much of the military data is still
classified. One of the legacies of the previous misleading information
system and the distorted economic calculations prevailing in the sector
is that basic figures are still hazy and contradictory. Although military
budget figures have been published regularly over recent years, there
is still evidence that military-related expenditures are concealed under
other budgetary headings, as was the practice in the 'good old days' of
state socialism.

The picture is not much clearer in respect of military producers. The
number of factories and the size of the workforce involved in military
production are constantly being altered. In addition, the official figures
generally exclude the vast circle of subcontractors who supply both the
defence industry and the armed forces with raw materials, machines,
instruments, vehicles, food and clothing. This 'snowball' nature of military expenditures gives calculations a slightly hypothetical nature.
According to Andras Brody's estimations, about five times as much
intake should be taken into consideration.

All this means that conversion is a larger and more complex undertaking than it seems at first sight on the basis of available military
industry figures.

Main Structural Features

The foundations of the Czechoslovak arms industry were laid down in the 19th century, as part of the industrialization of the Czech and Moravian lands. In a later wave of modernization, between 1920 and 1926, the three major arms industry centres were established: Skoda (Plzen), specialized in artillery weapons, tanks and ammunition; Ceskoslovenska Zbrojovka (Brno) produced infantry weapons and ammunition; and CKD (Prague) made tanks and armoured vehicles. Another important production profile was the production of combat aircraft, based in the Avia and Aero concerns (Prague).

During World War Two, under German occupation, the Czech lands served as a major military supplier of the German army. The existing enterprises were expanded and some new military firms were built in Moravia (Vsetin, Uherski Brod, Slavicin, Boykovice) and in Slovakia (Dubnica, Povazska Bistrica). Even though some of these factories were destroyed by the end of the war, most of them survived and the defence industry as a whole was larger and more efficient than ever before. After World War Two, some of the military enterprises shifted to civilian production. (Artillery production at Skoda-Plzen was replaced by turbines and electric train engines.) However, when Czechoslovakia joined the Warsaw Pact in 1955, new military enterprises were established, producing among other things aircraft technology, radio-electronics, radio sensors, optical instruments, training aeroplanes and anti-tank mines. In Slovakia huge heavy weapons factories were built.

Within the framework of the Warsaw Treaty Organization (WTO) division of labour, small arms, aircraft, armoured vehicles, cars, electronic equipment and ammunition were produced to local designs. The rest, mainly tanks, artillery weapons, fighter planes, bombers and rocket technology, was under Soviet licence. Soviet licences became regularly available to enterprises some time after their products were introduced to the Soviet armed forces. Czechoslovakia had to pay high licence fees, even for its own patents used within the Warsaw Pact. It also had to pay for each further development of a certain licence.

There was a specific internal division of labour within the country as well. The bulk of the Soviet-licensed heavy weaponry was produced in Slovakia. Here, as in most Warsaw Pact countries, relatively little local (and Czech) technological capacity and know-how was employed, except in the case of a handful of products such as engines, optical instruments for tanks or the processing and documentation of Soviet licences. In the Czech lands, in contrast, locally developed, more sophisticated military products were manufactured in addition to heavy weapons and ammunition.

Most military enterprises were dual-purpose factories: they produced for both military and civilian use, often using the same technology. This was partly to disguise military production and partly to cushion the significant fluctuations of demand. Military production represented more than one-fifth of the total output in only one-third of the factories. Even in Martin, one of the classical strongholds of the heavy weaponry industry, the share of military production varied between 50 and 70 percent. In theory, the technological diversity creates favourable preconditions for conversion, specifically in the case of a gradual diversification towards civilian production. In practice, however, it was typical in the past that the heavily subsidized and fairly lucrative military production financed civilian production carried out on the premises of military enterprises. Therefore, even though demand for arms production has declined, most firms maintain the, now much less remunerative, military production in order to develop the civilian branches.

Another characteristic of the defence industry was its high regional concentration. Roughly 32 percent of the workforce employed in the sector were located in the Central Slovak region, 23 percent in Southern Moravia and 17.4 percent in or around Prague. In cities like Martin, Dubnica, Boykovice, Slavicin or Uherski Brod, military and military-related production was the main, sometimes the only, employment possibility. Concentration was much heavier in Slovakia, where the different character and development patterns of the military industry created huge enterprises with thousands of employees. There were 30 000 workers in the military triangle of Martin, Detva and Dubnica, while the largest concentration of factories in Czech lands, in Slavicin, Boykovice and Uherski Brod, employed 10 000 people. The biggest Czech factory, Tesla Pardubice employed only(!) 6–7000 workers at peak capacity.

The Crisis

The first significant cuts in defence production were implemented in 1988–9, following the dramatic fall in Warsaw Pact – mainly Soviet and East German – demand. The fall in export demand caused a major setback for the defence industry, since arms sales represented a significant export item, the bulk of which traditionally went to the Warsaw Pact countries. In 1989–90, after the 'Velvet Revolution', the new leadership's revised security and military concepts led to further reductions. At the same time several third world customers became insolvent or politically undesirable business partners, which contributed to a further decrease in export demand. In June 1991, Czechoslovakia had accumulated claims of $1 billion for unpaid arms exports. An additional blow came when the Gulf conflict escalated in late 1990 and early 1991. The embargo affected the military sector's trading and cooperation partners in the Arab world, the country's main customers after the collapse of the Warsaw Treaty Organization. Owing to the embargo on Iraq, Czechoslovak exports and joint ventures for manufacturing ammunition, tanks and L-39 aircraft had to be suspended.

The effects of the unfolding crisis hit the military sector hard. Production fell to Kcs 16 billion ($500m) in 1990. According to Czechoslovak sources, output in 1992 was expected to be about 30 percent of the peak production in 1987. Particularly badly hit were 48 factories, 21 in the Czech Republic, 27 in Slovakia. Estimated total losses were twice as high in Slovakia as in the Czech Republic. According to the companies, 70 percent of the losses was caused by unsold stocks and capital assets and the rest was due to bad debts. In addition to direct support for conversion, the state allocated Kcs 2.6 billion in 1990 to buy up part of these reserves of raw materials and stocks and sell them at public auctions.

Defence workers were particularly hard hit by the crisis. According to official data the highest defence-related unemployment reached 15–18 percent in Slovakia and 5–8 percent in the Czech lands.[2] A further blow to the workforce was the almost total elimination of its special status and advantages that in the past made defence-related employment so attractive for many.[3] This lowered status created serious tensions within the traditionally well-trained, motivated workforce, which is strongly attached to military production. The fear of losing the military sector's elite workers was one of the major concerns of the government and the enterprises. In order to preserve this intellectual capital, despite the military expenditure cuts, the state continued to subsidize some development projects, for example covering 50 percent of the costs of a new radio sensor (which eventually could be used for civilian purposes as well) and a trainer aircraft, as early as 1991.

In 1991–2, government policy was apparently to let about half of the defence industry go bankrupt or be converted, depending on its ability to adjust to the new market requirements. The rest of the enterprises could be rescued with state support, in view of their strategic importance or their potential profitability. Seemingly still completely committed to conversion, policy makers kept an eye on potentially profitable business enterprises, even if they were military-based. What determined the selection of enterprises doomed to perish or to be resurrected was unknown and the government's policy still seemed unpredictable. In the absence of a clear policy for the future, military enterprises on the verge or already in a state of bankruptcy either resorted to simple survival techniques or tried to engage in renewed political lobbying to secure their positions.

Although the majority of defence industry firms are highly indebted and seem to be unable to face radical restructuring, there have been only a few bankruptcies. The general economic crisis has been unfolding fairly 'smoothly', mainly owing to the fact that the bankruptcy law went unenforced, even though it was passed by the federal Parliament in spring 1991.

CONVERSION

The first significant step towards conversion was taken in 1989, when the Communist government, led by Prime Minister Ladislav Adamek, suggested that tank production be gradually phased out. When Vaclav Havel became President, the new cabinet 'adopted' the idea and decided to reduce and halt tank and armoured personnel carrier production. At the beginning conversion was a decision driven by the strong moral commitment of the new government led by former dissidents like Vaclav Havel and Jiri Dienstbier. 'Economic disarmament' aimed to diminish losses caused by the fall in demand witnessed in the late 1980s, radical military expenditure cuts and the collapse of the WTO military market. The overall reduction plans envisaged a 85–89 percent cut (compared to the 1987 peak level) in military production by the end of 1992, with deeper cuts in Slovakia.

Between 1985 and 1993, a 'Special Technology Fund' existed to finance conversion projects. Until 1991, state support took the form of direct transfers to the enterprises. However, most of this money was spent as a simple state subsidy. This is why, in 1991, the government decided to finance specific projects and not enterprises and expressed its view that conversion support 'will have to be spent rationally, conforming to market criteria'. From 1991, the sum allocated by the federal budget for conversion (Kcs 1.5 billion) was managed through the 'Fund for Structural Changes' and was aimed at special conversion projects. This Fund finances long-term projects of structural adjustment, such as environmental programmes, energy-saving projects and conversion. According to Ministry of Economy figures, the federal government's financial support for conversion was as shown in Table 7.2.

Table 7.2   *Financial support for military conversion (Kcs, billions, current prices)*

	1989	1990	1991
Total	0.4	1.2	1.5
CR	—	0.35	0.3
SR	0.4	0.85	1.2

Source: Ministry of Economy, Prague, 1992.

In addition to subsidies aimed at financing conversion projects, in 1991 the federal government provided Kcs 2.266 million to reduce damages caused by the halting of military production and Kcs 6.5 million for requalification. Plans for 1992 originally allocated Kcs 1.5 billion to already existing conversion projects.

Conversion Competition

In 1990, a large-scale conversion competition was announced, and 98 enterprises and research institutes presented 304 projects (186 from the Czech and 118 from the Slovak Republic) to a special committee appointed by the federal Ministry of Economy. The committee consisted of representatives of the federal Ministries of Economy, Finance, Foreign Trade and Industry, as well as regional ministries and banks. It ceased to exist after the competition was completed and state subsidies were pledged.

In general, the conversion projects were elaborated by the enterprise management and white-collar workers, in some cases with the help of foreign trade companies or specialized research institutes. Successful applicants could receive state subsidies and/or apply for special loans from the regional banks. Bank credits were pledged only if the plans had already received official approval. Altogether, 125 plans were approved: 60 in the Czech lands and 65 in Slovakia. The projects were divided into two groups: those with a budget over Kcs 50 million and those under. From the first group, four large-scale projects were chosen by the federal government: the Hannomag and Lombardini projects at Turcianske Strojarni in ZTS Martin, the mobile hydraulic cranes project at ZTS Dubnica and the chassis production project in Detva. The first three projects aimed to convert heavy weaponry production, whereas the fourth was to replace special military engineering products. All of the projects were based in Slovakia. Their aggregate costs reached Kcs 4.185 billion, out of which the state would cover 453 million. The federal Ministry of Economy selected more than 100 smaller projects and in a handful of cases Czech regional banks decided to finance the projects without central participation.[4]

State subsidies could only be used to purchase new technology, licences and to pay interest. Although the ceiling of the state's contribution was limited to 30 percent of the project's total costs, in exceptional cases, when the project implied global technical restructuring, it could reach 50 percent. In theory, a state contribution was only given if the factory was able to cover 70 percent of the project's total costs. However, according to the representatives of the Czech Ministry of Industry, there was no recorded case of a regional bank refusing to pledge credits for an enterprise at least nominally involved in conversion. Given the dire financial state of the enterprises, however, it was quite unlikely that the enterprises could really meet these requirements. The fact that no application was rejected by the banks also shows that the conditions for financial support in reality were rather soft.

The proposed new products fell into three categories. There were projects based on the extension of already existing civilian production lines, for example producing hunting guns instead of machine guns (hand-weapons factory, Uherski Brod) or consumer electronics in Tesla, Pardubice. Another group of projects aimed to create new profiles to complement existing civilian production, for example to produce machinery for the civilian production already going on in the same firm. (These included textile machinery, small tractors in the Vlazske engineering factory (Slavicin) and in Zbojovka (Vsetin); pneumatic equipment and electromagnetic horns (Policka), sliding meters and motorcycle brakes (Zeveta in Boykovice).) The third group of projects tried to find market niches and create totally new types of products. The factory Zeveta Boykovice, for example, suggested producing metal-cutting instruments, toys and civilian bridges instead of grenades, rockets and anti-tank weapons; the Povazska engineering factory (Povazska Bystrica) proposed agricultural machinery, small cars and ecological equipment, replacing jet aircraft engines, and the Slovak Shipyards (Komarno) containers instead of military transport equipment.

Results

The selected conversion projects were due to begin in October 1991. Out of the 60 projects originally accepted, about 30–40 had been implemented in the Czech lands by mid-1992. According to Slovak Deputy Prime Minister Roman Kovac, there were 11 conversion projects under way in Slovakia in early 1993, covering about half of the fall in military production.

The most documented conversion programme was in ZTS Martin in central Slovakia. The main factory in Martin employed 17 000 workers in the 1970s and was originally constructed to produce 800 tanks in a 'normal' year and 950 in an emergency. Conversion efforts date back to 1988, when ZTS signed a contract with the Hannomag company (Germany) to produce tractors and construction machinery. In 1990, another agreement was completed with Lombardini (Italy) on the establishment of a small diesel engine plant. In addition to being expensive, conversion presented another problem for the factory, specifically concerning marketing and the workforce. According to the licence agreement with Lombardini, for example, the factory can sell its engines only to Eastern European markets, which, at present, are unable to absorb the huge volume produced. The international market for large engines, tractors and construction materials is also near saturation. The difficulties stemming from the unfavourable external environment were multiplied by the need for fundamental structural reorganization and a radically different managerial approach, both of which were postponed while the management awaited a government decision on the enterprise's privatization.

In the case of the other large military enterprise in Slovakia, ZTS Dubnica and Vahom, where infantry fighting vehicles were produced, the original conversion plans envisaged mechanical gearboxes and machinery for rubber, chemical and food production. The enterprise searched for potential business partners who could have provided the capital, know-how and markets for new civilian products. In the end, out of roughly 2000 potential foreign investors, only one, Reda Corp. (Oklahoma, USA) was interested and signed a contract to transfer technology for drilling pumps that could be sold to Russia in exchange for crude oil. Between 1989 and 1993, the workforce dropped from 16 000 to 7500 and the revenues from $164 million to $89 million. The military production's share in the revenues fell from $89 million to $23 million, and in 1992 it was limited to producing spare parts and completing existing contracts.

The cases of the Meopta Optical Works in Slovakia and the enterprise Adast in the Czech lands seem to be somewhat more convincing conversion success stories. In the past about 50 percent of Meopta's output was military-related. Over a period of five years, the company's total output dropped by two-thirds and the military production's share fell to about 10 percent. The workforce shrank from 2500 to 500 by early 1993. The enterprise produces overhead projectors and other optical instruments for educational purposes, for example a self-designed project that projects images directly from a computer. Thanks to its dynamic market strategy, Meopta has succeeded in penetrating the international market, although the management is worried about future sales perspectives.

This case confirms one of the general concerns of conversion, namely that even a relatively successful transformation requires major cuts in both production and workforce. The absence of feasible regional development projects that would be able to address these problems discourages the enterprise-centred managements from making real commitments to conversion. The directors of the Martin factory, for example, refused to undertake even elementary reorganization projects for fear of having to lay off workers, which would cause major social tensions in a town that is completely dependent on the firm. Meopta's situation is easier since it is located on the outskirts of Bratislava which, even in these times of crisis, is able to offer more employment opportunities.

Adast used to be one of the oldest Czech military factories that produced mechanical parts for bombs and rockets. According to the enterprise's general director, there was no military production at all by 1993 and even the machinery and premises kept for 'cold capacities', that is in case of mobilization in time of war, were used for civilian purposes. The company extended its already existing civilian profile, the production of printing machinery, and introduced new lines, such as oil pumps. Although it has not yet reached the profitability of the years when military production was predominant, the enterprise is in a relatively solid financial state and produces and exports civilian goods all over the world, from China to the USA.

There are some other successful transformations to note. The Ceska Zbrojovka (Uherski Brod) factory has begun to produce sports and hunting guns and Blanicke Strojirny in Vlasim extended its rubber pipes production in place of bombs and introduced new lines for tools and small tractors for vineyards. Both companies started by extending their already existing civilian production, which means that the difficulties of retooling and retraining were considerably smaller than for a company launching an entirely new profile.[5]

There have been allegations that financial support for conversion was often used to reduce the enterprises' debts or even to continue military production.[6] Unfortunately, for many indebted defence industry enterprises, conversion was simply a desperate attempt to obtain further state and bank resources. In the summer of 1992, the Ministry of Control began a wide-ranging investigation to monitor how conversion subsidies were spent. The results were not made public, but representatives of the respective ministries and some outside sources claim that the specific government funds allocated for conversion were used properly.

There is no doubt that the bulk of factories have been radically cutting their military production. Military output fell on average by 70 percent in three years, with some companies stopping altogether, most of them reducing their defence-related production. However, a simple drop in output does not mean conversion. In most factories, particularly in Slovakia, both technology and the workforce became idle but not converted, causing further economic losses and increasing social tensions.

The obvious pains of conversion and the relatively modest financial and technical assistance provided for it made the majority of military enterprises uninterested in or hostile to the whole process. Paradoxically, in reality little conversion has actually been taking place. The main blows to the military sector – the gradual decline in demand, the radical defence expenditure cuts, the growing difficulties of third world customers and the collapse of the Warsaw Pact – happened before the launching of the state-sponsored conversion projects.

Despite some positive experiences, both governmental and industrial circles have gradually come to the conclusion that the conversion programmes gathered momentum too slowly and presented too many unsolvable problems. Most difficulties (or failures) were attributed to the lack of financial resources and markets which the major decision makers seemed unable to address properly. Although military production has been steadily decreasing since 1987, conversion became a scapegoat for all the defence industry's ills. Rejecting conversion served as a justification for 'easy' solutions: instead of restructuring, rescue military production; instead of facing domestic and external market challenges, return to state protection.

The slow pace, few convincing results, possible abuses, the industrialists' resistance and the fundamental political changes that have been taking place in Czechoslovakia made the government change its conversion policy by mid-1992. Growing mistrust and lack of interest, in some cases open hostility, made the government not only reduce the amount of state contribution, but rethink its whole strategy. A report on conversion by Vladimir Dlouhy, federal Minister of Economy, presented to the Federal Assembly in the spring of 1992, suggested that only those factories which halted arms production altogether should receive subsidies for conversion: 'I do not want the present policy going on, which allows a tank producer to receive state subsidies for conversion only because it simultaneously started to produce Italian diesel engines as well. . . . Only in the long run, when all developed countries will indeed stop arms production, will we join them.'

Since even the enterprises most committed to conversion envisaged a gradual transformation, with a steady diversification of the product range, the government's decision was undoubtedly a blow to conversion efforts. In addition, the parallel liberalization of arms exports served as an incentive to continue producing and exporting weapons. The most blatant statement concerning the revised relationship of economic development and military production came from Vaclav Klaus, (then) federal Minister of Finance: 'Our foreign policy should first and foremost be profitable for us. I am against cheap gestures. We should not be the most peaceful country in the world, which does not sell a single bullet or gun to anyone. These ideas sound nice, but they are forced upon us by countries that themselves export arms to the whole world.'

The Future: Revival or Bankruptcy

Despite their precarious economic state, most defence industry factories intended to maintain production at whatever price, even producing for stock. They used reduced work time, obligatory holidays, lower salaries and inter-enterprise indebtedness to diminish the running costs of production. They continued to absorb and waste the scarce resources of the country, although at an undoubtedly lower level than in the past. Many enterprises were led by sheer inertia, but many sensed the significant changes on the Czechoslovak political scene and decided to 'wait and see'. Rising unemployment made outright closures increasingly risky and politically undesirable.

As early as 1991, a 'revivalist' current had emerged among representatives of the defence industry and the attached ministries. Their arguments were taken up in the 1992 election campaign, both by the Czech and the Slovak political elites. It seems that short-term economic and political considerations or sheer inertia both at the macroeconomic and enterprise level make the idea of revamping the defence industry more attractive than the challenging, complicated, timeconsuming conversion programmes. The 'revivalists' claim that the post-1989 period was a time of naive humanism, brutally abused by other arms-producing countries. When Czechoslovakia unilaterally withdrew from the lucrative armaments market, its place was immediately occupied by Western, Eastern European and Chinese exporters, selling weapons not only to Czechoslovakia's former clients, but to countries under international embargo as well, including what used to be Yugoslavia. According to this view, the damage caused by the federal government's conversion policy and ban on arms exports could only be repaired if the country was to regain its position on the international military market. The new policy of 'pragmatic realism' envisages a 'rational armaments production' operating on a commercial basis. The best way to revamp Czechoslovakia's military production is cooperation with Western military firms, both by widening already existing contacts with the USA, France, Britain and Germany and by finding other partners. Another suggestion, formulated back in 1991, was to create an armaments producers' association in order to improve the situation of the defence industry enterprises. Since then the Federal Union of State Enterprises and Joint Stock Companies has been established with 31 participants and in Slovakia the Union of Engineering Industry has been set up, both representing enterprises involved in military production. Before this new policy direction was formally accepted, the federal Ministries of Economy and of Foreign Trade decided to act as mediators between Czechoslovak and foreign arms producers to promote further cooperation.

Aero Vodochody (Prague) is one of the success stories of the already revived Czech military industry. In cooperation with US and Canadian firms (among others, General Electric) the company has modernized its L-39 jet trainer, 90 percent of which in the past was produced for Soviet markets. Owing to the new, modernized version, the factory's products sell extremely well. The main buyers are Nigeria, Egypt, Thailand, the Philippines and another, unspecified, Southeast Asian country.

In addition to major political changes, the future of the defence industry in the former Czechoslovakia will be determined by the continuing privatization process. Large state-owned enterprises were to be privatized in two waves during 1992, partly within the privatization programme, partly by centralized, case-by-case methods. The latter was suggested as the preferred method to privatize the military sector's enterprises, mainly using closed or semi-closed bids. Most military factories were transformed into (still state-owned) stockholding companies, in preparation for privatization.

It is still difficult to assess the impact of privatization on military production. The general experience is that the prolonged period of preparation causes general insecurity, which in turn contributes significantly to the erosion of defence industry enterprises. The best employees leave the sector, while the remaining management is reluctant to take any substantial decisions because they cannot envisage the company's (and their own) future, not even in the short-term. As far as already privatized firms are concerned, it is still too early to tell whether ownership changes created major improvements in economic management.

Many military producers and representatives of the related ministries would like the state to keep majority shares in military factories even if they were privatized. A significant percentage of shares (or a symbolic golden share) would guarantee the state's right to interfere in decisions concerning military production or conversion. It was also suggested that large military enterprises should be first decentralized and sold in units, with the state keeping the military-related assets. Some, for example the research group of the Academy of Science, argued that the Ministry of Defence should be directly involved in decisions concerning the privatization of military-related enterprises and should retain its right to ask the government to keep some of the factories, since the armed forces lack resources to import new military technology and spare parts.

Although the state is still the most important actor in the whole military economy, it did not specify openly what kind of role, if any, it was going to play in the future defence industry. This means that, in theory, the new private owners could decide either to continue military production or to pursue conversion projects. Since the government is apparently disillusioned by conversion and potential new private entrepreneurs are more likely to be attracted by alternatives promising quick and high returns than by a long-term, not immediately profitable transformation process, the prospects of conversion are certainly not very encouraging.

ARMS TRADE

Arms trade has traditionally been one of the most important and lucrative sectors of the Czechoslovak economy. The country was the fifth largest arms exporter between the two world wars. During the late 1980s, it ranked as the seventh largest arms exporter in the world, representing approximately 1.5 percent of world arms exports and 0.9 percent of the sales to the third world. The bulk of military exports went to the members of the Warsaw Treaty Organization, mainly to the Soviet Union and the GDR, and, according to the general WTO rules, the income was used to cover arms imports within the organization. In some sectors, for example in the production of heavy military trucks, nearly the total output was exported.

According to Ministry of Defence data, arms exports represented an average 7–8 percent of total exports (Table 7.3) in the 1980s.[7] In November 1989, when the political transformation took place, arms sales represented 6.5 percent of the hard currency earnings of the country.

Table 7.3 Arms exports as percentage of total exports

1966	1968	1970	1975	1980	1985	1989
11.8	9.8	10.4	6.9	7.1	8.7	7.2

Source: Ministry of Defence, 1992.

In the 1970s, several third world countries began to buy Czechoslovak military hardware. They were attracted by the relatively high-quality and comparatively cheap weapons, while their main appeal from the Czechoslovak side was that they paid in hard currency, although, as the data on unpaid claims prove, their performance was fairly uneven. The main partners were the Middle East states and some African countries, such as Nigeria, Ethiopia, Tanzania and Zimbabwe. After the collapse of WTO, these countries represented the principal market for the Czechoslovak arms industry. Arms exports outside the Warsaw Pact earned the country an annual average $850 million in cash or other essential resources, such as oil, in the 1980s.

Compared to the 1986 figures, by 1990 arms exports fell by 47 percent. Deals with non-WTO countries declined by 77 percent. In this period the industry's main markets were Libya, India and Iran. In 1991, arms sales dropped further, to about 12 percent of sales in the previous year. Warsaw Pact sales figures were not made public, but exports to the third world dropped from $8 billion in 1986 to $1 billion in 1991.

After the Havel government came to power, arms exports were initially banned, but later on they were cautiously liberalized again. The original argument for liberalizing arms exports was that the earnings could be used for conversion or to import military equipment for the Czechoslovak army. Later on it became clear that arms exports were too lucrative to renounce, particularly in an economy undergoing major restructuring.

Together with the new regulations, some fundamental changes were introduced in the organizational infrastructure of weapons trade. The monopoly of the state-owned Omnipol Company, which until 1989 was the only trader of arms, was broken and arms-trading licences were issued to other, state and private, firms. In 1991, Omnipol's Slovak counterpart, Unimpex, another state-owned arms trade company, was established. Omnipol has also been modernized and now trades in medical equipment as well.

In 1990, the federal Ministry of Foreign Trade established a new department to authorize and supervise trade in military products and materials. The department issues licences for general commercial activity, including arms. Up to April 1992, 27 general licences were given, mainly to military production enterprises which were allowed to sell their own products. In addition, limited licences were issued for individual transactions. Many small and medium-scale companies involved in foreign trade managed to obtain licences to trade in weapons as well.

In 1991, only 10 percent of total exports was military-related. No finished product was sold to ex-Warsaw Pact countries; trade only included spare parts.[8] According to Western sources, the 'big deals' of the Czechoslovak arms trade during 1990–92 were 250 tanks sold to Syria and 200 sold to Peru. An agreement with Iran for the sale of 1518 surplus tanks (to be reduced according to the Conventional Forces in Europe (CFE) agreement) was completed in 1990, but was later cancelled. After Iran threatened to suspend its $2 billion worth of civilian trade with Czechoslovakia, a compromise was agreed with Baksay, Minister of Foreign Trade, to sell other, more developed, military equipment instead. There are numerous rumours about other weapons deals in the country, but these are very difficult to verify.

The general slump in the international arms market, specifically the insolvency of Middle East buyers and the proliferating black market, makes it even more difficult to sell ex-Czechoslovak products. Despite their generally good reputation, according to Glezgo of the Federal Ministry of Foreign Trade, they are difficult to introduce on the West's established military markets. The solution proposed by ministry representatives is to develop cooperation with Western military producers and sell on third markets. Most joint ventures and cooperation agreements with Western partners promise secure markets, although in several cases the former Czechoslovak side only provides spare parts, which means that the end-products are marketed under foreign brand-names.

Apart from official arms traders, there are many illegal or semi-legal companies selling weapons. Legislative proposals to control the proliferating weapons market were rejected because of the resistance of Slovak MPs, who considered them another example of 'Czech centralism'. The prevailing Slovak opinion on the question of arms exports was summarized by the 'impartial' director of Omnipol, Kozeny: 'The first priority of the new Slovak Prime Minister will be to maintain standards of living. And in Slovakia this is linked directly to allowing the arms factories, the republic's main hard currency earners, to sell.'

The relative looseness of arms trade regulations makes it possible for some companies to sell weapons even to countries embargoed by UN decisions, for example the former Yugoslavia and Libya. In early 1992, the government published the list of countries where it was forbidden to sell arms in order to prevent such transactions. Owing to the legal loopholes, the federal authorities can stop, but cannot prosecute, illegal traders. Nevertheless, the decision created a significant uproar. As an official put it: 'Publishing the list of the countries where we cannot sell arms was embarrassing, because it indicated that we did not trust these countries and will most likely have a negative impact on our civilian trade with them.'

In mid-1992, the government again reformulated its arms exports policy. It waived the general ban on arms exports, allowing individual (private or state) enterprises to produce and sell arms, without any state intervention, thereby allowing exports to those countries which are not on the state's embargo list. The government's decision can be understood as a recognition that it was no longer able to resist the pressure of the representatives of the arms industry and the increasingly radical Slovak opposition to federal regulation of the arms trade.[9]

THE ROLE OF CONVERSION TO THE BREAK-UP OF THE FEDERATION

While the break-up of Czechoslovakia involved a complex set of political, economic and historical factors in which the post-1989 transformation was decisive, the regional pattern of the defence industry became a key factor in determining the fate of the Federation. The development of the defence industry took different directions in the two parts of the country. After the communist take-over in 1948, the Czech and Moravian lands continued the pre-war traditions of the arms industry and took up production under Soviet licence, mainly as a complementary activity. In Slovakia, in contrast, as in the other backward economies of Eastern Europe after World War Two, the development of a Soviet-style weapons industry was seen as an easy means of rapid industrialization.

In some respects the two parts of the Federation represented two separate development patterns. Slovakia functioned as any other 'ordinary' member of the Warsaw Pact 'brotherhood' and used Soviet licences. The Czech lands enjoyed slightly more independence because of their higher level of development. The Slovak arms industry was subordinated to both Czech and Warsaw Treaty Organisation needs, and it is paying a double price for this now. Its oversized military industry seems to be unable to cope with the devastating effects of the crisis and the challenges of conversion, but at the same time, unlike its Czech counterparts, it seems to be unable to attract Western investors to modernize its enterprises and break into lucrative military markets.

As the size and nature of the defence industry was different, conversion problems were also somewhat different in the two parts of the country. Slovakia, where the military sector was more concentrated, less diversified and developed, was hit by the crisis more severely than the rest of the country. The decision to halt tank and armed personnel carrier production and exports was made by the federal government in 1990. After long constitutional disputes about the Republics' competencies, the Slovak government, led by Carnogursky, regained control over military production in early 1991. It decided to continue a limited amount of tank production and export, in order to ease the growing social tension due to massive lay-offs. At the same time, Slovakia also became involved in conversion programmes. In January 1992, it published its own document, 'On conversion of arms production in industrial enterprises in Slovakia', which attempted to lay out a comprehensive strategy to address the problem. The idea gained support among regional and local organizations as well. Regional and municipal authorities, mainly in Martin and Dubnica, tried to work out proposals to resolve the grave problems caused by the defence industry's crisis, in cooperation with the factories, regional developers and representatives of the emerging private sector.

The Czech government did not confront the question with such vigour. The situation in the Czech lands was certainly much less dramatic. According to the Ministry of Defence, there were only two seriously affected companies: the ammunition factory in Boykovice and the Adamovski in Brno. Czech sources did not report significant job losses due to conversion either, claiming that the alternative civil production absorbed the redundant workforce.

The federal institutions were unable or unwilling to address conversion in its complexity. Labour, regional, market or industrial policy dimensions of the problem were not seriously addressed. There were no policy decisions on direct and indirect economic means that could have facilitated conversion, like preferential credits, tax allowances or specific wage regulations, which all fell within the federal government's competence. Conversion and the whole set of related issues had no 'patron'. Once the federal government decision was made, the task of promoting and monitoring the whole process was distributed among several federal and regional ministries and government agencies. In the end, no one party was clearly responsible for conversion or able to handle its specific requirements and immediate consequences.

The conversion problem and the conflicts it triggered were used as a pretext to fuel separatist ambitions both on the Czech and the Slovak side. Although it was hardly ever expressed openly, there was some resentment on the Czech side about the large sums of federal money being spent on Slovak military producers. The slowness and the growing problems of conversion alienated the Czech side even more. Dlouhy's statement about 'fake' conversion obviously refers to Slovak enterprises. According to the Slovak interpretation, Prague was eager to promote conversion in Slovakia and let the Czech and Moravian branches survive, having in mind from the very beginning the idea of a possible NATO membership, which would require a strong, modernized army.[10]

In the meantime, in the campaign of the emerging Slovak nationalist opposition led by Vladimir Meciar, conversion became the general scapegoat for all the dramatic consequences of the unfolding economic crisis. With an original linguistic twist, enterprises became 'hit by conversion' and the state was pressed to take care of them. Since the federal government was unable (and somewhat reluctant) to do so, the 'genuinely national' movement promised to undertake the issue. Prague's continued insensitivity to Slovakia's specific problems convinced many Slovaks that Meciar's promise of autonomy in the form of a confederation would resolve their economic hardships. Before the June 1992 elections, in an absurd end-game, arms production and exports became the symbol of Slovak national sovereignty, worth defending at any price.

At the same time, the Czech leadership seemed unwilling to take into account the growing social and national tensions and began to envisage Slovakia as an unwanted handicap which was not only expensive, but slowed down the desired union with the developed Western world. The Czech decision makers at the same time 'discovered' that they too needed lucrative arms exports and they could capitalize on the advantages of their relative development during the state socialist period and on their pre-war military traditions. This made conversion another unwanted remnant of the immediate post-1989 agenda.

After the divorce, both sides revealed the real motives behind their lobbying for separate countries. The separation not only cleared the path towards fulfilling the deep aspirations that the 'other side' seemed to hinder, it also gave an evident boost to build up national armies and therefore to rescue what was left of the respective defence industries. In one of his first interviews, the new prime minister of Slovakia, Meciar, declared that 'arms production will be resurrected wherever possible'. In a meeting with representatives of the Ministry of Defence he promised that 'the Slovak army will have enough means to guarantee its efficiency, even if these means will have to be provided at the expense of other budget items'. According to the new policy guidelines, the resurrection of the military industry is needed to generate export earnings, but also to feed the new Slovak national army facing the 'threats' of neighbouring Hungary. However, after Meciar's first belligerent statements, major actors in the Ministry of Economy and the defence industry declared that massive investment in reviving the defence industry would be a futile exercise. Independent of further decisions on military production, the Slovak government agreed to provide KS 1.500 million for conversion projects already under way.

The Czech Republic did not initially have any specific conversion policy because the new leadership considered the support provided by the previous federal government to be sufficient and was convinced that, in the new market environment, factories have to cope with their difficulties by themselves. In extraordinary cases enterprises can apply to the Ministry of Industry for specific funds, to be provided on an individual basis. Similarly, if military producers have viable (and, it is hoped, exportable) development projects, they too can ask for state-guaranteed loans.

The developments that have been taking place since 1 January 1993, when the division became formal, seem to confirm the gloomy predictions about the future of the two independent republics. In the fairly precarious state of the Slovak economy, arms sales seem to be an easy and viable means of earning hard currency. Instead of conversion and radical restructuring, heavy weapons production resumed, not only in Martin, but in some other major factories as well. Slovakia delivered its last instalment of 250 T-72 tanks to Syria and began negotiating new deals with Syria, Pakistan, Egypt and several other Arab countries. The Slovak Republic was the first former Warsaw Pact member country to produce new artillery equipment, with calibre compatible with NATO standards. This means that even significant R&D costs must again be provided for enterprises engaged in military production.

The Czech Republic is busy promoting arms sales and streamlining its army in the hope of a quick integration into NATO. In addition to keeping up its already established trade links with several Western and third world countries, it negotiated a controversial deal to sell weapons to Iran. The most significant development, however, is the creation of a new, private consortium, the Research and Development Group, to design, produce and market Czech military products. The group that unites the most important defence industry firms is headed by the general director of Skoda-Plzen, an enterprise that decreased its military-related production to 5 percent by the early 1990s, but which made plans to increase it again in 1993.

It is likely that military production will be restored in both republics, at about 20–30 percent of its peak level and with some sectors, principally those with export potential, promoted intensively. Conversion will continue to burden those enterprises that will be unable to recover a high level of defence-related production; therefore it will remain a source of major economic and social imbalances. The break-up of the country not only set back development in both regions and created significant, unnecessary losses and pains, but also led to a boost in arms production and exports in both republics.[11] These consequences are sinister enough to make clear the importance of a well-founded, convincing and properly implemented conversion project in the countries of Eastern Europe.

CONVERSION DILEMMAS

Problems with the Conversion Projects

The conversion projects accepted by the conversion committee and implemented by the respective enterprises were fairly innovative in technical terms. Many of them were the fruits of the unique creativity of workers and engineers working under the permanent shortages and malfunctions of the command economy. However, they were not genuine conversion projects in a broad sense. They failed to take into consideration the global context in which conversion was to take place and the way it was expected to be accomplished. The prevailing industrial structures and forms of management were taken for granted and the ideas of technological innovation were accommodated within this framework. Most of them shared two important shortcomings: they did not address the implications for the workforce and lacked wider-scale economic considerations.

Being principally engineering creations, the bulk of the conversion projects neglected the problems of the workforce. Even if there were sufficient resources and reserves, and technically it was possible to create new lines of production, the workers had to be retrained, redeployed and some of them inevitably made redundant. For most firms this came as an unpleasant surprise which they were not equipped to handle. To complicate the problem, the ministries nominally in charge refused responsibility as well; representatives of the Ministry of Industry assigned the problem to the competence of the Ministry of Labour, which sent it forward to the Ministry of Defence, and so on; federal government agencies passed it to local offices and vice versa.

Most projects were designed by the enterprise management, in cooperation with their white-collar personnel or outside experts, but rarely included representatives of the workers of the plants themselves. Except in some rare cases, the human factor, the need for employee and union participation, was missing from both the plans and the actual management of the conversion projects. This can explain why, on the whole, workers have not been very supportive of conversion in the former Czechoslovakia.[12] They were the first losers of both the contraction of the defence industry and the immediate difficulties of conversion. At the same time, they were not involved in the process of solution seeking and often were not even informed about the projects. Instead of a long-term, viable alternative to an obsolete and wasteful industrial system, they have experienced conversion as a direct threat to their jobs or habitual work tasks. One of the major shortcomings of the whole conversion process in the former Czechoslovakia was the lack of motivation and support for those most affected, a sad testimony to the democratic deficit of the 'Velvet Revolution'.

Another weak point of the conversion projects was that they were not complemented by economic feasibility studies. They appeared as a 'leap in the dark' and, understandably enough, most of them crashed. They failed to take into consideration the wider economic environment, financial, cost, marketing and investment dimensions. This certainly contributed to the fact that even those projects that were accepted by the conversion committee and received state support have been struggling for survival.

A common problem was an almost absolute neglect (or ignorance) of market realities. Products were designed on a technical basis and not confronted by the actual needs and opportunities of the domestic or foreign markets. In the Policska ammunition factory, for example, the management examined 100 conversion proposals and selected 10 plans to be produced. Some of them, for example spare parts for hydraulic brakes, sell relatively well, but most of the new products have problems with marketing. Simple durable consumer goods, like vacuum cleaners or household mixers, can hardly sell because of lack of effective demand, while more sophisticated products, like pneumatic equipment, have to face competition from well-established Western firms.

Problems at the Enterprise Level

At the enterprise level the defence industry's firms are even more unsuited to adjusting to changing external conditions than the civilian ones. During the long decades when they enjoyed a special status and were provided with almost unlimited resources, a fairly predictable environment, 'reliable' five-year plans, huge, stable markets and other special advantages, they rarely faced economic efficiency criteria or the necessity to adjust to external changes. At the same time, they were also condemned to isolation because of the strict rules of secrecy that surrounded the sector. This left military producers much more vulnerable than their (similarly shocked) civilian counterparts when they had to cope with 'normal' economic conditions. Most enterprises, but specifically the military ones, lack such basic skills as industrial design, double accounting, marketing or flexible management. Moreover, they also face specific technical problems. Owing to the requirements of military production, most firms have special physical conditions: huge buildings, established generally in remote territories, surrounded by concrete and double-wired fences. They had to be able to cater to emergency situations, therefore they were oversized and over-equipped. They were also burdened by huge stocks and material reserves, specialized machines and technology, which proved difficult to sell or convert.

The resistance to change is fairly typical of the whole obsolete, overweight heavy industry in Czechoslovakia, which should have been restructured long ago. However, in contrast to other seriously hit enterprises of the heavy industry, defence-related firms have been able to lobby successfully and postpone, at least for the time being, the unavoidable adjustments. The members of the military establishment have always been powerful negotiating partners, because of their political connections and their weight in the economy, particularly in Slovakia. After the political turnover, top management was changed in most defence industry factories and there were also significant changes in personnel in subordinate posts. According to several observers, however, there are indications that these alterations served the formation of a new, now multi-party-based nomenklatura, rather than a more efficient management.

Although the bulk of defence-related enterprises are on the verge of bankruptcy, only a handful of them have been shut down and relatively few have succeeded in restructuring or introducing reforms in management, internal organization, accounting systems, market strategy or changing profile. Many firms did not even use the modest support provided by the state if it implied genuine restructuring efforts. Only

10 of the Slovak defence-related companies took the opportunity to write off their single-purpose military machinery. In 1992, the federal budget provided Kcs 116 million for retraining, but only Kcs 8.5 million was requested by the enterprises and only Kcs 6.5 million was actually used.

The enterprises' half-hearted approach explains why a significant amount of money earmarked for conversion could be used for other purposes. The 'flexible' conditions for obtaining additional credits facilitated the postponement of radical changes within the enterprises. Conversion subsidies and conversion-purpose credits could be used as financial injections to maintain ailing military or civilian production. The idea of 'seed-money' can hardly be employed in an economy in which most companies are insolvent, there is a general lack of capital and the old patterns of enterprise 'problem solving' – such as false accounting, inter-enterprise indebtedness and mobilizing informal personal networks to gain access to scarce resources – remain unchanged.

Problems at the Macroeconomic Level

One of the major problems hindering conversion in East Central Europe is the fact that it is taking place parallel with a major economic and social transformation of the region. This uneasy historical transition to a fully-fledged market economy is made even more difficult by the deep crisis that has been unfolding in the last decades but became acute and visible from the late 1980s. Even without conversion, the crisis produces unemployment, drastically falling living standards, social tensions, growing inequalities, masses of enterprises in a state of virtual bankruptcy, and major sectoral and regional disequilibria. Conversion, at least in the short run, aggravates these problems. Since the two processes unfold simultaneously and their consequences are interwoven, it is very easy to mix them up, especially if it serves short-sighted political interests.

The strict neo-liberal stabilization measures taken in order to overcome the crisis and establish the new economic model have inevitably created further difficulties for conversion. As a result of the restrictive monetary policy, credit is in short supply and public expenditures are radically curtailed. This makes financing conversion projects very difficult. The sudden withdrawal of most state subsidies and the parallel increased tax burdens have pushed most military enterprises into a sudden financial collapse. The lack of liquid resources has created a complicated system of mutual indebtedness among enterprises.[13] The emerging new barter-like exchange system fosters the conservation of existing structures both within and among enterprises, calling into question the chances of radical change, envisaged by conversion programmes.

At the same time, the high taxes and high interest rates indiscriminately levied on private enterprises restrict the chances of survival of the potential new private firms that could be set up using the premises and assets of former military enterprises or employing the workers made redundant. The restrictive monetary policy has also led to a drastic fall in both private and public consumption which, further squeezing the effective demand, limits the marketing opportunities for newly developed civilian products.

The provision of functioning market economy institutions, such as a stock exchange, flexible factor markets or a well-developed, multilayered, versatile bank system, could partly compensate for the lack of state-provided financial assistance. Converting enterprises would require medium- and long-term credits allowing them to get through the difficult transition period from military to civilian production. Unfortunately decentralized regional banks, specialized sector banks, and small or medium-size banks that would be able to help converting enterprises are either absent or undercapitalized. The credit policy of the central bank and main commercial banks at the same time is specifically short-term, owing to the volatility of the economic situation and the monopolistic position they still enjoy.

Another aspect of the transition to the market economy is that, in pursuing a 'pure' free-market ideology, the social consequences of the drastic changes have been overlooked. The unexpectedly high costs of the 'shock therapy' implemented in the defence sector were justified by the envisaged positive impact of 'healthy market forces'. This neglect of social consequences, however, created a strong backlash and in the end led to a complete policy reversal, inspiring a return to state protection, mostly in Slovakia but to some extent in the Czech Republic as well. (The free-market ideology is also used to prove that weapons are 'neutral' products like any other, therefore no economic or moral discipline should prevent them from being produced and sold if they are profitable.)

Financing conversion is one of the key problems of the whole issue. The question is who finances it, what should be financed and from what resources. The cost calculations presented in the original conversion projects were exaggerated in themselves, but specifically in the light of the possibilities of the economy in transition and the already overstretched state budget. Aggregating the estimated losses of the defence industry due to the loss of markets plus the total costs of conversion (calculated on the basis of the original plans) plus costs of the suggested alternative projects (which would have needed some time for maturation before yielding benefits), the proposed sum would have exhausted the bulk of the state's resources.

The calculations seem even more unfavourable in comparison with the immediate gains expected from arms exports and the (presumably) lower costs of modernizing the military industry, in the hope of future expansion. (The problem with these calculations is that they reflect short-term and enterprise-centred rationality. In the long run and in global economic terms, defence industry innovation and development requires huge investments, but these costs are spread over the whole society and not covered directly by the military factories.)

The pressing needs of the overall economic restructuring require enormous resources. Although in 1989–90 conversion was a priority political target, the economic resources allocated for this purpose were fairly limited. Later, parallel to the shift in the country's foreign policy from endorsing a neutral, collective European security system to advocating NATO membership, conversion gradually 'slid down' in the hierarchy of the economic and political targets. This meant even fewer central state resources and more half-hearted decisions to push for it.

Political and Social Problems

After the 1992 elections that brought a devastating defeat for the Civic Movement, the main grouping of dissidents who led the 'Velvet Revolution', a new force of 'technocratic elite', represented by Vaclav Klaus, emerged. The creation of a collective pan-European security system based on the CSCE was abandoned in favour of NATO membership and an exclusive Western orientation. As far as the defence industry and conversion was concerned, the 'idealistic' policy to cut radically defence expenditures, arms exports and arms production capacities gave way to the 'pragmatic' orientation of reconsidering the importance of the national army (specifically as a hopeful NATO member), the national defence industry (as the army's main supplier and also as an attractive branch for foreign investments) and evidently the still fairly lucrative weapons sales.

In 1986, Vaclav Havel in his essay, 'An Anatomy of Reticence' wrote:

> the sole meaningful way to genuine European peace – and not simply to some armistice or 'non-war' – is the path of a fundamental restructuring of the political realities that are the roots of the current crisis. This would require both sides to abandon in a radical manner their defence policy of

maintaining the status quo (that is the division of Europe into blocs) as well as their policy of power or superpower 'interests' subordinating all their efforts to something quite different – to the ideal of a democratic Europe as a friendly community of free and independent nations.

After his election, President Havel and his close collaborators launched several initiatives to strengthen the CSCE as a pan-European security forum that would replace both NATO and the Warsaw Pact. They also emphasized the importance of Eastern European cooperation, both in the political and the economic sphere, taking part actively in the Visegrad process (Poland, Czechoslovakia and Hungary cooperation) and the intentions to develop the Pentagonale group into a regional security system. However, since NATO did not disappear after the demise of the Warsaw Pact and the alternative political and security forums failed to gain importance, the Czechoslovak policy gradually moved towards participation in NATO and other established Western European institutions, most importantly the European Community. Instead of creating or reinforcing Eastern European structures, the emphasis shifted to redefining national interests, in the wider context of a desired Western European integration.

On the occasion of his first visit to the NATO headquarters in Brussels, already as President of Czechoslovakia, Havel said: 'we believe that an alliance of countries united by the ideals of freedom and democracy should not be forever closed to neighbouring countries that are pursuing the same goals. . . . NATO's defence of democracy and freedom has served as encouragement for Eastern European countries and has been a source of hope for millions of people.'

An additional political obstacle to viable conversion projects has been the absence of a new defence strategy, which would determine what kind of weapons and how many the armed forces would need in the future. It could define the scope of indispensable military production, the size of cold capacities and reserves, and would make it possible to design plans for the remaining part of the defence industry. The absence of this concept is explained by political reasons, both internal and external. Eastern Europe has become an extremely unstable region, which makes a good argument for new military build-ups. Mutual lack of confidence pushes states in the region towards rearmament and the consequent restoration of the military industry, instead of searching for cooperation and common security measures. The extreme nationalist ideologies that have re-emerged throughout the region provide ideological 'justification' for these intentions.

The emerging renewed military lobby, a powerful representative of this new ideology, is one of the few coherent pressure groups in the crisis-ridden, disunited society and therefore it has the potential to shape society much more than its actual size or economic importance would suggest. In the present critical and contradictory situation, it can build alliances through an extremely wide spectrum, including ex-Communists and 'liberal marketers', the management of moribund military factories and those who became prosperous thanks to the new opportunities of privatization and cooperation in the military sphere, and the embittered and insecure workforce, which is not offered any other alternative than an escape to the past.

Conversion: State v. Market

Each period of transition contains elements of the previous and the emerging new systems. In transforming Czechoslovakia, the rules of both market and bureaucratic coordination function side-by-side. In the sphere of arms production a rare, 'selective laissez-faire' policy has been introduced. There has been alternately a quasi-free market regulation or state intervention or a mixture of the two, depending on the interest of the strongest pressure groups and the twists of government policy. 'Pure economic' arguments were used to prove the impossibility of conversion: 'national security'-based, non-economic considerations emerged to justify state intervention to maintain arms production.

The new official policy, adopted in early 1992, was presumably 'laissez-faire', and basically meant that defence industry enterprises could not count on the traditional forms of state intervention: subsidies or other forms of preferential financial constructions and direct resource transfers in exchange for 'fulfilling' the state's policy incentives. However, the state would not disappear completely from the scene. It would intervene in arms exports if politically undesirable trade partners were involved, when state mediation was required to find lucrative markets or when state financing was pledged to develop new weapons and keep the chosen military enterprises alive. The criteria for state intervention became fairly amorphous. Although in theory arms producers could only receive state subsidies if they produced weapons vital for the country's defence, in the absence of a valid military doctrine the limits of 'vital' could be modified arbitrarily.

A 'pure economic' argument was employed to show that to meet the country's defence needs it was cheaper to produce weapons locally than to import them. Once arms production was allowed, the state was not expected to interfere because that would harm market discipline. 'In order to achieve efficiency, the industry will need to produce more and will have to export the surplus,' reasoned Nemec, a representative of the Czech Ministry of Industry. Evidently, it was never mentioned that it was the state that was expected to invest significant amounts of capital to pull bankrupt military enterprises out of the crisis and stimulate R&D and renewed production.

The increasing resistance to conversion also used 'purely economic' arguments. The federal government's original decision to halt tank production and exports was later interpreted as 'violent state intervention'[14] and continued state help for conversion was judged both unprofitable and incompatible with the new market principles. Paradoxically enough, although there was state commitment and financial help at the beginning, conversion basically was left to be accomplished by market forces. One of the general lessons of conversion in Czechoslovakia is that market forces are not sufficient to carry it out, in particular not recently introduced ones that naturally gravitate towards short-term gains. Conversion requires specific promotion: a more comprehensive state policy that takes into account the predictable negative side-effects of the restructuring period, more substantial but much more focused financial incentives and assistance, abundant (possibly preferential) credits and markets for the newly created civilian goods. It should be complemented by wide-reaching regional development projects and clear, long-term government strategies in areas such as labour, industrial and housing policy. Unfortunately, all this was missing.[15]

The Czechoslovak case underlines the fact that conversion is not a simple technical matter. It requires the conversion of the whole present way of thinking and social acting, ranging from new security concepts to a really democratic way of policy making. It requires flexible and efficient state management, able to motivate and collaborate with regional authorities and the private sector. It is only viable when it includes a wide range of active participants on different social levels: central government agencies and local authorities, civil movements, enterprise management, counting on the active participation of the workers and unions. This type of multi-level, 'interdisciplinary', flexible and democratic approach that conversion requires is absent in the transforming societies of Eastern Europe. Promoting conversion therefore is a way of learning to build a genuinely democratic society as well.

The Global Dimension

Eastern Europe's dramatic transformation takes place under conditions of a deep, worldwide recession. This means that, even if its importance is acknowledged, conversion (and in reality the whole restructuring process) has to take place with much less foreign financial help than was envisaged at the beginning. Until now, the most important external (Western) support for conversion has arrived in the form of technical expertise and advice. Even though a significant amount of foreign capital was invested in Czechoslovakia, (more than 70 percent in the Czech lands), it was much less than originally expected and than was necessary to give a genuine boost to restructuring. Foreign investments accomplished in the defence sector in most cases aimed at modernization and cooperation in military production instead of conversion.

Foreign aid and more technical assistance for conversion could have been crucial in bridging the transition period between mid-1990 and mid-1992, when military producers veered between falling back to old patterns or advancing towards conversion. Representatives of the defence industry often complain that, although there have been many seminars and conferences organized on the topic in the last three years, they received fairly little effective help in the form of aid, investment, facilitating enterprise networking, know-how exchange or market research. There have been some important undertakings, for example a substantial study on the Slovak arms industry, financed by the PHARE programme, a number of consultant projects, mainly concentrating on technical assistance, and a joint Institute for East–West Studies and the Helsinki Citizens' Assembly project to develop the Martin region, but they were unable to make a significant impact.

In addition, owing to the long, global economic recession and the increasingly protectionist policy of the major Western economic powers, including the 'uniting' Europe, potential foreign markets for the fruits of conversion prove to be limited also. But even if they were more welcoming, in most developed countries the markets for durable consumer goods and other typical products of conversion, such as agricultural and construction machinery, are either near saturation or are spheres of intense competition. And although the enormous markets of the former Eastern bloc could happily absorb all these products, they are difficult to reach or present insoluble financial difficulties in the present conditions of crisis and chaos.

One of the bitter lessons of the Czechoslovak case is that conversion should be pursued as a genuinely worldwide project. Partial conversion, as well as partial disarmament, leaves open the possibility of reversal at any time. The complaints about the counties that immediately occupied the abandoned Czechoslovak positions in the arms market and earned huge profits that the economy badly needed are unfortunately justified. However, while conversion should be proposed globally, in the meantime viable proposals should also be elaborated by the affected communities, their respective governments, outside experts and international agencies. These projects would present new types of products, a different enterprise structure and management culture and would be integrated with the development projects of the affected regions. They could serve as a positive example to show that a new form of participative management, following a long-term global survival rationale, instead of temporary profit and political interests, can be both attractive and remunerative.

NOTES

1. Western documents quote different figures. The *Financial Times* mentions 70 000 workers employed in Slovakia alone; according to a Deutsche Bank publication, altogether 250 000 people were employed by the defence industry, 100 000 directly. Most Czechoslovak sources used to quote one set of figures, until the present crisis of the sector, when numbers became 'inflated' in both the press and official publications.
2. The *Financial Times* quotes a 12–13 percent unemployment rate in Slovakia and 3–5 percent in the Czech lands (22 March 1992).
3. Dangerous workplaces, such as ammunition and explosives factories, were allowed to keep some of their privileges.
4. The state budget was unable to accommodate these requests.
5. Unfortunately, the former has been under investigation, accused of illegal arms exports, violating the ban on selling to crisis areas, possibly including the former Yugoslavia.
6. The attitude of several enterprises during the conversion competition was fairly revealing in this respect. Some of them simply applied for state subsidies, without even bothering to design a conversion plan.
7. According to other sources, arms trade counted for 47 percent of all foreign trade until the end of the 1980s, although its share was decreasing.
8. According to the *Financial Times*, exports between January and August 1991 reached $6.54bn.
9. Long before the separation, the Slovak government, violating the existing legislation, shipped a prototype armoured personnel carrier to Sudan and declared its intention to sell more. (See *The Economist*, 28 November 1992.)
10. 'The current plan of defence industry conversion is widely resented and interpreted as an insidious plot to stab the Slovaks in the back. Allegedly it is the great catastrophe that the Slovak people has had to endure since the Turkish invasion of the country in the 17th century' (*Forum*, 10 April 1991, quoted in Ulc, 1992, p. 24).
11. Events taking place since the separation confirmed predictions. The two countries are not only developing their remaining defence industries, but also competing fiercely on international markets. The latest evidence is the presentation of a Czech and a Slovak version of a T-72 tank, modernized with the help of West European arms producers, at a fair in Brno, in June 1994.
12. This is quite contrary, for example, to the experience of the Western part of Germany, where the first conversion initiatives came from grass-roots union and employee organizations.
13. According to estimates, inter-enterprise indebtedness in 1991 affected 83 percent of

the firms and reached 10 percent of GDP (Ulc, 1992, p. 25; *Financial Times*, 7 November 1991).

14. This occurred specifically in Slovak nationalist circles, where it was denounced as 'foreign' intervention as well.

15. By way of excuse, it has to be said that conversion on such a scale is an unprecedented project. The complexity and depth of the problem was simply unknown. In an article published in 1991, Dr Vrany, from the Institute of International Affairs in Prague, claimed that conversion would only require Kcs 2 billion and of the 111 military enterprises only 13 would need substantial subsidies and state support (Vrany, 1991, p. 6). The original government decisions could have been based on similar assumptions.

BIBLIOGRAPHY

Adast (1993), visit to the Adamovske Strojirny factory and interview with Jan Dosek, general director, 7 April, Adamov.

Baker, Stephany (1992), *Martin Report*, Prague: Helsinki Citizens Assembly (HCA).

Batt, Judith (1991), 'The end of Communist Rule in East Central Europe. A four-country comparison', *Politicka Ekonomie*, (Prague), no. 11–12.

Bautzova, Libuse (1993), 'Will military expenditure increase?', *Ekonom*, no. 8, February (in Czech).

Begg, David (1991), 'Czechoslovakia', *Economica Policy*, October.

Benda, Vaclav (1992), 'On the problem of the CSFR military doctrine', *The Revue*, no. 10 (in Czech).

Blaha, Jaroslav (1992), 'L'économie tchécoslovaque en 1991–1992. L'an I de la grande réforme', *Le courrier de pays de l'Est*, no. 369, May, Paris.

Borovicka, Michael (1992), 'The renaissance of arms trade?', *Noviny*, 29 May (in Czech).

Cechak, O., Selesovsky, J. and Stembera, M. (1993), 'Czechoslovakia: reductions in arms production in a time of economic and political transformation', in Herbert Wulf (ed.), *The Arms Industry Limited*, Oxford: SIPRI, Oxford University Press.

Cooley, Mike (1991), *European Competitiveness in the 21st Century*, London: FAST.

Daly, Brenon (1992), 'The flip side of peace', *Prognosis*, 4–17 September, Prague.

Deutsche Bank (1991), 'The peace dividend – How to pin it down?', report, Frankfurt.

Dienstbier, Jiri (1991), 'Report to the Parliament on CSFR and European security systems', December (in Czech).

Dlouhy, Valdimir (1992), 'Interview', *Novini*, 29 May (in Czech).

Dobrovcic, M. (1992), Head of Department of Social Relations, Federal Ministry of Defence, interview carried out by the author, 13 April, Prague.

Dobrovski, Lubos (1991a), Minister of Defence of the CSFR, 'Interview', *International Defense Review*, no. 8.

Dobrovski, Lubos (1991b), 'There is no future for tanks', *International Defense Review*, no. 8.

Droppa, Karel (1993a), 'History of armament production in Czechoslovakia', paper presented at a conference organized by the Slovak Academy of Science and the Friedrich Ebert Foundation, Bratislava.

Droppa, Karel (1993b), Head of Department of Special Production, Slovak Ministry of Economics, interview carried out by the author, 1 April, Bratislava.

Extract directory of Czechoslovakia's defence industry (1991), *Military Technology*, no. 7.

Financial Times (1991), 'The Czech and Slovak Federal Republic', 7 November, London.

Fucik, Josef (1991a), 'The Czechoslovak armament industry', *Military Technology*, no. 7.

Fucik, Josef (1991b), 'Conversion: The outline for "economic disarmament"', *Hospodarske Noviny*, no. 20 (in Czech).

Fucik, Josef (1992), Head of the Department of Defence Economy in the Federal Ministry of Economics, interview carried out by the author, 15 April, Prague.

Gennillard, Ariane (1992), 'Question of arms points up Czechoslovak divisions', *Financial Times*, 11 March, London.

Glezgo, Stefan (1992), Director-General of the Department of Military Production, Federal Ministry of Foreign Trade, interview carried out by the author, 14 April, Prague.

Havel, Vaclav (1986), *Living in Truth*, London: Faber & Faber.

Havel, Vaclav (1991), 'Speech at NATO Headquarters, 21 March, Brussels', *Atlantic News*, 22 March.

Havel, Vaclav (1992), 'New Year's Address', *East European Reporter*, March–April.

Ivanek, Ladislav (1991), 'Economic and social problems of conversion in the CSFR', manuscript presented at the seminar on Financial and Technical Assistance for Arms Conversion in the Aftermath of the Cold War, 2–4 December, Stirin.

Janda, Jaroslav and Chromec, Stanislav (1991), 'The strategic context of our defence', *Mezinarodni Politika* (in Czech).

Jonas, Jiri (1992), 'Disarmament and the structural changes in Czechoslovakia', *Politicka Ekonomie*, Prague, no. 4.

Jurak, Jiri (1992), 'The economic context of the transformation of the Czechoslovak army', *The Revue*, no. 7 (in Czech).

Kaldor, Mary (1992), 'A town called Martin adjusts to peace', *The Guardian*, 5 May, London.

Kaliar, Stepan (1993), 'Regional issues of conversion: The case of Dubnica', paper presented at a conference organized by the Slovak Academy of Science and the Friedrich Ebert Foundation, Bratislava.

Kominkova, Zora and Schmognerova, Brigita (1993), 'Conversion of military production: Comparative approaches', paper presented at a conference organized by the Slovak Academy of Science and the Friedrich Ebert Foundation, Bratislava.

Martin (1993), visit to the ZTS Martin factory and meeting with members of the management in a joint HCA & EWSS Seminar on Conversion, 29–30 March, Martin.

Matousek, J. and Ivanek, L. (1992), 'Conversion of military industry in Czechoslovakia', *Peace and the Sciences*, Vienna.

Meopta (1993), visit to the Meopta Bratislava factory and interview with Jan Chovanec, managing director and Laurenc Svitok, commercial director, Bratislava.

Mikusova, Karolina (1993), 'Fiscal and credit policy of the government: Impact on the conversion of military production', paper presented at a conference organized by the Slovak Academy of Science and the Friedrich Ebert Foundation, Bratislava.

Nemec, Vladislav (1993), Department of Technical Policy, Federal Ministry of Industry, interview carried out by the author, 8 April, Prague.

Novotni, Karel (1991), 'Defence doctrine', *Narodni Obrana* (in Czech).

OECD (1991), *Czech and Slovak Federal Republic*, Paris: OECD.

Policska (1992), visit to the Policska strojirny factory and interview with general director Pospisil, Bohumil, Policska.

Renner, Michael (1992), 'Environmental dimensions of disarmament and conversion', in K. Cassidy (ed.), *Converting the Military Economy and Building Peace*.

Sauerwein, Brigitte (1991a), 'Focus on the Czechoslovak defense industry', *International Defense Review*, no. 8.

Sauerwein, Brigitte (1991b), 'Reforming Central European defense', *International Defense Review*, no. 8.

Schmognerova, Brigita (1993), 'Behaviour of the arms producing enterprise in conversion: the comparative approach', paper presented at a conference organized by the Slovak Academy of Science and the Friedrich Ebert Foundation, Bratislava.

SIPRI (1990, 1992), *World Armaments and Disarmament*, Stockholm International Peace Research Institute, Oxford: Oxford University Press.

Slimak, Anton (1991), 'Interview', *Defense News*, 11 February.

Sutton, Oliver (1992), 'Czechoslovak industry re-orientates', *Aerospace World*, June.

Ulc, Otto (1992), 'The bumpy road of Czechoslovakia's Velvet Revolution', *Problems of Communism*, May–June.

Vojenska doktrina Ceske a Slovenske Federativni Republic (The military doctrine of the Czech and Slovak Federal Republic) (1990), Prague: Kancelar Federalniho shromazdeni CSFR.

Vrablik, J. *et al.* (1991), 'The conversion of arms production', research carried out by the Central Institute of National Economy with collaboration of external researchers, Prague.

Vrablik, Jan (1992), Central Institute of National Economy of the Czechoslovak Academy of Science, interview carried out by the author, 14 April, Prague.

Vrany, Jan (1991), 'Conversion: Transferring resources from military to civilian pursuits', *Peace and the Sciences*, December, Vienna.

World Bank (1992), *World Development Report*, Oxford: Oxford University Press.

Zamitt, Ann and Dharam, Ghai (1992), *Czechoslovakia: Which way to the market?*, Geneva: UNRISD.

8. Hungary

Yudit Kiss

The radical changes that followed the elections of 1990 in Hungary were the culmination of a process of gradual transformation that has been taking place over the last three decades. Owing to its long history of economic and political reforms, the Hungarian transition to a market economy and pluralist society has been smoother and less dramatic than those of the neighbouring Eastern European countries. Although there are major social and political tensions, these do not seem to undermine the country's integrity and are not likely to lead to disintegration, explosive ethnic conflicts of paralysing economic crisis to the same degree as in other ex-socialist countries.

Hungary's army used to be the smallest within the Warsaw Pact; the country's defence industry was never as important as that of the former Czechoslovakia; its military power was not paraded in public as was that of the former GDR. The army has never played such a significant political and social role as in the Soviet Union or in Poland. All in all, by the end of the cold war, Hungary appeared to be a 'normal' case, without strong specific features that would influence the way demilitarization and conversion would take place, but nevertheless a fairly typical example of the problems of transition. This 'regular path' of peaceful transformation within Eastern Europe promised to provide useful lessons for the rest of the region. This chapter presents the changes concerning security and military issues in the first years following the change of political system in Hungary.

THE IMPACT OF THE POLITICAL CHANGES ON SECURITY AND MILITARY ISSUES

New Foreign Policy Orientation

The political changes of 1989–90 brought a radical shift in the foreign policy orientation of the country. One of the key words of the new political discourse is 'European' meaning West European and the main ambition has become full membership of the European Community (later European Union).

In the late 1980s, Hungary took several important steps towards major Western institutions. Hungary's first step towards the North Atlantic Treaty Organization dates back to 1986, when correspondence between the Hungarian Parliament and NATO leaders began. In late 1990, the country became an associated member of the NATO Parliamentary Committees. Together with representatives from Bulgaria, Czechoslovakia, Poland and the Soviet Union, Hungarian delegates were able to take part and intervene in meetings, but had no right to vote. Hungary was accepted into the (GATT) General Agreement on Tariffs and Trade in 1973 and joined the International Monetary Fund (IMF) in 1982. In January 1988, a trade and cooperation agreement signed with the EC came into force, followed by an application for associated and eventual full membership in 1990. In 1990, Hungary became the first ex-socialist bloc country member of the Council of Europe.

Having been a pathbreaker of radical political and economic transformations, Hungary used to enjoy a special reputation in the West. After the domino-like collapse of the former Eastern bloc and in a climate of increasing competition among the once 'fraternal' countries, Hungarian politicians tried to capitalize on this fact. In his speech at a conference organized by the Council of Europe in May 1990, Prime Minister Antall boldly declared that the West had a moral duty to help the emerging democracies of Eastern Europe, 'because we won the Third World War for you without the loss of one soldier on your side'.[1]

The other fundamental current in Hungary's new foreign policy orientation is the *rediscovery of the nation*. According to the newly established official ideology, state and nation do not coincide in the present geopolitical situation. The fact that the 'borders of the nation and those of the state do not overlap' is considered one of Hungary's major external problems today. In his official speech, Prime Minister Antall made it clear that for him the real borders were the ethnic ones, calling himself prime minister of 16 million Hungarians, including those living outside the official borders. This approach has a significant effect on security policy. On the one hand, it increases a feeling of vulnerability through the problems of Hungarian minorities in the neighbouring countries, for example in Romania or, more recently, in the rump Yugoslavia. On the other hand, the minority problem can be interpreted as Hungary's right to intervene in other countries on behalf of its minorities' interests. This idea often surfaces in political circles, in various formulations. One military expert declared: 'Our long-term strategical aim is to guarantee humane living conditions for the Hungarian minorities outside Hungary.'

Representing the interests of ethnic minorities can be constructive or hostile. An example of the former is a minority code, created together with the Ukrainian government, to protect both the Hungarian and Russian ethnic minority. This can be considered as a viable model for the whole region. A much less constructive approach was manifested during the 1993 discussions of representatives of the governing coalition, who fervently opposed the ratification of the cooperation agreement with Ukraine, because of a clause that ruled out territorial demands on both sides.

The other crucial institutional development that followed the end of the cold war in Eastern Europe was the *end of the Warsaw Pact and the end of the Council for Mutual Economic Assistance (CMEA)*. For Hungary the most important element of the process was the withdrawal of the Soviet forces from the country by 30 June 1991. The last Soviet soldier's farewell was celebrated with an hour-long chiming of bells and ferocious honking, but behind this political event there were serious economic problems waiting to be resolved. After the treaty on the Soviet withdrawal was signed, a special committee worked on the economic implications. Their task was fairly difficult, because there were no formal contracts about the stationing of foreign troops in Hungary. In long and rather difficult negotiations, the Hungarian side demanded compensation for the deterioration of the installations used by the Soviet army and for ecological damage (mainly contaminated soil), unpaid bills (for services and purchases) left behind by the troops. The Soviet side asked for reimbursement for the more than 600 buildings, barracks and other establishments they built during their stay in Hungary.

The surprisingly rapid end of the Warsaw Pact created a political and military vacuum in Eastern Europe. In 1989–90, most ex-Warsaw Pact member-countries went through a quick revaluation of the importance of their national armies and simultaneously decided to apply for NATO membership. In June 1991, NATO was still rather cool towards these Eastern European advances, seeking to avoid further 'destabilization' in the Soviet Union. After the failed coup in the Soviet Union in August 1991, however, the NATO stance changed remarkably. Although full membership or military protection provided by the organization was still excluded, multiple forms of collaboration were elaborated.

The collapse of military-based cooperation had a multiplier effect on the former member-countries and the Soviet Union itself. The end of the CMEA military market, particularly the decline of Soviet and GDR demand, led to the bankruptcy of the large Hungarian suppliers and a loss of stable income for the whole economy. Apart from the specifically military-related changes, the disappearance of the CEMA had a complex impact on the whole Hungarian economy. Exports fell by about 60 percent and Comecon-related industrial production fell by about 70 percent. In the short run, this was compensated by a spectacularly rapid switch of foreign trade to Western countries. By 1992–3, however, it became clear that a Western export-led economic recovery was unrealistic and trade and cooperation with the former Eastern partners needed to be re-established. Even in the case of Western investments growing dramatically and the easing of EU import restrictions, Eastern European economies will need each other as cooperation partners and markets. This realization is mirrored in the 'Visegrad process' – the efforts of Poland, Czechoslovakia and Hungary to create new types of regional cooperation.

The New Security Concept

The significant political changes necessarily left their mark on the new Hungarian concept of security. It was the first time since the early 1930s that an independent security policy was elaborated in Hungary. However, although it was one of the first items destined for the new legislation and several alternatives were published, neither a crystallized security concept nor a new defence doctrine had been 'officially' formulated by the end of 1993. At this time, the country was in the process of a hectic, contradictory and unprecedented social transition, making it difficult to find consistent ideas and policies concerning even fundamental issues. Different parties, fractions within the parties, the army, the ministries, social movements and other pressure groups presented their different (and rapidly changing) concepts, which, following the complex cycles of the political power game, may prove to be decisive or totally irrelevant. The coalition government itself was far from united and became engaged in a permanent struggle to define and defend its own policy both outside and inside the country.

There were, however, two important common points that all interpretations of the new Hungarian security concept shared: security was no longer defined with reference to a potential enemy, and it was no longer simply military security – it was taken in a broader sense, including economic, social and environmental aspects. While this concept was broader than the previous one, since it was based on the idea of a new collective European security, as expressed in the 1990 Paris Treaty, it was also narrower in so far as the bloc security was replaced by national security.

Excluding a possible attack by an unidentified enemy, the possible threats to Hungarian security were seen as 'the economic collapse of Eastern Europe, ethnic tensions and a wave of refugees' (as the vice-president of the Hungarian Parliament put it in 1990). The new Hungarian security policy aimed at creating guarantees against such eventualities. According to another interpretation by the state secretary of the Ministry of Foreign Affairs in 1991, the main dangers threatening Hungary's security were 'environmental dangers, the limits of a society's tolerance and the state of the economy'. These are internal factors, except for the environmental risk, which, as seen in the case of the Danube dam, can create serious political and even military tensions.

Hungary's security is to be guaranteed through a 'security network' of bilateral, regional and global European security agreements. Economic security is considered a priority because it is expected to pave the way to the European Union and it also helps to avoid possible internal social tensions stirred by a worsening economic crisis.

The New Defence Doctrine

In harmony with the new security concept, a new defence doctrine was elaborated. Its main guidelines were outlined in a government communiqué, issued on 14 February 1991. The new strategy is strictly defensive and excluded an attack against any other country. There is no defined enemy. The aim is to solve conflicts by political means, within the framework of a global, cooperative European security system. Hungary does not have weapons of mass destruction and will not allow any country to deposit such weapons on Hungarian territory. It intends to maintain its defensive capacities at the necessary level, without, however, generating a feeling of threat in any other country.

The core of the new Hungarian military concept is the concept of 'circular defence'. The idea of 'the enemy in possible attack' on which the previous military doctrine was built has been abandoned. The aim of the new strategy is 'to exclude the possibility of an attack by an enemy against which Hungary has no chance of winning, and to be prepared to demonstrate genuine determination to defend ourselves in case of an assault by a possible (but by no means identifiable) enemy of the same military potential within the region'.

The new military concept based on circular defence was made public almost immediately after the political changeover. It suggested that, instead of expecting an attack from the West, as before, the Hungarian army be prepared to defend itself from a possible blow 'from anywhere around its borders'. The new strategy implied the reallocation of military units, until then concentrated on the western borders, demonstrating that there was no longer any possible threat from the West. At the same time, the precarious situation of the neighbouring countries and the increasing flow of refugees raised concerns about the security of eastern borders.

While there is growing competition and open manifestations of formerly suppressed mutual resentments among Eastern European countries, fortunately there is also a recognition that regional stability is a principal precondition for any kind of progress in the region. Several months after discussing the army's concept of circular defence, the idea of 'circular relation building' was launched. Since then, several bilateral agreements have been signed with neighbouring countries.

Military Expenditure Cuts

Data on Hungary's military sector began to be published in the late 1980s, but detailed budget figures were not available until 1988. In 1988, the military budget was officially estimated at Ft 42 billion; in 1989, 39.8 billion; and in 1990, 40 billion. This represented about 2.1 percent of GDP according to Karoly Janza, chief economist of the Hungarian army.[2] A new element of the 1990 budget was that Ft 35 billion was allocated by the central budget and the rest was expected to be earned by the Ministry of Defence.

After a temporary retreat, following the radical political changes in Hungary, the army demanded an increased budget for 1991. In the parliamentary discussion of the 1991 budget, the Ministry of Defence originally applied for Ft 71 billion, but finally Ft 42 billion was approved. This sum, claimed the military, was hardly enough for subsistence, because the minimum amount necessary simply to maintain the armed forces was Ft 55 billion. By the end of the summer of 1991, the military had already expressed its desire to be allocated a 'minimum 3–3.5 percent of the GDP, with a 40 percent share of development'. During the parliamentary debate on the 1992 budget, the military were even more forthright. They lobbied for a Ft 67 billion budget and received 59.5 billion, out of which Ft 1.1 billion was allocated for development. Later in the year the armed forces received another Ft 1.1 billion to cover the unexpected costs due to the security hazards related to the Yugoslav war. The 1993 budget was Ft 64.5 billion.

It is still not clear what is included in the military budget under the heading of defence expenditure and what should be there but is missing. It is well known that in the past a significant part of military spending has been hidden in the budgets of other economic sectors, under different headings, which always made it impossible to trace. Since glasnost began, the military claims this method has been abandoned, but there are certain problems that indicate that this might not exactly be the case.

A 1992 State Accounting Office investigation revealed that, in the period examined, 1987–90, the sector had a growing amount of 'off-budget' funds, kept on several secret bank accounts. Originally, the money was taken from unused budgetary funds and was multiplied by illegal financial transactions. The sum involved was Ft 738 million in March 1988 and Ft 3.5 billion in March 1990, about 8 percent of the budget for that year. It was used to improve the armed forces' economic situation, support defence industry factories and speculation, which involved other ministries (for example the Ministry of Finance) and other official and private organizations (for example, the Technika Trade Company, a couple of canneries catering for the military and a military enterprise, the Godolloi Gepgyar). According to documents published by Tamas Wachsler, opposition FIDESZ party MP, the abuse continued in 1991 as well, despite a general outcry and the Defence Minister's denials (Wachsler, 1992a, 1992b).

In several articles, Andras Brody, a leading Hungarian economist, argues that, because expenditures are hidden in the budgets of other sectors, the defence sector absorbs much more than the officially published data indicate. Calculating for the year 1980, when the military officially received 2.5 percent of GDP, he deduces an approximate 20–25 percent real share, derived from indirect contributions, such as military-related production, services and disguised resource allocation. Another problem in judging the real military expenditure is that the calculations are made on the basis of distorted prices. The army's main local suppliers' prices and those of imported products, for example weaponry, were calculated by an utterly unsuitable and fundamentally different system from that used to determine the civilian sector's prices.

In addition to resources received from the central budget, the Hungarian army owns a significant amount of property, consisting of land, infrastructure, houses and other buildings, transport facilities and reserve supplies. It is difficult to assess the actual size of this property. In an interview, Lajos Fur, the minister of defence, quoted a survey from the mid-1980s that gave an estimate of Ft 180–190 billion. This sum did not include the value of about 100 000 hectares of military forest and several thousand hectares of land occupied by military installations, barracks and other buildings, nor was the total value of weapons and technology and the reserves for 60 days taken into account.

Although the military budget was cut by 30–35 percent, military experts unanimously claimed that about 50–60 percent of the possible gains driving from these cuts would be lost, as a result of the losses stemming from the collapse of the defence industry and arms trade. Apart from the direct consequences of the radical budget cuts, the military suffered from the consequences of the overall economic crisis and the collapse of the Warsaw Pact. The Ministry of Defence calculated a Ft 9.5 billion loss due to the switching of trade to hard currency among the Eastern European countries, meaning a threefold price increase for the military.[3]

The cutback in compulsory military service meant an additional Ft 1.5 million loss for the army, because certain services previously undertaken by conscripts would have to be paid for and because the same amount of ammunition and amortization would be used in a shorter time. At the same time, the armed forces are especially hard hit by inflation because of the relatively high share of food and energy in total consumption.

The army's capacity to generate income was apparently overestimated by the budget planners. It was originally proposed that the army raise a part of its own budget through the sale of unused equipment, military instruments and real estate, offering services to the civilian sector and renting flats and resort houses. Apparently owing to bureaucratic obstacles and lack of demand and experience, the military was unable to fulfil these expectations.

The New Economic Management of the Defence Sector

The major impact of the change in the security concept in Hungary was a radically different economic approach towards the military and the defence sector. During the period of 'socialist construction', the idea of maximum military security enjoyed absolute priority over economic considerations. To achieve maximal security or (during the worst years of the cold war) maximum possible military protection at whatever price was the underlying logic of major economic decisions.

With the new political set-up the emphasis has changed radically. Economic security has gained priority and consequently the military sector is now placed within economic realities. As one of the army's economic experts remarked: 'there is a very strong correlation between military policy and economic policy, even if today the latter is dominant. Our share in the state budget can only be as much as the economy can afford.' After long decades of enjoying uncontested priority, this 'residual character' of military finances might appear slightly humiliating for the representatives of the army and prove difficult to put into practice. Managers of the defence sector, the army's economic experts and the whole professional staff have to learn very quickly 'new' concepts of economic calculation and new types of management governed by market laws.

THE NEW HUNGARIAN NATIONAL DEFENCE ARMY

The Hungarian military enjoyed significant social and economic privileges in the 1950s and 1960s. It could count on almost limitless resources allocated by the system of national planning, including large-scale greenfield investments to cater for its multiple needs. The army represented the 'cream of the socialist youth', it had fairly high social prestige and was one of the strongholds and symbols of the political system.

Even in the late 1980s, the majority of military personnel were Party members and the army's public manifestations mirrored absolute loyalty towards 'existing socialism'.[4] The army remained identified with the system and as such was feared and despised. Hungary's participation in the 1968 invasion of Czechoslovakia further undermined the army's reputation and reinforced the image of a hardline, efficient military, which acted as a dominant agent of the system.

The role of the armed forces changed slightly in the period of liberal Kadarism, from the late 1970s. In order to preserve social peace, the Party made a private deal with the military, as with other important social groups. The army kept a fairly low profile in society and mainly confined itself to the barracks where it enjoyed almost absolute freedom. Its internal problems, such as economic mismanagement and abuse of power, were never publicly addressed. The army's tendency towards seclusion and the absence of any social control over it made possible the maintenance of an extremely loose and lavish internal economy which, among other ills, was the hotbed of widespread corruption.

The army became more closed, secretive and increasingly alienated from the rest of the society, which at the same time prevented it from becoming a real, visible power-holder, able to challenge or dictate to the Party. There were strong personal loyalties between the Party and the military, but apparently the military's power was not overwhelming, so it was used to negotiate rather than to dictate. The Hungarian army acted at the same time as a mediator between the Hungarian Party leadership and the Soviet armed forces 'stationed temporarily on Hungarian territory' which in turn mediated with the Moscow Party headquarters. This role of 'translating' the Soviet Union's approval or disapproval in key internal issues must have given the army further importance and opportunities to intervene in the country's management.

The Hungarian armed forces were strictly subordinated to the Soviet army. The internal hierarchy of the Warsaw Pact guaranteed Soviet leadership in every key position. Major decisions where taken in Moscow and in certain cases the member-countries were not even informed about them. An example of this unequal relationship was the case of nuclear weapons which had been positioned in Hungary, apparently without the Hungarian military leadership's knowledge. The Soviets held exhaustive, detailed information about the national armies of the member-countries, which made tough control over them possible. The member-countries, it seems, had no control at all and received very scattered information about the size and movements of the Soviet military stationed on their national territories. In addition, Hungary had the smallest army within the Warsaw Pact (49 700 professional staff) and a relatively large Soviet presence (60 500 soldiers; together with families and auxiliary personnel, about 100 000 people).[5]

The new political system would like to give the army a radically different image. The armed forces have been renamed the 'Hungarian Defence Army' (*Magyar Honvedseg*) instead of 'Hungarian People's Army' (*Magyar Nephadsereg*). The new name expresses a symbolic break with the army's socialist past and evokes associations with previous armies which played heroic roles in the country's history. In contrast to the old 'socialist' and 'internationalist' army, the new Hungarian army is bound to be national – both in form and spirit. It has a new name, a new seal, a new parade step, new terms of address (instead of 'comrade', 'fellow-soldier') and other patriotic symbols.

While the Hungarian People's Army was used as the Hungarian Socialist Workers' Party's tool, the new Hungarian army is presented as clearly non-political. As early as 1989, important structural changes took place within the military, including the separation of the Ministry of Defence and the Armed Forces. According to a constitutional amendment, the civilian president became the supreme commander, and the armed forces were placed directly under Parliament's supervision. In 1989, when political organizations were banned from workplaces, the highest ranks of the Ministry of Defence and the armed forces were purged of staff presumably committed to the previous political system. Only 44 generals out of 87 remained in place, most of the military attachés were changed and in the Ministry of Defence alone 186 political officers were dismissed.[6]

There were significant cuts in military personnel as well, although the published numbers are slightly confusing. According to data released in 1989, the Hungarian army consisted of 106 000 soldiers. Following radical redundancy plans, their number should have dropped to 75 000 in two years, mainly via decreasing the number of conscripts. In his first interview in office in summer 1990, the new minister of defence, Lajos Fur, said that the size of the armed forces would drop from 120 000 to 90 000 by 1992, out of which 75 000 would be official soldiers and the rest civilian employees.[7] The defence spending cuts involved a reduction of compulsory military service from 18 to 12 months for armed service and another 10 months as reservists. (The reserve call-up age limit was also lowered from 55 to 50 years.) Non-armed service within the armed forces was set at 15 plus 7 months, whereas civilian service is for a continuous 22 months.

There were also important reforms concerning the army's internal life. The soldier is now treated as a uniformed citizen, enjoying civil rights, including the right to create representative institutions to defend his interests. Such organizations were strictly forbidden in the past, because they were considered as a threat to the army's internal discipline. This change is very relevant for conscripts, who in the past had no defence against the abuses of their superiors. Another important measure, crucial for the official staff, liberalized travel to the West, allowing them to undertake secondary income-earning activities. The internal composition of the army was also to be revised according to the new requirements. The new armed forces were to be smaller, stronger and more modern and there was to be a major internal reorganization.

There were also important changes in the army's economic management. The contraction of military expenditure strongly affected the distribution of resources. Of the 1990 budget, 25 percent was spent on personal tax and social insurance (welfare contribution); 50 percent on personal expenditure (wages, food, clothing). The sum allocated for development of military equipment was reduced from 17 percent in the late 1980s to 9 percent by 1990. In the years before the political changes, the proportions were approximately 40 percent for development and 60 percent for maintenance.[8] Trying to avoid further losses of personnel, the military management decided to save money on maintenance and not on wages, which meant a dramatic drop in financing military social services, hospitals, cultural institutions, crèches, kindergartens, military schools and colleges.

A comprehensive reform of the whole system of economic management within the army was also planned. The military's internal finances have always been a taboo topic in the past and they are still rather enigmatic. Apparently, one of the big internal contradictions was that, while the Ministry of Defence has control over the budget, only the headquarters of the armed forces has detailed information about the army's real assets, reserves and current finances. It also appears that different divisions within the army still have different types of economy: forces of the Technical Division still function according to the old-style quantitative norms, while units of the Armoured and Vehicle Division have introduced the rules of a monetary economy.

The Ministry of Defence has also engaged in commercial activity, leading to the Hungarian military's active or retired officers taking part in 11 limited liability companies. One of them, the Militex, sells civilian products used by the military (clothes, instruments, tools) under direct Ministry of Defence supervision. Another source states that the Ministry of Defence or other military organizations held stakes in 14 economic companies.

Problems in the Army

Despite significant internal changes, the army's actual situation is still fairly problematic. In addition, thanks to the greater freedom of the press, the general public is now much more aware of it. The former People's Army's distance from the society meant that its 'image' was rather far from reality. Occasional stories from conscripts and infrequently published news suggested that there were serious problems but, in the absence of reliable sources, this information remained at the level of gossip and jokes, which are rather efficient channels of information in East Central Europe. This is why, during the period of political upheaval, society was quite surprised to see that the army did not lift a finger to save the collapsing old system, despite its supposed total loyalty. The other shock came when the first reports about the armed forces' real physical state were published. It became known that the army's equipment was obsolete, its internal discipline was crumbling, its political profile was unclear and it had a deeply troubled, as some military experts themselves put it, neurotic personnel.

Although no detailed information is available about the level of the Hungarian armed forces' technical know-how and its equipment, there is a wide consensus that the army's material conditions are very poor and that, without major financial injections, it might soon collapse. The present tight budget – as the Ministry's spokesman put it – only makes it possible to tinker with the obsolete technology, instead of undertaking genuine development.

Another astonishing public revelation referred to the living and working conditions of the soldiers. Some 10 percent of the official staff lived below subsistence, 18 percent near poverty, 50 percent in the lowest strata of middle-income households and 9 percent above it. In addition, unlike the overwhelming majority of the population, they (and in most cases their spouses) were not allowed, until the latest reforms, to find additional sources of income through second jobs or forming small enterprises.

According to an interview with army spokesmen after the political changes, the professional officers' average age was 35 years, but their life expectancy was 58.9 years, six years less than the (rather low) male average. One in four soldiers had to retire earlier than retirement age (55) because of health problems. According to a 1990 survey, most of the professional soldiers suffer from insecurity, difficult work conditions, separation from their families and low wages, and 90 percent of the officers suffer from moderate or strong nervous tension.

The army's deep crisis was also manifested in the erosion of its internal order. Instead of the previous decades of large-scale corruption, after 1990 ordinary crimes, riots and internal clashes began to proliferate within the ranks of the military. According to the chief of the military court, crimes committed within the army rose by 30 percent in 1990 (a 50 percent rise was reported in the civilian sector).

THE HUNGARIAN DEFENCE INDUSTRY

After World War Two, the Hungarian military industry was rebuilt upon the foundations of the pre-war period, most significantly the 1938 'Programme of Gyor' that aimed to arm the country in preparation for the war. The first large-scale post-war reconstruction took place between 1950 and 1954, in the early years of the cold war. The reconstruction of the defence industry was part of a forced industrialization programme, adopted by the country's political leadership. The aim was to build up a powerful economy, based on heavy industry: metallurgy, chemicals, machinery and cement production, a genuine 'country of iron and steel' according to the political slogan that was current at the time.

After the creation of the Warsaw Pact in 1955, the member-countries followed a rather intensive specialization and cooperation, which by and large served the interests of the bloc security whose centre of gravity lay in the Soviet Union. According to the prevailing division of labour, each of the members produced huge amounts of traditional military equipment for each other but mainly for the Soviet Union. Military R&D and high-tech production was concentrated in the USSR and some local centres, under strict Warsaw Treaty Organization (WTO) supervision. After the collapse of the Warsaw Pact, this 'colonial-type' division of labour left the former member-countries with an overspecialized local military sector and significant dependence on imports of spare parts and other inputs. It also created enormous excess capacities and reserves which the respective countries are finding it rather difficult to convert or get rid of today.

There were two major structural guidelines within the Warsaw Pact cooperation: no product was allowed to contain parts imported from the West and all products were manufactured under Soviet licence. There was an internal division of labour that assigned each member-country to specialize in a certain area or product. This assignation was made by the highest WTO leadership, which in practice meant the Soviet authorities.[9] Bulgaria, for example, specialized in radio and computer R&D and production, telephone and switchboard centres were produced in East Germany and Hungary carried out research in telecommunication and related military techniques. This means that at least part of the production was based on local R&D. Some sources confirm local technological development, others claim there was no independent research, but only licence-based mass-production in Hungary, although these also give examples of Hungary's own military technical development capacity.

Since 1968, the Hungarian defence industry has been defined as consisting of only those end producers whose weapons, military equipment and other military-related output represent about 10 percent of the company's output. Suppliers and other enterprises that cater to the military's multiple needs, such as utensils, uniforms, raw materials or food, are not included. The scope of these activities and the involvement of the enterprises in question are also unknown. Andras Brody estimates that even the costs of the strictly military activity are five times higher than the published data suggest.

In 1988, the most successful year of Hungarian military production, some 70 factories were involved in the defence industry.[10] There were 17 enterprises whose military output was higher than 5 percent of their total production (ranging from 7.1 percent to 82.2 percent) and these accounted for 93 percent of the country's military output. The rest was provided by another 50–60 enterprises. Only in five companies, in MN Godolloi Gepgyar, Mechlabor, Finommechanika, PVG and Labour MM, did defence production surpass 50 percent and there was only one factory, Godolloi Gepgyar, specializing in armoured vehicles and weapons repair, whose entire production was military. The bulk of defence industry producers were characterized by dual technology, both in a technical and an output-oriented sense.

In 1988, military production represented 3 percent of the total industrial output and an estimated 1.5 percent of the processing industry's output. The sector's full productive capacity was an estimated $400 million. In 1988, when the defence industry reached record production levels, its output was $370 million (Ft 20 billion), almost reaching full capacity. The sector employed 30 000 people, approximately 2 percent of the economically active population. Estimates of other sources oscillate between 20 000 and 35 000. Communication electronics and precision instruments represented 75 percent of the whole military output; the rest was made up of 12 percent weapons and ammunition, 8 percent vehicle and aeroplane repair and 5 percent other goods such as chemical and textile products.[11]

During the decades of Warsaw Pact cooperation, major decisions about the size and structure of the Hungarian military industry were made in the Moscow headquarters. However, to be able to fulfil them special internal regulations were elaborated. After the reorganization of the military industry following the 1956 uprising, Hungary did not have a separate Ministry of Military Production to supervise the sector. With the exception of the above-mentioned Godolloi Gepgyar, which functioned directly under the Ministry of Defence, all military producers were subordinated to the Ministry of Industry. The most important 20–25 factories were under strict state supervision, with managers appointed directly by the minister.

Despite more or less radical changes in the Hungarian economic system since the 1968 reforms, the defence industry remained an almost untouched residual of the classical command economy. Its activity was strictly secretive. It was developed and managed by detailed five-year plans (disaggregated into one-year plans) whose prescriptions were obligatory. Fulfilment of these plans (in theory) enjoyed priority over other economic goals, being secured by special regulations and allowances. All major ministries related in some way to military production had a special 'closed department' whose function was to plan and coordinate military-associated activity. These special departments presumably had separate funds within the respective ministry's budget, given that one of the common ways of 'hiding' military expenses was to integrate them into other sectors' budgets. The Ministry of Industry, for example, used to have a special yearly fund of Ft 200–300 million for military development projects. (In 1990, this source was used to finance conversion projects with sums of Ft 25–30 million per project).

The defence industry was a highly privileged sector of the economy. Enterprises engaged in military activity could get special credits for investment and development, with extremely soft conditions, low interest rates or in some cases interest-free. Part of the extremely high debt burden most military producers carry today dates back to this practice. In addition, given that the defence industry output reached record levels in the second half of the 1980s, there were many new investments, covered mainly by state and bank loans that the factories are now unable to service. The defence industry workers received an additional 10 percent wage 'complement' and enjoyed other privileges, made possible through special state subsidies. In exchange, the mobility of the sector's core workers was restricted both within the local labour market and when travelling abroad.

Defence sector enterprises also had the advantage of having producers obliged to cater to them, a rather beneficial element in an economy short of internal productive discipline and underdeveloped infrastructure. Non-official sources and some individual cases suggest that they also received special import subsidies. They could also count on steady markets assured by state-guaranteed bilateral contracts. These markets proved to be rather rewarding, mainly owing to a fairly unusual way of determining prices. It consisted of an intimate, two-sided bargaining between state representatives of consumers and producers. The producers' profit was automatically calculated regardless of costs and productivity. The bargain was 'ratified' by a special 'military price-setting committee'. As a whole, the military sector reached an average 10 percent higher profit margin than that of civilian producers.

Although the defence industry was privileged, it was restricted too. Defence industry enterprises were tightly bound to their supervising agencies and the military, with elements of both coercion and bribery. Indeed, until the mid-1980s, participation in military production was obligatory. However, even afterwards, enterprises were seen to take part in it. The situation of defence enterprises was very different from the general conditions of enterprise operating outside the military sector and it was certainly barely affected by the economic realities of the country. This is the reason why most enterprises were unable to foresee or even to allay the effects of the unfolding economic crisis. They became virtually paralysed and, instead of trying to cope with a dramatically new situation, acted as if nothing had changed, pleading to their superiors for economic support and protection.

Crisis

After a record year in 1988, 1989 brought a drastic reduction of military orders. There were significant military cuts in the Soviet Union and consequently export orders dropped. At the same time, owing to Hungarian military budget cuts, both imports and local consumption declined. Hungarian military orders fell by 30 percent in 1989, mainly owing to the contraction of exports.

The combined effects of the decline of the WTO military market and the internal military budget cuts shook the sector deeply. In addition, all this happened at the same time as the unexpectedly rapid collapse of the CMEA civilian market, which had devastating effects for the whole Hungarian economy and the civilian profile of the military-related enterprises. The present acute situation of military producers is due both to their specific features and to the general crisis involving the majority of Hungarian enterprises.

Despite the apparent signs of crisis, there were no fundamental changes in the military sector's structure or method of functioning in 1989–90. The most important change was that production became slightly more concentrated. In 1989, the most important 17 producers provided 96 percent of the total military output. The enterprises' performance suggests that 1989 was still not (or was not considered) a crisis year. Two of the companies increased military production, while cutting back on civilian output. Four enterprises decreased military output by more than 10 percent; 13 of the 17 enterprises increased civilian production, most of them by more than 10 percent.

Apparently, the military enterprises did not feel or did not want to realize the fact that their room for manoeuvre had dramatically changed. Whether they still enjoyed the protective cushioning (as did most state enterprises) and hoped to keep enjoying it, or they were led by sheer inertia, is difficult to tell. The inevitable collapse of the sector took place between 1990 and 1992. The drop in military orders led to a 25 percent fall in Hungarian military production between 1988 and 1989, and to a further 25–30 percent by 1990. In 1991, military output was an estimated Ft 3–4 billion, 20 percent of the 1988 production. Although no enterprises closed down, 5–6000 workers were already made redundant by early 1991. Data provided by the Military Industrial Office illustrate the depth of the crisis (see Table 8.1).

Table 8.1   Hungarian military production, main indicators

	1988	1991
Output (Ft billions)	20	3.7
Employed (thousands)	35	6.3
Enterprises	45	4.5
Share of military production in output (%)	20	4.7
Share of military production in industry (%)	3	0.5

Source: Military Industrial Office.

The case of DIGEP, Diosgyori Gepgyar, shows how the combination of external and internal impacts led the company to bankruptcy. In 1988, firearms and other weapons production reached 29.3 percent of the enterprise's total output, which represented 6.3 percent of Hungarian military production. The first economic difficulties due to stricter economic regulations and higher production costs appeared by mid-1988, before the military's sector's crisis became visible. The firm issued bonds to generate resources for a civilian restructuring programme. In 1989 came a new blow: the contraction of Soviet export orders. The enterprise's military production shrank by more than 40 percent, but total production fell by only 2.5 percent owing to a 14.1 percent increase in civilian output. Fighting against bankruptcy and trusting the 'almost totally convertible' capital stock, the enterprise tried to issue more bonds and attract foreign capital. However, the loss of civilian export opportunities, the contraction of the domestic market and internal difficulties in the enterprise's management led to bankruptcy in 1990.

After a two-year-long liquidation process, the enterprise was divided into one military and several civilian divisions. Although the military division has not had orders since the collapse of the WTO, it was not liquidated. The civilian divisions produce mechanical spare parts for, among others, Volvo, Fiat–Iveco and US firms. In March 1993, the military division was sold to Hungarian private entrepreneurs who aim to maintain military production for the armed forces and for export.

Between 1990 and 1993, defence industry enterprises had to face organizational chaos, decentralization and further difficulties created by the new challenges of the economy in transition. Most of them went through multiple stages of transformation of legal form and internal organization and were divided into smaller, quasi-independent enterprises or limited companies which, although still mostly state-owned, were prepared for future privatization. Some of the enterprises, even if they managed to survive the collapse of the military production, went bankrupt as a result of the abrupt liberalization of imports that crowded out Hungarian consumer goods from the shrinking domestic market. Such was the case of Orion (13.1 percent telecommunications and precision instruments) which succeeded in shifting to a civilian profile after losing its profitable WTO markets, but was unable to compete with major Western producers of television, video and other telecommunications equipment.

Owing to the fact that, by 1990, most military producers had become insolvent, the majority ended up under the supervision of a state-owned liquidation agency. Some enterprises, or parts of them, where privatized. The impact of privatization on the firms' management and the future of military production is not yet clear. There are cases where privatization is no more than a formal change of legal status, without major restructuring, and there are others where it leads to a genuine transformation. In some cases it is the means of getting rid of the (now) burdensome military production and in others it is a way of preserving it, in the hope of future orders. In some cases state supervision hinders efficient decision making and prolongs the agony of the enterprises, in others it functions as a guarantee to lure potential foreign investors or receive some kind of financial support.

Examples are FEG (17.5 percent artillery and infantry weapons) and MN Godolloi Gepgyar (100 percent vehicles). After a lengthy process of reorganization and transformation, the weapons-producing division of FEG was separated from the main enterprise and became a state-owned limited company. The rest of the firm carries out entirely civilian production (gas boilers and heating equipment) and was recently bought up by a group of Hungarian entrepreneurs. In the similar case of MN Godolloi Gepgyar (the factory that used to be a 100 percent military producer under the Ministry of Defence) the military profile, the production and repair of armoured vehicles, was maintained under the supervision of a state-owned liquidating company. The rest of the productive capacity became a joint venture with the US Caterpillar company and produces construction machinery.

One of the complicated and fairly typical cases was that of the Pestvideki Gepgyar, PVG (59.7 percent military production in 1988, military vehicles and aircraft repair). The enterprise enjoyed a monopoly position in the Hungarian market and was situated near a former Soviet military air-base, which can be converted into a civilian airport, The company went bankrupt in June 1990 and was scheduled to be liquidated by Reorg, a commercialized state agency in charge of the liquidation process of bankrupt state-owned enterprises. In February

1991, Line Up, a British firm, bought the enterprise, but was unable to pay for it, so the deal fell through. In March 1992 the Eldorado Foundation, representing a group of private individuals coming together to 'promote youth culture and sport activity' won the new open tender for the company. Subsequently, Parliament's Defence Committee and the Ministry of Defence protested against privatizing such a crucially important military enterprise. When the Foundation's financial assets were scrutinized, it turned out that it did not have sufficient capital and was probably acting on behalf of a non-specified foreign (allegedly Swedish) interest group. After this scandal, this deal too was cancelled; in June 1992, 572 of the former 945 employees created Dunai Repulogepgyar Ltd in order to manage the firm until its final liquidation or sale. Twenty-six percent of the company's assets were transferred to the AVRt, the state holding company set up in 1992 to manage the national assets which were not expected to be privatized, and which guaranteed to preserve the state's stake and its influence in major decisions.

The history of Videoton of Szekesfehervar, which used to be the largest military producer (in terms of value added), provides another representative example. Despite several warning signs of an approaching crisis in the Warsaw Pact-oriented military (and civilian) production in the late 1980s, the enterprise continued increasing its military output in 1989. Neither the management nor the supervising authorities were able to elaborate a viable crisis-managing strategy and decide about the future of the company. The company went bankrupt in 1991.

There are other indications that the sector's privatization taking place would involve foreign capital, which, at least in some of the published cases, happen to be Western military producers. Alcatel, Thomson, Philips and Mitshuba are among the interested companies.

Changes in the Management of the Defence Industry

Until 1989, military production was supervised by a special Defence Committee. After the political changes a Coordinating Bureau, working with a rather restricted staff and responsible to the Council of Ministers, took over this function. The Price Setting Committee, other institutions and special regulations that used to guarantee the military sector's privileged position, were all abolished.

In late 1991, the first signs of a new government policy appeared. In May 1990, Lajos Fur, Minister of Defence had said in an interview that Hungary did not need an independent defence industry because it could satisfy its armed forces' needs through imports. However, a year later he stressed the necessity of Hungarian arms production in order to supply the army. On 1 January 1992, a Military Industrial Office was set up to coordinate and promote military production and related activities. The office was an independent state organization, financed from the Prime Minister's Office budget and its director, Jeno Laszlo, had a state secretary rank.

Among the office's plans was the establishment of a military industrial holding by transferring the assets of 10 main military producers from their state supervisory agencies. This would have created the core of the renewed Hungarian military industry, which would have been financed directly from the state budget and other, independent sources, such as the Fund for Technical Innovation.

In summer 1993, Laszlo became a victim of factional struggles within the governing MDF and was removed from his position. The Military Industrial Office was dissolved, with some of its personnel and departments being transferred to the Ministry of Industry. They were left with the same task of coordinating and representing military producers, but very restricted administrative and financial power to fulfil it.

Conversion

Conversion in a narrow sense implies the release or sale of military-related products, materials, installations for the civilian sector and the transformation of productive capacities for civilian-purpose production.

Surplus products

The legal market for Soviet-licensed second-hand military hardware is fairly restricted. Potential buyers in the former state socialist countries face similar problems of liquidity and unusable stocks and the increasing regional tensions require political caution. The traditional partners in the Middle East and North Africa became insolvent and new partners are difficult to find, because of the sharp competition which is characteristic of the sector. Interest in developed Western countries is rather limited.

There are also problems on the sellers' side. In the absence of a valid security concept, it is still unclear what the country's defence precisely requires and which part of the military-related stock is indeed superfluous. The sale of cold capacities, for example, is still only possible with the individual approval of the respective ministries. The new bankruptcy law states that, even in a case of privatization, 'emergency reserves' are untouchable. Despite all these difficulties, the Hungarian army managed to sell a certain amount of its surplus military hardware.

Following conversion guidelines, non-saleable military equipment should be destroyed or converted for other purposes. According to technical experts, the latter solution is still a fairly expensive one. For example, to cut into pieces an armoured tank cost Ft 300 000 in 1990 and the result fetched only Ft 40–50 000 for recycling. A small private company, Bakonymetall of Varpalota, specialized in converting tanks, military vehicles and other equipment 'thrown out' by the Soviet and Hungarian armies. The same firm, in cooperation with other companies, was involved in cleaning up the former Soviet barracks. Undoubtedly, until now the most successful case of this type of conversion has been the making of the equipment used to extinguish the fires of the Kuwaiti oilfields during the Gulf War.

Unused military products which cannot be sold or converted are a heavy burden for the enterprises and the army that have to store them. One indication of the high cost of storage is the considerable contribution received by military-related enterprises for the maintenance of cold capacity.

Installations

A relative easy form of conversion would be the conversion of the installations left behind by the withdrawing Soviet army for civilian purposes. According to the original plans, 80 percent were to be given to local municipalities and 20 percent were to remain in the hands of the State Property Agency to be sold. Unfortunately, the former barracks and other installations need major investments to be cleaned and restored. Local municipalities generally lack the financial resources needed to maintain or convert them. The Hungarian private sector is also short of capital and is often discouraged by legal and bureaucratic uncertainties. Most foreign investors seem to be more attracted to less troublesome and more fast rewarding investment opportunities. According to a Ministry of Defence source, until early 1992 only one of the 2000 ex-Soviet military barracks had been converted successfully: into an 'Incubator and Centre of Innovation' for new private enterprises.

The history of a former military airport in Sarmellek demonstrates some of the difficulties of the conversion process. The State Property Agency announced an international bid to sell the seven Soviet military airports in Hungary in January 1991. The international market proved to be uninterested, but none of the Hungarian private sector bidders was successful either because the Agency preferred to postpone privatization, expecting the large foreign airlines to become interested. Half a year later the Hungarian private entrepreneurs nevertheless managed at least to rent one of the airports in Sarmellek at a fairly low price.

Now it functions as a weather forecast station and private airport, providing easy service to Lake Balaton, one of the country's major tourist attractions.

Productive capacities

As far as productive capacities are concerned, their conversion is not an easy task either. It can only be conceived as part of the overall restructuring of the whole economy, which itself is slow and painful. The specific military profile makes restructuring even more difficult, owing partly to the physical conditions required for (mainly heavy) weaponry production and partly to the enterprises' specific mentality, which is fairly difficult to change. Moreover, conversion would imply an overall technical reconstruction, requiring huge capital investments that at present neither the enterprises nor other economic agents seem to be able to provide. The existing old-style dual-purpose capital stock can at the most produce obsolete consumer durables, whose market, at least in Hungary, is limited.

In 1990–91 the Ministry of Industry allocated some state budget funds to promote conversion. According to the Ministry of Finance, the relatively small amount of money used for this purpose demonstrated that the defence-related companies failed to elaborate viable conversion projects.

Since the difficult period of the sector began, only a handful of successful cases of conversion have been registered. Some of the few companies that managed to avoid the most devastating effects of the crisis, such as Danuvia, Bakony and Gamma, did so by reorienting production for civilian purposes at an early stage. A report on Hajdusagi Iparmuvek (a company which has never been listed as defence-related) claimed that one of the reasons the enterprise was able to survive was that, after the collapse of its military market, it managed to switch to civilian consumer durables (*Nepszabadsag*, 3 March 1992).

There is a series of related economic and social problems to resolve even if conversion is successful. In Ozd, in north-east Hungary, for example, the demise of military-related production at the metalworks led to substantial redundancies. Since the redundant workers could not find other jobs, new faculties were opened at the local high school to provide retraining opportunities. However, in another similar case, when uranium mining came to a halt in Pecs in the south of the country, no solution was found.

The contraction of military production does not mean conversion. The historical dual-purpose character of the Hungarian military sector makes it more difficult to distinguish real conversion from temporary retreat in the hope of a future reconstruction. There are two major tendencies concerning the future of the defence industry, using the nationalist arguments and the government's increasing efforts to recentralize both economic and political life. The other tendency is the urge to privatize, which could also make it possible to rescue military producer enterprises, using the arguments of profitability and potential export-led growth, in which military products would play an important role.

ARMS TRADE

Exports

The expansion of Hungarian military production depended on its capacity to export, because the Warsaw Pact countries had a barter-like commodity exchange system: a certain type of product was exchanged for the same type of goods. Arms exports were paid for by arms imports, so the needs of the Hungarian army were met through military sales, mainly to the Soviet Union. In 1986, a typical year, the Hungarian army bought altogether 3 percent of the local military production, 2–2.5 percent was purchased by other armed organizations and the rest was exported.

Until 1991, two state-owned companies, Technika Export–Import Company and Industrialexport had a monopoly on arms trade. The former administered 98 percent of the deals, whereas Industrialexport's share was a symbolic 2 percent. FEG, one of the major weapons producers, also used to have export rights, but rarely used them. Technika Company was mainly a broker firm, under strict state control. Its general manager was nominated by the Ministry of Foreign Relations and Exchange, and each of its deals needed permission from a special committee set up by representatives of the Ministries of Defence, Interior, Foreign Affairs and International Economic Relations. Similar to the practice followed in the defence industry, arms sales were meticulously worked out by five-year plans. In the last of these plans, which covered the 1986–90 period, the planners prescribed a $500 million income, of which around half was 'fulfilled' by 1990.

In 1988, the peak year for Hungarian arms sales, $130 million worth of weapons were sold to the third world.[12] Export earnings dropped to $50 million by 1990 and were planned to reach $45 million in 1991; $30 million was earned by the end of that year. In the past, the primary aim of arms sales was to obtain weapons for the Hungarian army and other armed organizations, although in the last decade their importance as a hard currency source became increasingly significant. Hungary's traditional arms trade partners used to be the allied countries of the Warsaw Pact and 'socialist-minded' systems in the third world, with whom deals were not conducted on a commercial basis. Important buyers used to come from the Middle East as well, but, owing to political and liquidity problems characteristic of the region, countries of the Far East and Western Europe became more important. Technika has been selling Hungarian military products on Western markets since 1985.

Before 1989–90, arms exports were not primarily determined by considerations of profitability. Because of the special barter-like system, arms prices were artificially kept down within the Eastern bloc, because 'it was not in our interest to increase export prices, which would have automatically pushed up the prices of imports'. Today 'arms are products like anything else in the market', unperturbed by moral or political considerations. One of the main Hungarian 'conversion experts' argues for 'neutral' arms sales: 'Why should we not sell weapons to our neighbours if it is a profitable business? The income could be used for military development, which would strengthen us and the buyers' need for spare parts would make them dependent on us.'

Parallel to the general liberalization of the economy, arms trade was also liberalized. Technika has been undergoing a complicated process of decentralization and commercialization. According to a 1990 regulation of the Council of Ministers, every single arms deal has to be approved by a special committee, comprising highest level representatives of the Ministries of Foreign Trade, Defence, Foreign Affairs and Interior and the state secretary of the National Security Office.

The country's geographic position and the high profitability of arms sales might explain why Hungary has become a centre of illegal arms trade in recent years. Non-official sources claim that the departing Soviet army was deeply involved in arms sales, following the venerable tradition of selling food and other consumer goods to the local population on the black market. Their role was taken over by private firms, often with extended links in other Eastern European countries, who are difficult to stop or prosecute. In a published case, for example, several million dollars' worth of 'hospital equipment sent from Chile' was detected at Budapest airport. According to investigations, an international network of arms dealers was involved in the business. Another infamous case came to light at the beginning of the war in Yugoslavia when high-level Hungarian state officials were involved in the sale of 10 000 Kalashnikovs to Croatian forces. The affair took place despite the fact that the above-mentioned 1990 legislation on arms sales strictly forbids arms sales to countries at war or in crisis areas.

According to an anonymous military expert, the bulk of the income generated by the armed forces is derived from arms sales. The shipments are generally addressed to a distant third world country (even if they are in fact sent to neighbouring countries) and behind the civilian merchants there are always military experts. Very few cases become public, generally as the result of some accident, like one in which a significant consignment sent to Nigeria was stolen in the Polish port of Gdynia (*Nepszabadsag*, 4 and 9 December 1991).

Imports

In the past most imports came from the Soviet Union and Czechoslovakia, the two major arms producers of the ex-Comecon group, and were arranged through Technika. As a result of the defence budget cuts in all the respective countries and the significant drop in Hungarian military exports, imports shrank considerably. Given that the bulk of the Hungarian military equipment was still Soviet-made or licensed, the country had to maintain military cooperation with the Soviet Union. In 1990, the two countries signed a 10-year agreement, according to which Hungary continues to receive defence equipment, mainly support and spare parts from the Soviet Union.

Another important development was the agreement reached on outstanding debts with the former Soviet Union. In a visit to Budapest in November 1992, President Yeltsin promised that the debt taken up by Russia would be partly paid by $800 million worth of military equipment and spare parts. The shipments also contained several *MIG*-29 aircraft and T-72 tanks. The value of this contribution was almost the total military budget for 1992. Another major, investment-free military acquisition was a German 'gift' of military equipment from the former GDR arsenals. Hungary asked Bonn to sell its arms one month before German unification, relying on the goodwill created by Hungary's role in the reunification process. After several twists, declarations and refutations, by November 1992 it seemed to be confirmed that unspecified quantities of unused military spare parts were to be given to Hungary, in order to improve the country's defence capabilities.

According to the reorientation of Hungarian foreign policy and the country's desire for future NATO membership, interest in Western military products and collaboration is increasing. There have been negotiations about buying military products from some West European countries, but, since the army's financial resources are fairly limited, for the time being the main form of cooperation is exchange of information, official visits and training.

CONCLUDING REMARKS

The economic structure of post-war Hungary was built on the Soviet model, which was a classical type of war economy – war economy in a double sense: the way the economy is managed and the fact that its main targets are shaped by military needs. The economy is constructed to be able to cater for the military machine in case of war and peacetime is used for preparation for the 'unavoidable' war. The whole notion of a command economy emerges from this primordial model; the ability to concentrate and allocate resources and to centralize and redistribute income, the highly centralized decision making and the punishing, not rewarding, nature of economic stimulation all originate from this model.

During the post-war period and the early 1950s, when the foundations of the state socialist economy were laid down in Hungary, this logic of a forthcoming war and permanent military threat had a decisive impact. The structure of production, the preponderance of heavy industry, the strongly centralized economic direction, the strict discipline regulating the labour force and the campaign-like organization of the economy were all designed to prepare the country for a possible military mobilization. The Hungarian economy has gone through significant changes since the first major economic reform package was introduced in 1968 and was followed by consecutive waves of reforms and counter-reforms. However much the military grip has loosened and the economic system altered, important elements of the model are still present. It is like an imprint in the deep structures of the system, very hard to overwrite.

The basic structural proportions, the overwhelming power of the centre, the political embeddedness of the economy, the military-style forms of management, the still campaign-like organization of macro-economic projects and the special role of the military sector are all legacies of the original military-centred economic system. In addition, until very recently, both the army and the defence industry functioned as untouchable enclaves of the classical command economy, absorbing important development resources and distorting the economy's development.

Using Andras Brody's metaphor, the military's interests are 'frozen' into the economic system; military logic influences the system's deep structures, affecting even clearly civilian decisions. In Brody's examples the Budapest underground was built much deeper than was technically necessary; the country's western highway network, heavy metallurgy and chemical industry, and wheat cultivation were specifically developed (and consequently other sectors, such as intensive agriculture, services and infrastructure were deliberately neglected) with a possible westward military mobilization in mind (Brody interview, *Figyelo*, 1990). Following the lines of Brody's argument, one can envisage the whole Hungarian economy as a dual-purpose system, convertible (reversible) to a classical war economy if necessary.

Owing to the nature of the topic, it is hard to find evidence to prove these statements, but it is also true that it is impossible to disprove the role of the military influence behind important economic decisions, especially if both the decision-making process and the results remain behind a protective veil of secrecy. (Several large-scale investment projects that seem irrational or counterproductive when judged by purely economic considerations can be easily explained by following the logic of the military.)

Although the military sector's actual size is relatively limited, it still enjoys certain preferences. It is enough to compare its share in the state budget with that of other sectors of social consumption, like health, housing and education. The 1990 *World Development Report* shows the military's share in government expenditure (which itself represents 58.3 percent of the GNP) in 1988. Defence is allocated 4.8 percent, while education receives 2.1 percent and housing 1.7 percent.

Despite the proclaimed changes in the military's management, some remnants of the military's 'extraterritoriality', which was so characteristic of the 'golden years' of classical war economy, are still recognizable, mostly in spheres which apparently have nothing to do with the military. The government's different privatization and restructuring projects put the defence sector and arms trade enterprises into a separate category of economic management and aim to maintain them under direct state control. This might be a form of (necessary) political control, but might also lead to the reproduction of earlier unproductive patterns of mutual dependence and protection.

Although it has lost most of its former privileges, the military industry, at least in some cases, can still count on the helping hand of the central authorities. Given the dire situation of its enterprises, it might have priority in receiving new loans for restructuring, resources which would be badly needed for the readjustment of the civilian economy as well. 'They might be first among equals,' as one of the Ministry of Industry spokesmen put it (*Figyelo*,13 April 1989). The recent efforts to save military production under the protection of the Military Industrial

Office confirm that the defence industry succeeded in keeping its special status (at least in the eyes of the high-level economic decision makers).

The end of the cold war seemed to open up an era of new politics and economics where cooperation and peaceful problem solving would become dominant. It also promised to capitalize on the enormous social energy accumulated in skills, talent and hopes in Eastern Europe which, once set free, could create new types of societies in the region. The first wave of radical social changes in East Central Europe in 1989–90 envisaged a quick and unquestioned shift from a modified war economy to a peacetime economy. They called for a radical reformulation of security policy, placing emphasis on defence and peaceful cooperation, substantial military expenditure cuts, elimination of the military's privileges and conversion. Instead of this, the dawn of the 'new world order' was marked by a worsening economic and social crisis, war in Yugoslavia, several other wars and a violently disintegrating society in what used to be the Soviet Union, with thousands of refugees forced to abandon their homes. Eastern Europe, mainly the Balkan peninsula, became a major crisis area, representing a considerable security risk for the whole world. The real dangers of this suddenly very volatile situation have unfortunately activated the worst historical reflexes in the 'post socialist' systems of the region. Instead of trying to find common security guarantees and the widest possible economic, political and cultural cooperation, they all tend to close in and play the nationalist card in their efforts to gain legitimacy. This leads to increasing tensions both within and among them.

In Hungary as well, the government has been using nationalism as a major means of legitimization. The army, eager to reconfirm its position in society, became a fairly responsive partner in this undertaking. With its reconstructed identity it presented itself as an objective, metapolitical force, which was able to embody the recently rediscovered national unity. According to the system's new ideology, this 'genuinely national' army and the security of a redefined nation state might deserve special sacrifices and the society (again) must understand and accept the burdens stemming from this. Once the armed forces' special status was re-established, the arguments for maintaining and supporting the local defence industry became enforced and influential again. The cycle was ready to run again – at a lower level, maybe even with more efficiency, but following the same, devastating logic.

The first period of significant economic and political changes did not bring a fundamental difference in the way military-related issues were treated in Hungary. There have been many, very important changes, but the basis approach was not essentially altered. The following years confirmed this trend. After a short period of crisis and uncertainty, both the army and the defence industry found a new identity and new arguments for justifying their existence within the changed political system. The armed forces have appealed for additional financial resources in order to be able to protect Hungary from the new security threats the destabilizing Eastern Europe might pose. They have also presented themselves as a precursor of Hungary's European integration, in the form of the possibility of joining NATO. After 1992, the army fought each year for an increased military budget and, even though it never received the requested sum, it always succeeded in getting more than was originally planned. Despite their precarious financial state, the armed forces managed to purchase some new, high-tech military equipment, for example IFF systems from the United States.

Although the bulk of the defence industry failed to manage its crisis successfully and is still in the red, and weapons production continues to decrease, there are significant political forces in Hungary that exert pressure for significant government intervention to revamp the sector. Now the arguments are based on 'purely economic' grounds, like the lucrativeness of potential arms sales, the replacement of weapon imports by cheaper local production, the fight against unemployment and the protection of the domestic industry. In its latest proposal to the new government, elected in May 1994, the Military Industrial Office proposed special treatment for 80 selected companies and some macroeconomic measures to facilitate the reconstruction of the defence sector.

Back in 1989, when the Berlin Wall fell, symbolizing the end of the cold war era, it seemed that Hungary would be a quick and easy case of radical demilitarization and conversion in East Central Europe. It had relatively small armed forces with a low social profile. In its relatively small defence industry, electronics and telecommunication equipment production was predominant, which meant favourable technological conditions for a potential radical conversion. The fact that both the army and the defence industry managed to maintain a special position in the new social–economic system is a disquieting sign, both for Hungary and for the whole region, since it represents a general tendency. What began as an extraordinary period of peaceful, humane transformation might easily end up with a new rearmament race, reconsolidation of authoritarian politics and further pain and sacrifice of the civil populations in the countries of Eastern Europe.

NOTES

1. He referred to the German exodus to the West via Hungarian borders in the autumn of 1989.
2. Western sources suggest the share of GDP was higher than this. According to *International Defense Review*, the Hungarian defence budget accounted for 3 percent of GDP.
3. For some reason, the loss to the military stemming from the switch to dollar account-ancy is larger than that suffered by the civilian sector.
4. Thus 50 percent of the soldiers, 80 percent of the medium-level officers and 100 percent of the Ministry of Defence staff were members of the HSWP, the Hungarian Socialist Workers' Party.
5. In the former GDR, there were 360 000 Soviet soldiers; in Poland, 50 000; in Czecho-slovakia, 73 500.
6. This is quite a significant number, especially if we take into consideration that, after a 90 percent cut and personnel reallocation to other related institutions, the minis-try's staff was reduced to 150.
7. Another interview claimed that by 1991 the armed forces had 110 000 soldiers, including 25 000 professionals, the number of which would not be further diminished.
8. According to another source, in 1986 the ratio was 43:57 while, in 1991, 9 percent went for development and 91 percent for maintenance.
9. It is a common complaint in ex-WTO military circles that the national armies had to pay high licence fees even for their own products.
10. Basic figures on military production, output, export, import, the number of enter-prises involved and workforce employed are constantly changing. This is due partly to the surviving traditions of secrecy, partly to the fact that real economic data were fairly difficult to obtain in the highly distorted economic system characteristic of the whole sector. The dominance of dual-purpose enterprises also makes accounting slightly hypothetical.
11. This listing is unusual because light industry is not supposed to be counted within the military sector. Csobay (1990a) quotes 66.7 percent telecommunication elec-tronics and precision instruments, 13.8 percent vehicles, 10.8 percent weapons, 6.9 percent 'other products' and 1.8 percent ammunition.
12. The identity of the recipients is not specified.

BIBLIOGRAPHY

Annus, Antal (1991), 'Interview', *Tallozo*, 24 April.

Babus, Endre (1991), 'Felfegyverzo mosoly', *Heti Vilaggazdasag*, 16 February.

Balazsy, Sandor (1991), 'Bekejobb a hadiiparnak', *Figyelo*, 26 September.

Brody, Andras (1990a), 'A hon vedelmerol', *Valosag*, No. 6.

Brody, Andras (1990b), 'Interview', *Figyelo*, 20 December.

Csabai, Gyorgy (1991), 'A biztonsag es a biztonsagpolitika gazdasagi dimen-zioja', *Uj Honvedsegi Szemle*, no. 3.

Csapody, Tamas (1990), 'Civil polgari vagy alternativ katonai?', *Tarsadalmi Szemle*, no. 11.

Csobay, Jozsef (1990a), 'Valsagban van-e a magyar hadiipar?', *Vilaggazdasag*, 21 September.

Csobay, Jozsef (1990b), 'A magyar hadiiparrol, penzugyi szemmel', *Penzugyi Szemle*, no. 1.

Csobay, Jozsef (1991), 'Megjegyzesek', manuscript, Budapest: Ministry of Finance.
Deutsche Bank (1991), *Rebuilding Eastern Europe*, Frankfurt.
Eller, Erzsebet (1991), 'Volt, nincs hadiipar', *Figyelo*, 14 February.
Fur, Lajos (1990), 'Interview', *Nepszabadsag*, 3 December.
Fur, Lajos (1991), 'Interview', *Heti Vilaggazdasag*, 20 April.
Fur, Lajos (1992), 'Interview', *Nepszabadsag*, 14 February.
Gyarmati, Istvan (1990), 'A hadsereg a demokratikus tarsadalomban', *Valosag*, no. 5.
Hajdu, Laszlo and Levay, Geza (1991), 'Az europai hagyomanyos erokrol folytatott CFE targyalasok egyezmenye', *Uj Honvedsegi Szemle*, no. 4.
Janza, Karoly (1990), 'Interview', *Heti Vilaggazdasag*, 8 December.
Janza, Karoly (1991a), 'A haderoreform ara', *Tarsadalmi Szemle*, no. 8–9.
Janza, Karoly (1991b), 'A vedelemgazdasagrol', *Uj Honvedsegi Szemle*, no. 10.
Janza, Karoly (1992), 'Interview', *Magyar Hirlap*, 29 February.
Katona, Tamas (1990), 'Interview', *Nepszabadsag*, 30 December.
Kiss, Mariann (1993), 'Orion, A Marketing Case Study', manuscript, Budapest: Privatization Research Institute.
Kiss, Sandor (1991), 'Politikarol es biztonsagpolitkarol', *Uj Honvedsegi Szemle*, no. 5.
Kiss, Zoltan (1991), 'Uj rendszer – uj nemzeti hadero', *Uj Honvedsegi Szemle*, no. 2.
Kovacs, Attila (1990a), 'A leszereles es a haditermeles konverziojanak hatasa a magyar gazdasagra', *Aula*, no. 1.
Kovacs, Attila (1990b), 'Interview', *Magyar Hirlap*, 10 October.
Kriston, Istvan (1990), 'Egy uj magyar honvedelmi koncepcio es kritikaja', *Kapu*, no. 1.
Laszlo, Jeno (1992), 'Interview', *Nepszabadsag*, 10 June.
Laszlo, Jeno (1993), 'Interview', *Nepszava*, 21 April.
Lemaitre, Pierre (1987), *Hungarian Concepts of Security Policy and the Security Policies of Hungary*, Copenhagen: Centre of Peace and Conflict Research.
Medgyesi, Janos (1992), Office of Military Industry, interview carried out by the author.
Mernyo, Ferenc (1991), 'Onkoros vedelem', *Heti Vilaggazdasag*, 13 April.
Moricz, Gabor (1991a), 'Interview', *Uj Honvedsegi Szemle*, no. 5.
Moricz, Gabor (1991b), 'Interview', *Magyar Honved*, 7 June.
Palankai, Tibor (1990), 'Conversion: The Hungarian Case', *Disarmament*, no. 2.
Palankai, Tibor (1992), 'Conversion: national case studies', paper presented at the IIP Conference, Vienna.
Pataki, Istvan (1991), 'Gyokeresen uj katonai doktrinara van szukseg', *Uj Honvedsegi Szemle*, no. 1.
Radvanyi, Laszlo and Szabo, Jozsef (1991), 'A partallam hadseregetol a nemzet honvedsegetig', *Magyar Honved*, 14 June.
Reti, Pal (1989), 'Merre huz a hadiipar?', *Figyelo*, 13 April.
Sauerwein, Brigitte (1990), 'Hungary's national defence', *International Defence Review*, no. 11.
SIPRI Yearbook (1992), Oxford: Oxford University Press.
Szilas, Istvan (1991), 'A hon vedelmeben. Valasz Brody Andrasnak', *Valosag*, no. 8.
Szucs, Laszlo (1991), 'Honvedsegunk alapjai', *Uj Honvedsegi Szemle*, no. 4.

Vamosi, Zoltan (1991), 'A (volt) Varsoi Szerzodes es a valtozo nemzetkozi viszonyok', *Uj Honvedsegi Szemle*, no. 5.

Wachsler, Tamas (1992a), 'A miniszter csak hallgat', *Nepszabadsag*, 24 February.

Wachsler, Tamas (1992b), 'Interview', *Beszelo*, 7 March.

Walki, Laszlo (1991), 'Megbizhato vedernyo kerestetik', *Nepszabadsag*, 28 October.

9. Russia

Yevgeny Kusnetsov and Alexander Ozhegov

In 1988, at the end of the cold war, military hardware represented 62 percent of the machinery output of the former Soviet Union, estimated in world prices, with capital goods 32 percent and consumer durables 6 percent. The central role of defence industry adjustment in the course of short-run stabilization and long-run industrial policy makes Russia distinct from any other country where the defence conversion debate is normally relatively independent of the economy-wide restructuring and development.

In this chapter, which adopts an explicitly evolutionary approach, defence reductions will be examined, not in terms of reallocation of resources from military to civilian use, since this is based on the assumption that resources are fungible, but in terms of the release for civilian use of latent resources locked into defence production. The most important of these resources – entrepreneurial routines and high-tech production processes – are also the most military-specific. Thus certain incentives and pressures are needed to shape their evolution in a commercially viable direction; this will be a long process of tacit learning-by-doing.

The structure of the chapter is as follows. The first section surveys changes in the Russian defence sector, paying particular attention to the macroeconomic effects of the drastic cuts in defence procurement in 1992. In the second section we try to uncover 'hidden rationalities' of defence enterprise behaviour in 1992, both those that facilitate and those that inhibit defence sector transformation. The macro analysis of the first section and micro approach of the second section are combined in the third section to outline three stylized scenarios of the Russian defence sector transformation. We argue that one of these, the 'open economy' scenario, was pursued briefly in the first half of 1992 but then abandoned in favour of a more interventionist approach, allegedly aimed at civilian export performance. The third alternative considered is 'selective import substitution'. In view of the numerous linkages of the Russian defence–industrial complex to the whole economy, the fourth section discusses the general economic problems of industrial restructuring.

MACROECONOMIC CONDITIONS FOR CONVERSION

The starting conditions for defence industry transformation were rather unfavourable. By the beginning of 1992, defence enterprises had already had four years' experience in conversion in the former Soviet Union and, in most cases, this was negative. The defence industries in the former Soviet Union were already considerably diversified and traditionally produced civilian as well as military output. It is noteworthy that all civilian aircrafts and vessels, all radio-electronic equipment (including computers, means of communication and so on), up to 70–80 percent of all refrigerators and washing machines, most motorcycles and about 10 percent of motor cars were manufactured at defence enterprises. Consumer durables manufactured within the defence sector amounted to 50 percent of their total output in the country. The technological level of the defence sector was much higher than that of the civil sector because the defence sector always received priority in the allocation of all kinds of resources. At the same time, the orientation of the Soviet system towards the fulfilment of military potential was associated with autarky and overemphasis on military technologies. In the context of the growing inefficiency of the entire economy, this resulted in the technological heterogeneity of the defence sector.

The leading Soviet position in aerospace (thanks to an extensive commitment of human and material resources) as in some other defence branches, coexisted with extreme backwardness in micro-electronics, radio-electronics and telecommunications – indeed, the whole field of information technology.

The fact that almost all advanced technologies were developed inside the defence sector inevitably led to large-scale product spin-off; almost all science-intensive civilian production was manufactured in the defence enterprises. But, at the same time, there was no technological spin-off from the defence sector to the civilian branches of the economy, so the gap between them continually widened. Moreover, the product spin-off was quite specific and limited because of the low priority given to the manufacture of civilian products in defence enterprises. Some civilian products were identical to military products; for example, civil aircraft were designed like military transport planes. Others were produced out of substandard components which did not meet military requirements – this was the case for consumer microelectronics.

From the very beginning, the transformation process was aimed at extensive diversification into the civilian sphere. Civilian capacities were to be developed through new investments and physical resources, rather than through redistribution of existing manufacturing resources (raw and operational materials, productive capacities). The cutbacks in military programmes and the release of labour resources were, in practice, accompanied by negligible releases of operational equipment and capacities. As a rule, these were conserved within the framework of the programme for defence industry mobilization readiness. Under such conditions, conversion was becoming, not the engine of economic growth, as the political leaders of the country had hoped, but another serious burden for the economy.

Within the framework of the State Programme for Conversion, defence enterprises were forced to manufacture goods which did not fit their profile. They were required to manufacture a wide range of equipment for the agricultural sector and food-processing industry. Already by the end of the 1980s, this resulted in the rapid increase in prices for civilian machine-building production. This was due to the fact that defence enterprises were induced to include the expenditure connected with preserving defence production in their prices.

The curtailment of defence orders began in 1989 and initially concerned tanks, aircraft missiles and artillery procurement. Space programmes (in particular, *Energy-Buran*) were given serious reconsideration and the construction of some large radar installations was suspended. As compared with 1988, in 1991 the output of aircraft was 1.8 times lower, tanks 2.1 times, strategic missiles 2.4 times, ammunition 2.8 times, and infantry machinery, landing machinery and armoured carries 4.2 times.

Some programmes not only escaped being cut but were even substantially expanded. This was true first of all for aircraft carriers and large nuclear submarine building.[1] Nevertheless, the general reduction of financial expenses for military equipment and for defence R&D was quite noticeable. In 1991, the budgetary assignments to armaments and military hardware procurement and to R&D were only 71 percent and 78 percent, respectively, of the 1988 level in real terms. In view of the disintegration of the Soviet Union, it is rather difficult to estimate the size of the military budget decrease; the cuts were probably even greater.

According to official data, general defence expenditures for the former Soviet Union in 1989 amounted to 77 billion roubles. In 1990, these were reduced to 71 billion roubles in comparable prices (or increased to 96 billion roubles in current prices). These figures do not, however, accurately reflect the actual changes, as the structure of the domestic prices in the former Soviet Union economy differs considerably from that of world prices. In particular, prices for most types of weaponry in the former Soviet Union in roubles were from six to 14 times lower than the price of corresponding types of armaments in dollars.

The conversion efforts made in 1989–91 did not fundamentally change the situation. After the disintegration of the USSR, the government took a new economic course aimed at price liberalization accompanied by drastic toughening of financial policy. Price liberalization was, in particular, supposed to bring the structure of domestic prices in line with the structure of world prices and also to reduce the budgetary deficit. Drastic reductions in defence spending were announced. In 1992, budgetary assignments to defence in Russia amounted to 718 billion roubles, plus 115 billion roubles for armaments and military hardware, 76 billion roubles for military R&D and 20 billion roubles for the defence expenditures of the Ministry of Nuclear Industry. But, taking into consideration the abrupt rise in prices in January 1992 and increasing inflation, this meant a drastic reduction of expenditure for weapons procurement and R&D. (According to official estimates, by December 1992, prices had risen 20 times and according to expert estimates many prices had risen 100 times and more compared with the year before.)

According to data provided by First Deputy Minister of Defence A. Kokoshin, the cutback of spending on armaments and military hardware amounted to about 68 percent of the level of 1991. The purchases of conventional armaments and military hardware were almost halted in 1992 and the main part of procurement consisted of strategic missile forces. As for R&D expenses, their share in total expenditures for defence decreased from 17–19 percent in 1989–90 to 10.5 percent in 1992.

The slump in military orders was not compensated by civilian orders or by a financially backed policy for defence enterprises or for the military-related scientific sphere. Moreover, drastic curtailment of state demand drove even those few former conversion projects which had been on the way to realization to the verge of collapse. Let us take as an example a conversion programme for medical equipment. Within the scope of the State Programme for Conversion, various types of medical machinery and equipment had been developed and tested by 1991 at some of the defence enterprises, mainly at space and missile enterprises. However, the disastrous condition of state-run medical care, and the impossibility of promoting a rapid growth in insurance and private medical service, caused cuts in the output of the new production. Support on the part of the state, so essential during the transition period, proved to be insufficient to overcome the poor state in which programmes for development of civil aviation and shipbuilding, space and other programmes of conversion found themselves.

As a result, the idea of conversion, rather unpopular in the military–industrial complex even before that, was totally discredited. The slump in military demand in 1992 was called 'avalanche' conversion. It was ruinous not only for Russian defence industry, but also for the whole science and technology potential of the country. Technological discipline at defence enterprises deteriorated sharply and the personnel problem increased.

The transition from hidden inflation to high open inflation was not accompanied by any noticeable rise in unemployment: the directors of enterprises tried to hold back the outburst of public discontent by continuing to pay the workers their wages even in the absence of orders; that is, hidden unemployment became a typical phenomenon. This was the case, above all, for the defence sector, in which, according to existing estimates, there were about six million people employed at Russian enterprises in 1992.

In 1991, approximately half of the operating personnel at defence enterprises in the USSR were involved in military production (see Table 9.1). Taking into account the fact that about 80 percent of all defence potential of the USSR was situated in Russia, by the beginning of 1992 this correlation could be considered as typical for Russia too. In 1990, some 300 000 employees of the defence sector were dismissed from military production. Out of these, some 228 000 continued to work on civil production at the same defence enterprises. In 1991, the corresponding figure were 380 000 and 300 000. A slump in military orders and derailment of many programmes for diversification into the civilian sphere in 1992 meant the loss of work for several million people. Taking into account the siting of defence enterprises, this could turn out to be a social disaster for some cities and even whole regions. For example, in the Urals region in Yekaterinburg and the area around it, of two million employed, 500 000 are working for defence.

At the beginning of 1992, the situation was complicated greatly, owing to the lack of coordination of government measures, which meant that enterprises continued working in accordance with old defence programmes, using bank credits for the purchase of spare parts and for paying wages to their employees. This resulted in a rapid increase in

Table 9.1   *Changes in personnel involved in civilian production as a share of total industrial personnel in the defence sector, 1989–91*

Industries	1989	1990	1991
Aviation industry	38.3	43.6	51.4
Defence industry	45.6	53.2	59.9
General machine-building (missile & space industry)	35.9	46.3	56.4
Shipbuilding	35.9	46.3	56.4
Radio industry	34.6	39.9	48.3
Electronic industry	52.7	56.3	64.1
Communications equipment manufacturing	30.2	35.1	43.6
Nuclear industry	46.6	50.6	55.4
Total for all industries of defence sector	39.5	45.5	53.0

Source: Smirnov (1992).

the amount of unpaid production. For example, by February 1993, new *MIG*-29 jet aircraft worth around two billion dollars were being stored on the Dementyev airfield of the Moscow Industrial Association. In 1992, not one aircraft was sold to the Russian airforce or abroad (and not primarily because of the lack of demand in foreign countries, but because of internal confusion and fighting between various factions within the military–industrial sector over rights to sell military hardware abroad).

Because it was impossible to realize a large part of their production in either world or domestic markets, enterprises were induced to gradually reduce working hours. The wages of workers at defence workshops were financed by government subsidies and 'conversion' credits, as well as by charging higher prices for civilian products. This emerging hidden unemployment at a great number of workshops was essentially a form of welfare. The outflow of top high-quality staff became inevitable under such conditions. Before 1992, the trend was to seek employment in the 'alternative' independent sector, that is to join cooperative and small business enterprises. New defence employees began to transfer to state-run enterprises in the other industries, where wages were higher. In many cases, this transfer was accompanied by an abrupt decline in quality requirements, especially for the staff at defence institutes and design bureau. The inevitable lagging of defence enterprises and scientific organizations in the light of the wages 'rush', which increased greatly during 1992, caused a powerful outflow of personnel. From January 1991 to January 1993, for example, the Mikoyan Design Bureau, which developed *MIG* jet aircraft, lost over 1500 employees: in October 1992, some high-quality programmers at the design bureau with monthly wages of 10 thousand roubles left for firms where they were paid 75 thousand roubles per month. In total, according to recent estimates, some 700 000 employees were released from military production in 1992 in Russia. This was almost twice as many as in 1991. Of these, about 200 000 were scientists.

Similar processes took place in the other most militarized state on the territory of the former USSR – the Ukraine. About 15–20 enterprises specializing in almost every branch within the defence sector were situated in the Ukraine, including large-assembly enterprises such as one of the most powerful missile plants in the former USSR, the South Engineering Plant ('Yuzmash', Dniepropetrovsk), in which the *Zenit* missiles were produced, and the Nikolayevsky Shipbuilding Plant specializing in aircraft carrier manufacturing. The cutback in defence orders was even larger than in Russia and required colossal subsidies and state credits. In other words, the Ukrainian government was induced to conduct a similar 'hidden welfare' policy. A serious blow for the Ukrainian enterprises proved to be the break-up of economic connections with Russia. This was caused by many factors, including the 'bank financial wars' and non-payment for shipped production; these problems have been repeatedly raised at Ukrainian–Russian summits.

Already during the first half of 1992, Russian defence enterprises had demanded that the government give definite answers to a set of questions, including those of a legislative nature. The 'Law About Conversion of the Defence Industry in Russia' was passed in March 1992; however, it was adopted earlier than other laws concerning defence which were to determine the fate of the defence industry ('The Defence Law', 'The Status of Defence Enterprises Law' and so on). In practice, this law concerned the problems connected with defence proper rather than conversion (the drawing up of state programmes for developing and manufacturing weaponry, the process of decision making regarding defence orders, the necessity of preserving the mobilization capacities withdrawn beyond the scope of conversion and so on).

Not being backed financially, this law has had a negligible effect in promoting the acceleration of the conversion process. Moreover, in some respects, it actually hindered or distorted the transformation process. To prove this fact it is enough to cite only two examples:

- According to the law, enterprises or structural subdivisions of enterprises which serve a mobilization purpose and are not involved in current manufacture cannot be privatized. Since any military capacities may be ranked as mobilization capacities (or, to be more exact, the plans for mobilization capacities to be preserved could include any workshops and equipment at defence enterprises), this article may cause privatization at any defence enterprise at any time to be vetoed.
- A compensation for part of overhead expenses is to be provided for those enterprises that undertake conversion at which equipment for agricultural and food-processing sectors is manufactured, in order to maintain a 'not higher than world' price level. This would inevitably stimulate inflation.

The absence of a definite short-run or medium-run perspective, even after the adoption of the 'Conversion Law', meant that by the beginning of 1993 defence enterprises faced the same problems they had to face a year earlier, that is the necessity to promote profitability and effectiveness of military orders, the difficulty of obtaining payment in full and on time for manufactured military hardware, the task of creating the economic conditions for supporting mobilization capacities to the optimum extent and a determined orientation towards military orders during the following two to three years. It is very important for the military–industrial sector that a definite military doctrine is established and that a certain number of 'public' (state-owned) enterprises are recognized, thus granting that others have the freedom to choose how to organize their work.

According to the report by First Deputy Minister of Defence A. Kokoshin, the long-term purposes and tasks of military–technical policy had already been formulated in April 1992. He stated that this policy

is to promote the science and technology basis of Russian Military Forces doing some preparatory research work, which will provide a foundation for the defence industry in Russia for the 21st century, to allow no serious lagging behind the most developed countries, to maintain the capacity for handling science and technology resources which will help level the effect of possible science and technology breakthroughs in other countries. (Kokoshin 1993).

By 1993, the Ministry of Defence had developed and confirmed the basic items of the programme for armaments up to the year 2000. The priority was given to maintaining defence strategic nuclear forces, high-precision weapons, communication systems, intelligence and war-management systems, and radioelectronic military equipment. The programme aimed to establish a balance between the systems of weapons and military infrastructure, innovations and armaments modernization, the level of fighting characteristics of systems and their operational qualities, and the development of military hardware and software.

The system of military orders was also to undergo change. According to the 'Defence Law', the Ministry of Defence obtained the right to conclude long-term contracts directly with the enterprises. For complex military hardware, the law provided for a system of advanced payment to be awarded to make up a substantial percentage of the total annual order.

According to the budgetary project for 1993, the total expenditures for defence would exceed 1500 billion roubles; however, taking into account increasing inflation, this amount was obviously to be recalculated. The government and the Supreme Soviet were supposed to perform a complex indexing of prices for military production in accordance with the actual expenditures of enterprises based on the concept of the Ministry of Defence. In general, defence orders for 1993 increased on the previous year by 13–17 percent. Such a rise can be explained by the radical cuts that took place in 1992 and the consequent fragility of the defence base and the necessity to update armaments in Russia. At the time that the USSR disintegrated, most manufacturing of new equipment was concentrated in the Ukraine and Belarus, so the percentage of some types of new weaponry (in particular, jet aircraft) is lower in Russia than in these states. Russia was also found to possess a large share of out-of-date weapons which, by world standards, are rather ineffective as fighting equipment and have proved to be too expensive in operation. Plans included a reduction in the number of different types of armament systems, as budgetary constraints curtail opportunities for duplicating or dispersing the financial resources.

To withdraw out-of-date weaponry requires rather high expenditures for utilization of weapons and ammunition. In 1992, almost nine billion roubles were allocated from the budget for the weapons liquidation programme. In 1993, the amount of such allocations was expected to increase noticeably. One of the reasons for this is the signing of the Russian–American START-2 Treaty (which was primarily to affect intercontinental ballistic missiles, the output of which is to be repeatedly reduced up to the year 2003), as well as the convention on prohibiting design, manufacture, storage and use of chemical weapons and their liquidation. In 1992, the reserve of chemical weapons in Russia amounted to almost 40 000 metric tons, compared to 31 400 metric tons in the USA. The cost of liquidation of chemical weapons was estimated at US$8 billion.

It is obvious that Russia's expenditures for weapons utilization and liquidation during the next decade will require the creation of 'reverse' technologies, which may turn out to be rather difficult given the disintegration of the science and technology potential within the defence sector. A key question which will determine the future of the military–technological policy in Russia concerns institutional changes as well as the behaviour of both the management and the staff of the leading military-related firms of the country.

ECONOMIC BEHAVIOUR OF MILITARY-RELATED ENTERPRISES

The behaviour of Russian enterprises in 1992 consisted of a number of puzzles, none of which is easy to explain. Why, for example, did government credits to facilitate conversion produce favourable consequences in some enterprises while delaying the unavoidable adjustment in the majority of the others?[2] Why did privatization, the presumed hallmark of efficiency-inducing measures, seem to divert the incentives of the top enterprise management even further from the goals of adjustment? Why were managers so reluctant to resort to lay-offs while nothing formally prohibited them? (There is nothing similar to the Polish workers' councils in the Russian enterprises.) Even more mysteriously, why did the desire to avoid lay-offs serve, in many instances, as a stimulus for restructuring?

Before proceeding to an explanation, let us take a brief look at the history of development studies. About 30 years ago, prompted by a puzzle as to why the Nigerian state railway service had deteriorated in response to increased competition from cars, Albert Hirschman formulated a theory of 'responses to decline in firms, organizations and states'. He introduced two types of responses to such problems: 'exit' to a better alternative, and 'voice', defined as 'any attempt at all to change, rather than escape from, an objectionable state of affairs'. Hethen (1958, 1970) introduced a whole series of paradoxical 'hidden rationalities' of firms' behaviour which are relevant here. For example, if, in a monopoly-ridden economy there is no serious threat to the organization's survival, the presence of competition does not restrain monopoly as it is supposed to, but comforts and bolsters it by unburdening it of its more troublesome customers. This happens because exit is ineffective as a recuperation mechanism. Competition succeeds only in draining from the firm its more quality-conscious, alert and potentially-activist customers and employers, thus reducing the power of 'voice'.

For the typical Russian military firm, bankruptcy in the conditions of continuing credit allocation is not a credible threat. 'Exit' is an extremely weak incentive to restructure. Military technology is so highly specialized that it is hardly possible for the Ministry of Defence to withdraw demand from one particular enterprise and switch to another. Civilian customers can theoretically undertake a search for a better supplier and switch their demand to other producers. In reality, even if an alternative producer does exist, such cases are rare. Both transaction costs to the customer to find a new supplier and entry costs for the potential supplier to start production are very high because of the rudimentary market infrastructure. High entry costs constitute the major indicator of lack of competition, rather than the share of output supplied by a single producer, which is the way the Russian Anti-trust Committee identifies monopolies.

This situation was well understood by the experienced Russian military enterprise management at the beginning of 1992, when defence contracts were sharply curtailed. Rather than reduce output in accordance with the diminished demand or start searching for new sources of demand (which would have implied real adjustment), enterprises continued to produce either civilian or military output which far exceeded effective demand. In the first quarter of 1992, there were only 6.5 billion roubles allocated for military procurement while enterprises produced more than 20 billions worth of output. Since the state did not pay for the output it had not ordered, the producers could not provide payment to their subcontractors. Inter-enterprise arrears began to rise exponentially, especially in the military sector, because during the whole first quarter of 1992, the defence enterprises continued to work according to military programmes adopted in 1991. In July 1992, total arrears reached one-half of GDP.

Every military enterprise was technically bankrupt. The government could not help but resort to the provision of credits to alleviate the arrears problem. Since profitability and enterprise efficiency became totally unrelated, the credits were allocated according to the bargaining power of the potential recipients. Enterprises in Moscow and St Petersburg were receiving credits (in reality, subsidies) fairly easily by relying on their numerous connections in the government. Approximately 55 percent of all subsidies received by defence enterprises in Russia in 1992 were used to maintain employment and wages (and partially to repay arrears); 25 percent to finance social infrastructure (medical facilities, housing and so on, which traditionally were the responsibility of enterprises particularly in military-related one-company towns); and only the remaining 20 percent to finance R&D and investments (Telnov, 1992). In spite of a reduction in military demand of more than 50 percent, out of approximately 1000 military-related enterprises only 21 stopped production (all of them small; in the majority of cases, former workers were not considered to be unemployed but were technically on vacation) and about 400 enterprises operated three to four days a week.

These subsidies created the following vicious circle. The amount was quite sufficient to raise significantly the salaries of the top management of enterprises. By the beginning of 1993, it became quite common for an enterprise director to be paid a monthly salary of about one million roubles. With the salary of an average worker at 15–20 000 roubles, the wage differential between top managers and 'average' workers which used to be two to one rocketed to fifty to one – still smaller than in the USA, but much higher than in Japan. To avoid conflicts, the top managers eschewed large-scale lay-offs and in certain instances were mobilizing the workers to show popular discontent over government policies in order to receive more subsidies. In addition, as we have already mentioned, high-quality workers who were interested in real restructuring started to leave defence-related enterprises because of the relatively low wages. The remaining low-quality workers and grossly overpaid top managers formed a powerful, hard-to-break coalition against restructuring.

If competition ('exit' mechanism) has failed to emerge, what are the incentives to restructure? Our case-studies in Samara and the St Petersburg region show that incitement to real adjustment typically comes from the charismatic manager of a (typically peripheral) plant who identifies himself with the plant; he directs and is fairly certain that, as a result of privatization, he will end up as effective owner of it. At the same time this manager, because of low leverage on the central authorities, has to rely on his firm's business revenues rather than credits. This is a Schumpeterian entrepreneur of the 19th century: he has a vision of the business future of his enterprise; his decisions are shaped more by this 'vision' than by current profitability.[3] He is the business loner: he does not share his vision with anyone else. This means that, as long as he is there, the enterprise is profitable; if he leaves, deterioration of the enterprise performance is unavoidable.

'Voice' of valued employees whom it would be undesirable to lose acts as a catalyst to restructure and diversify into civilian production. In contrast to the 'no adjustment' case, where the internal brain of the skilled human capital moves into redistributive activities (which, under high inflation, guarantee much higher income), the desire to avoid this 'brain drain' serves as an incentive to start civilian production (usually for export) and augment the real income of valued workers. Thus the incentive structure of defence enterprise management is very weak and fragile. Privatization is said to improve the incentives by creating the market for corporate control. However, the immediate consequences of privatization in the Russian defence industry are quite different from this long-term objective.

First, there are many claims on the plant's property. Workers, management, local authorities and federal government are the major claimants. The defence ministry itself imposes a number of constraints on privatization and may eventually veto it. All this creates a situation of the universal 'fight for shares' in which the time and energy of the management are increasingly diverted to bargaining with workers about which privatization scheme to adopt and negotiations with numerous agencies that regulate privatization. All the time that would have been spent in elaboration and implementation of the restructuring plan is increasingly devoted to this 'fight'.[4] Second, the tensions between the current management – would-be owners – and employees of the enterprise (who influence the decision on which privatization scheme to adopt) normally result in a situation in which management buys the loyalty of employees with a 'no lay-off' policy. The anti-productive corporatist coalition between workers and management becomes even stronger.

There is no doubt that, in the long run, as the securities market emerges and as the threat of bankruptcy becomes credible, privatization could provide the appropriate incentives for restructuring. But the first stage of privatization (clarification of property rights) has aggravated rather than improved incentive problems.

So far we have focused on the incentives for diversification into one civilian sphere and reduction of defence production. What about resources for restructuring? The underdeveloped banking sphere does not provide any medium or long-term credits (only credits for working capital) and the rudimentary equity market (on which only financial and trade institutions are able, and then to a very limited extent, to raise capital by issuing equity). These are the basic problems that hinder restructuring in the whole economy. Three sets of problems are peculiar to, or particularly acute in, the defence sector.

First, there is a problem of financing the reserve production capacities that are still kept in case of war (mobilization capacities). Fixed costs to maintain these capacities are high: the overhead costs at many defence plants reach 70–80 percent of total costs largely because of the fixed costs of maintaining reserve capacities. In the new law on conversion it is assumed that the government must reimburse to enterprises the costs of maintenance of these capacities. In reality, either this does not happen at all or reimbursement is negligibly small. Very high unit costs of civilian production (and consequently high prices) result in low sales and low (often negative) profit.

Secondly, there is a new tendency to finance the orders of the Ministry of Defence out of profit from civilian production (because of the runaway inflation, budget allocations cover only a fraction of military hardware procurement: the budget is not indexed). The positive outcome of the unfolding privatization process was expected to be the organizational separation of production units specializing in civilian output into independent firms. Civilian production traditionally subsidized military output on a large scale (Kuznetsov and Shirokov, 1989). The leadership of the Ministry of Defence and the Committee on Defence Issues consider such subsidization to be pivotal for military contracting and vetoed the majority of privatization schemes where civilian production units would have become financially independent. For example, the privatization scheme of the largest military plant in St Petersburg, Baltyisk'i Zavod, which was stalled by the Russian government because (1) the export contracts with German firms for the production of commercial ships were seen as potentially lucrative revenues for financing remaining military production, and (2) the increasingly civilian orientation of the plant would somewhat undermine the prospects for military shipbuilding. It is noteworthy that in 1993 military hardware was set to provide only 6 percent of the plant's aggregate revenues, and for 1995 and onwards there were no orders for military ships at all (ibid.) but, according to the Russian military establishment, military and civilian production units were to be held together 'just in case'.

In some instances the atomization of the production structure has been encouraged by the current privatization programme in the Soviet-type economy. The ministry rather than individual enterprise was the equivalent of a firm in the Western sense of the word. When the ministerial structure disintegrated, its unit enterprises that produced complex customer-specific machinery such as aircraft unexpectedly realized that many of their subcontractors supplying primary resources were more interested in selling to the world market than abiding by the previous contract structure.[5] As a result, sophisticated technological chains disintegrated virtually overnight.

The problem here is that primary resource exporters focus on immediate, short-term revenues while complex machinery manufacturing requires a long-term approach (there is a lag between investment and revenues). In an advanced market economy the contradiction between short-term interests and long-run goals is overcome by the appropriate structure of property rights, or (if the subcontractor has to make an investment that is customer-specific) by a merger of all relevant subcontractors in the single firm where the exchange is governed by transfer rather than market prices (and thus implicit subsidization is widespread).

The problem of the disintegration of the production structure is particularly acute for the military–industrial complex with its long technological chains and use of customer-specific, often unique equipment. In 1992, the prevailing tendency was towards disintegration and atomization of organizational units. Gradually, however, enterprise managers started to form industrial integrated conglomerates as an attempt to avoid further decline of output resulting from the breakdown of subcontracting. The evolution of such conglomerates (or company groups) is the single most significant feature of the current adjustment in the Russian military industry sector. This will be dealt with more fully in the next section.

Currently, neither the structure of incentives nor the financial resources available for enterprise restructuring ensure efficient transformation of the defence sector. There are exceptions to this rule which arise if enterprise managers are exceptionally motivated to overcome numerous obstacles to restructuring. The current constellation of sociopolitical forces in Russian society opens up the possibility for three ways out of the current deadlock. The first, the 'open economy' scenario, which is beneficial for the powerful energy complex, amounts to drastic reduction (as opposed to diversification and transformation) of the military sector. In the contrasting 'high-tech export promotion scenario' there are extensive subsidies to military enterprises to build on their strength. The intermediate 'selected import substitution scenario' is designed to diversify the military sector into the production of agricultural and previously imported machinery. It is beneficial for the newly emerging agricultural entrepreneurs and for the civilian branches of the Russian manufacturing industry.

THE IMPACT OF ARMS REDUCTION ON EMERGING RUSSIAN DEVELOPMENT STRATEGY: THREE SCENARIOS OF RUSSIAN RESTRUCTURING

The economy of the former Soviet Union in 1988 (the year prior to the beginning of economic disintegration) can be characterized as a dual economy with two leading sectors: the primary resources industry and the high-tech defence sector. Exports of oil, oil products and gas generated in 1989 about 17 billion dollars (Vnesnye Ekonomicheskye Sviazi, 1990, p. 28); exports of defence output in that year are estimated at 12.2 billion dollars.[6] Although the primary resource sector is explicitly export-oriented, both forward and backward linkages are underdeveloped. More than 50 percent of capital goods for oil, gas and timber extraction were imported, and the Soviet Union traditionally exported unprocessed primary resources.

The dual structure of the Russian economy, combining extreme underdevelopment (the Russian primary resource sector, not unlike settler colonies, is highly dependent on imports and exports) and 'overdevelopment' (unsustainably high concentration of skilled human capital in the defence sector) potentially permits a wide range of development strategies. The current acute foreign exchange crisis and institutional vacuum (not unlike the situation in East Asia after the termination of American aid at the end of the 1950s and Latin America after its protracted debt crisis) create the possibility that, because of the magnitude of the crisis, the change of development strategy from import substitution to some sort of export promotion will eventually take place.

This conclusion, emphasizing availability of the wide range of development strategies, is especially important given the widespread 'fracasomania' (failure complex) which perceives the Russian economy as 'Upper Volta with missiles', with extremely limited comparative advantages.

Stylized Scenarios

The open economy (Chilean 1973–88) scenario
Under this scenario, Russia strives to achieve unrestricted international trade with the minimum of government intervention, initially exacerbating the dual economy profile. Zhuravlev (1992) has attempted to calculate the static (that is, short-term) comparative advantage for the Russian economy. He estimates that not only is a substantial share of machine-building industry uncompetitive, but that even the primary resource processing industries (such as timber processing, light and chemical industries and, most importantly, agriculture) would be unprofitable as well because of their high energy intensity. Economic stabilization will presumably attract foreign investment in these industries with static comparative advantages, mainly oil and other primary resource sectors and certain segments of the military complex. In the meantime, however, the major share of the defence enterprises is

expected to go bankrupt, with the exception of those capable of exporting immediately. This may not be a negligible portion: Russian transport planes (not to mention military aircraft) were competitive even after the Russian government imposed export duties of 20 percent in 1992. Weapons and high-tech exports will not experience a surge, however, because producers of intermediate products will go bankrupt. Military-related unemployment rather than the redeployment of the defence industry assets is the crux of this issue.

Since this scenario results in the elimination of negative[7] value-added production processes, in the short to medium run, overall welfare is expected to increase rather than fall. There are two economic problems with this scenario, however. First, how will the population tolerate the fall in employment, even given a relatively high level of social security? The tolerance of unemployment is bound to be low, if only because of the prevalence of one-company towns and low regional mobility. Second, the prospects for the re-emergence of the manufacturing industry are rather bleak. Because of the high productivity of the natural resource sector and the (albeit small) high-tech export sector, the equilibrium exchange rate and real wage will be relatively high. Thus the switch from predominantly natural resource to low-wage manufacturing export promotion will be difficult. For all these reasons, orientation to Russia's static rather than its dynamic (potential) comparative advantages and the resulting deskilling of the human capital of the military–industrial complex seems problematic.

High-tech export promotion ('East Asian') scenario

Unlike the open economy scenario, which results in the monopoly of the primary resource sector as the only leading sector, this scenario emphasizes the promotion of dynamic rather than static comparative advantages and views the military–industrial complex as a dynamic export sector. While the presence of certain dynamic comparative advantages in the Russian defence sector is unquestionable, the costs of this strategy potentially far exceed its benefits. First, there are efficiency problems associated with the implementation of industrial policy. Furthermore, subsidies – the key instrument of industrial policy – are not only inflationary but create tremendous moral hazards; that is, they offer considerable opportunities for corruption, and currently provide disincentives rather than incentives for restructuring. Second, high-tech export markets are markets with very high entry barriers. Even if it were possible to convert high-tech defence production into high-tech civilian production with relatively low investment costs (a dubious assumption in itself) there is a problem regarding the marketing of potentially competitive machinery.

The first set of problems may be, somewhat unexpectedly, addressed by referring to Hirschman's linkages theory (Hirschman, 1958, 1981). Developed initially for the primary resource sector, it may also be applied to the transformation of the defence–industrial complex. The idea is to channel revenues from the weapons sector to create production and fiscal linkages that would promote competitive high-tech civilian export. In this way both the problem of pro-inflationary bias of industrial policy and its efficiency problems are at least partially addressed. The source of subsidies to high-tech civilian exports is assumed to be weapons export.[8] That implies that allocation of subsidies is the function of large diversified enterprises which combine civilian and military production rather than that of the government. If subsidies are allocated by the government, they are allocated by relatively easily forced criteria of reciprocity based on export performance. The only (far from negligible, however) problem is to ensure that subsidies really go to civilian investment rather than to the further promotion of military exports or to real wage maintenance.

This scenario is attractive because it allows Russia to retain the large human capital of the military sector and build on its strength. Furthermore, it strives to apply the lessons of East Asian export-led growth. However, to the extent that the initial promotion of military exports is instrumental in creating linkages to civilian high-tech export, the lessons of unsuccessful settler colonies are more relevant. The phenomenon of surging weapons export revenues, which in itself is a dubious assumption, in the same way as are primary resources revenues in Latin America, might only strengthen socioeconomic forces and interest groups already inimical to development. In Latin America these were oligarchic landowners interested more in luxury consumption than in investment linkages. In the current Russian conditions these forces correspond to that part of the old top management of the military enterprises unable to adjust to the changing market environment. In this case linkages from weapons to civilian export fail to emerge and in the long run the defence sector, with the unavoidable termination of subsidies, collapses, just as in the first scenario. However, because of the high level of inflationary subsidies, inflation will persist and even primary resource exports will fail to increase. There is a high probability, therefore, that the advantages of this scenario are illusory.

Selective import substitution: export-adequate strategy (North American scenario, 1870–1920)

Unlike the previous scenarios that maintain the current dual profile (manufacturing based on military sector v. primary resources export) of the Russian economy, this scenario is explicitly aimed at facilitating the growth of the integrated economy. Like the first scenario, it focuses on the primary resource sector and agriculture as the leading sector of the economy. Aggressive government promotion of civilian high-tech exports from the military industry is rejected. The deskilling of the human capital is assumed to be unavoidable. However, this scenario strives to preserve at least some segments of manufacturing which might otherwise go bankrupt in the laissez-faire open economy. The focus is on manufacturing capital goods for the leading sector – primary resources and agriculture and their processing – which given the current high import dependency, amounts to import substitution. Similar to the previous strategy, a substantial degree of government intervention is assumed to create temporary bias in favour of the consumption of domestic equipment produced with reliance on defence sector assets.

The adverse consequences of import-substituting industrialization are well known. Why then should the effects of import-substitution reindustrialization be different? First, we advocate only selective import substitution and a strictly limited period of fairly low (20–40 percent) effective protection. Second, capital market imperfections, which are the major justification for infant industry protection, are particularly acute in Russia. Furthermore, since privatization has just started and adequate incentives for the selection of appropriate technology are not yet in place, the management of the oil-producing firms is frequently strongly biased towards purchase of foreign-produced equipment because its import facilitates lucrative speculative foreign exchange transactions.[9]

In this scenario dynamic comparative advantages are supposed to be financially supported by joint ventures with relevant foreign partners rather than by the government. The state starts to intervene aggressively to promote high-tech exports only after a productive agriculture and primary resource sector with extensive linkages into processing is in place. What makes the above scenarios distinctly different from each other is the apparently different interests that support them in the current Russian reality.

POLITICAL ECONOMY OF THE DEFENCE INDUSTRY TRANSFORMATION

The above scenarios focused on the initial endowments of the Russian economy and the role of the defence sector in their promotion. The actual transformation, however, will be shaped by the constellation of socioeconomic forces. Thus the initial attempt of the Russian government to implement the first scenario was doomed almost from the start. It did not succeed in convincing the energy and fuel sector that orthodox stabilization and subsequent open economy policies would ultimately benefit them and for this reason this policy did not find support among industrialists. Beginning in the second half of 1992, credit creation to facilitate defence industry adjustment turned the macroeconomic stabilization strategy into our second scenario. The export successes of defence-related enterprises are relatively widespread. They are based, however, on the very weak rouble, which makes exports profitable irrespective of costs. Furthermore, civilian machinery export significantly reduces demand for skilled scientists and engineers in comparison with the previously produced defence output. The export of high-tech machinery such as medical equipment produced as a result of conversion is still rare.

Under the guise of high-tech export promotion, there is rather trivial rent seeking which retards rather than advances the transformation of the defence sector in commercially viable directions. The available evidence supports our initial hypothesis that the second scenario is not viable and will degenerate into strengthening the military–industrial oligarchy already inimical to development. The remaining, third strategy, emphasizing selective import substitution, is the weakest politically, because civilian industries which it is supposed to strengthen (agricultural machine building, capital goods for the primary resource sector) have never been influential in the Soviet economy and are politically unorganized (unlike the defence sector, which forms the so-called Union of Industrialists). There are currently no pressure groups which would push for this strategy.

The configuration of interest groups is influenced by the industrial structure. The success of each of the outlined scenarios requires an appropriate industrial structure, which is currently being reorganized through the privatization campaign.

CONCLUDING REMARKS

After a period of disintegration of contractual relations, enterprises seeking to reduce their defence units and diversify into civilian production have started to form new industrial alliances. Industrial conglomerates are emerging either through cross-ownership of shares or around banks specifically organized to finance the conglomerate. The formation of industrial conglomerates starts from the inter-firm credit market. There is an inter-enterprise credit market which is specifically geared to enterprise restructuring. The Tuimen oil producers, for example, have substantial money balances waiting to be invested, as well as the need for the relevant machinery. On certain occasions, this combination has resulted in a short-term loan of these money balances by the oil producer to a prospective machinery supplier (usually the defence-related enterprise which has already displayed its ability to produce efficient manufacturing goods) to design and produce the relevant equipment.

Three characteristics of such loans are noteworthy. First, the loans are short-term (from three to six months) but extended again if they are 'to a certain extent' repaid by the output of the manufacturing enterprise in question, supplied directly to the oil producer, television sets being the typical example. Second, the criterion for extending a loan is more the personal trust in the ability to 'get things done' by the manufacturing plant manager (based on his prior performance) rather than the financial record of his enterprise. Third, there is a substantial degree of slackness in debt repayment and the real interest rate is often negative. The larger the personal trust, the more the slackness is pronounced. In other words, the string of short-term loans is viewed as a long-term subsidy to the manufacturing unit in the expectation that later the unit will be somehow acquired by the oil producer in question.

In some respects, the nascent Russian informal credit market resembles the credit market of developing countries. Among these are characteristically short maturity and personal trust as a means to overcome the fundamental informational asymmetries between borrower and lender. Nor is there anything peculiar in the reliance on short-term credits to finance relatively long-term projects. In Taiwan, for example, whole plants used to be built exclusively on short maturity loans. More perceptive observers, however, would interpret the informal credit market of the type described above as a transitory phenomenon signalling the emergence of diversified business groups based on long-term relations between vertically, and sometimes horizontally, integrated producers.

The future of the defence industry transformation depends upon specific configurations and motivations of the emerging business groups. If they were to compete, both selected import substitution and export promotion scenarios would be possible. If they were more geared towards financial speculation, none of the scenarios outlined would succeed.[10]

CONCLUSION

The success of defence industry transformation in Russia will depend upon the right balance between the market mechanism and the government's industrial policy. The exclusive reliance on the market mechanism attempted in the first half of 1992 resulted in failure: the defence complex proved to be unreceptive to market signals. The resulting policy shift towards more subsidies can be justified on the grounds of export promotion. The increasing popularity in government circles of our second scenario – 'aggressive export promotion' – by the beginning of 1993 indicates that subsidization will continue.

The overall picture is not totally bleak, however. There are examples of successful diversification into the civilian sphere and defence reduction. These successful examples indicate the primary importance of the informal market and emerging inter-enterprise business groups in restructuring. Evolution of such meso-level economic institutions will determine the particular future scenario of the Russian defence industry transformation.

NOTES

1. In particular, this narrowed the range of opportunities for redistribution of raw material resources involved in the defence sector, especially of ferrous and non-ferrous metals: for example, the manufacturing of only one modern submarine requires about 800 km of costly cables of various types.
2. The vivid example is the optic-electronic plant in Viborg (in the St Petersburg region, close to the border with Finland). In 1990, 80 percent of output was defence output; in March 1993, it was less than 15 percent. There were no layoffs (4000 workers are employed at this plant). Diversification into the civilian sphere was achieved through exports of intermediate, relatively simple goods for final producers in Finland and Sweden. Obviously, the extremely weak rouble made output for export profitable almost regardless of local factors, thus contributing to the success of adjustment.
3. It should be noted, however, that in the first quarter of 1992 no one (literally!) knew the size of effective military demand. For example, the Russian Ministry of Foreign Economic Relations was supposed to export in 1992 the completely unrealistic figure of $7.5 billion of weaponry (the preliminary estimate of the same ministry of actual

1992 exports is $1.8 billion (Felgengauer, 1992)). Enterprises received specific domestic orders for military hardware only in March of 1992, some of them even later. The state budget was only adopted in August 1992, with military procurement at the level of 115 billion roubles (1992 prices; the official index of inflation between 1991 and 1992 was 1700 percent). We are grateful to Ksenya Gouchar for this point.

4. Our arguments here resemble the arguments of neo-classical political economy on unproductive rent seeking which emerges because of government regulation and diverts time from productive activity (Krueger, 1974). However, in the Russian privatization case, the major policy advice of neo-classical political economy to abolish all government regulation would slow down the privatization. In Russia, it is the government that literally forces the privatization process. If it withdraws, privatization (or rather, at the current stage, clarification of property rights) would proceed at a slower pace akin to 'spontaneous' privatization in 1989–91.

5. The export of rolled aluminium (part of which was previously supplied to aircraft plants) is an example. The sudden Russian influx of aluminium into the world market depressed prices and made several Canadian firms bankrupt. Estonia, through whose ports it was exported, became the sixth largest world exporter of aluminium.

6. This is not equivalent to export revenues. Many weapons were transferred free as part of military assistance programmes to insolvent undeveloped countries.

7. The high degree of technological complementarity within the Soviet military industry does not allow uncompetitive and competitive segments to be dissected. This problem is particularly acute if the financial sector which normally performs this task is rudimentary.

8. In the current Russian conversion debate, this approach is advocated by the adviser to the president, M. Maley, and called 'economic conversion'. See, for example, Maley (1992).

9. For example, widespread over-invoicing of imported goods and under-invoicing of exported goods is unavoidable in times of high inflation and capital flight. Often such transactions provide the narrow circle of the top management with enough personal revenues for them not to have to worry about cost-effective import substitution.

10. Financial collapse in Chile in 1981, caused by the open economy policy conducted in an economy where corporate and bank interests were interlocked (such interlocking is emerging now in Russia), illustrates the potential dangers of conglomeration.

BIBLIOGRAPHY

Beliakov, R. (1993), 'Kosilki ... Grusherezki ... Ili Vsie-takiMIGi?' (Moving-machines ... Pear-cutters ... or Still MIGs?), *Krasnaia Zbezda*, 6 February, p. 3.

Felgengauer, P. (1992), 'VSE V Russia Hot at Torgovat Oruzhien' (Everybody in Russia wants to sell arms), *Nezavisimaia Gazeta*, 30 September, pp. 1–2.

Hirschman, A. (1958), *The Strategy of Economic Development*, New Haven: Yale University Press.

Hirschman, A. (1970), *Exit, Voice and Loyalty: Responses to Decline in Firms, Organizations and States*, Cambridge, Mass.: Harvard University Press.

Hirschman, A. (1981), 'A Generalised Linkage Approach to Development, with Special Reference to Staples', *Essays in Trespassing*, New York: Cambridge University Press, pp. 59–98.

Kokoshin, A. (1993), 'Voiennye Vyruchaiut Promyshlennost, Oboronshiki –

Armiu' (Militaries Help the Industry, Industrials the Army), *Izvestia*, 19 January.

Krueger, A. (1974), 'The Political Economy of the Rent-Seeking Society', *American Economic Review*, **64**, (3), June.

Kuznetsov, Y. and Shirkov, F. 91989), 'Naykoemkie Proizvodsva i Konversia Oboronnoi Promyshlennosti', *Kommunist*, 10, pp. 15–23. (English translation available: 'Science Intensive Output and Defence Industry Conversion', JPRS-UKO-89-016, 21 September 1989, pp. 8–13.)

Maley, M. (1992), 'Obornnyi Komplex moshet ne razoryat a kormit' (The defence complex can feed us rather than devastate us), *Izvestia*, 31 March.

Mamchur, Yu (1993), 'Ural Skazal Svoio Veskoie Slovo – Oboronnomu Kompleksu – Byt!' (Ural Said its Strong Word: The Defence Complex Has to be!), *Krasnaia Zvezda*, 6 February, pp. 1–2.

Nikiforova, N. (1993), 'Spor o voernom Zavode' (The Dispute about the Military Plants), *Izvestia*, 16 January.

Ozhegov, A. (1991), 'The Defence Complex: New Economic Problems', *Studies in Soviet Economic Development*, **2**, (1).

Ozhegov, A., Rogovski, Ye and Iaremenko, Yu (1991), 'Konversia Oboronnoi Promishennosti i Preobrazovanie Ekonomiki SSSR' (Defence Industry Conversion and its Role in the Transformation of the USSR Economy), *Kommunist*, 1, pp. 54–64.

Smirnov, V. (1992), 'Trudovye Resursy v Usloviah Konversii Voennogo Proizvodstva' (Labour Resources in the Conditions of Conversion), *Voprosy Ekonomiki i Konversii*, no. 2, pp. 40–53.

Telnov, V. (1992), 'Kredity na Konversiu Poluchat ne Vse' (Not Everybody Will Get Credits for Conversion), *Finansovye Izvestia*, 26 November, p. VII.

Tsherbakov, V. (1991), 'Perestroika bez Konversii Nerealna' (Restructuring is Unreal without Conversion), *Ekonomika i Zhizn*, no. 34, pp. 2–3.

Vinslav, Yu and Naumov, N. (1992), 'Kontseptualnye Podhodyk Perestrojke Sistemy Povyshenia Kvalifikatsii i Podgotovki Kadrov v Usloviah Konversii i Perehoda k Rynku' (Conceptual Approaches to the Restructuring of the Personnel Retraining System in the Conditions of Conversion and Transition to the Market), *VoprosyEkonomiki i Konversii*, no. 1, pp. 9–15.

Vneshnye Ekonomicheskye Sviazi SSSR v 1990 godu, Moscow, 1991.

Zhuravlev, S. (1992), 'Recession in the Economy of the Former USSR: General Regularities and Specific Features' (in Russian), *Ekonomika i Matematicheskye Metody*, **28**, (4), pp. 558–82.

10. The Need for New Institutional Arrangements

Mary Kaldor and Geneviève Schméder

There is, of course, a wide-ranging debate about which institutions are most appropriate to meet the challenges of the new post-cold war situation and how they need to be restructured. Even though some institutions, for example NATO, may be more burdened than others by the organizational and intellectual heritage of the cold war, all the existing institutions have lost their character in its aftermath.

The institutions and the rules of the game established during the cold war period no longer function, but new institutions and rules have not yet emerged. The institutional recomposition is in effect made necessary but also problematic by the decline of the hegemonic powers. The two great rival post-war economic and defence systems were characterized by a combination of convergent expectations and coded behaviour models. This does not mean that those involved systematically conformed to expected practices – both camps had their 'rebels' – rather, both systems included prescriptive elements and produced legitimacy. Both used a blend of coercion, cooptation and manipulation of incentives, although this varied according to the system, as the most efficient means of imposition was not one in which open and continual coercion was practised. The United States was able to promote advantageous arrangements through more subtle forms of leadership and manipulation than the Soviet Union, which simply did without the explicit consent of subordinate actors and the formal expression of the rules of the game. In this way, the USA did not need to exercise a strong constraint on the subordinate powers in order that these conform to the demands of the established order, dependency having not only a structural basis, but also a strong cognitive component.

The structural and far-reaching nature of the crisis in the West and in the East could be masked or ignored as long as the two blocs linked between them different countries and provided a framework for overcoming conflicts of interest. The discipline of the cold war did not only freeze the military and ideological status quo, it froze the economic status quo as well. It was not just by chance that, during the 1970s and 1980s, the structural character of the problems was systematically neglected or underestimated, especially by governments. Had these problems been properly addressed, it would necessarily have meant a reconsideration of the socioeconomic and security systems elaborated after World War Two. As a result, there were never any serious proposals for new and radical solutions to the problems of mass unemployment in Europe, of the American deficit, the huge indebtedness of the third world, or the stagnation of the East during the last decades. The only measures taken were fragmentary and unilateral.

Instead of improving things, these measures brought about the return of negative effects. All change introduced on one level modified the regulations in place at other levels; all partial change threatened the coherence of the global system. This was so because the interdependence of institutions is more important than their optimal character if they were to be considered separately. The problem now is how to take all dimensions into account simultaneously. All processes of recomposition force us to rethink the entire set of institutional forms in crisis (organization of production and distribution, relations between the state and the economy, commercial and financial regulations, and so on) and also to retain their global coherence.

In the absence of new rules for integrating different dimensions, nothing guarantees that potentially divergent evolutions will remain peaceful. There is a real danger that Europe, especially the eastern part, will degenerate into small, closed-in militarized and contested nation states facing a myriad of economic difficulties and conflicts. There is an alternative possibility of a much broader cosmopolitan approach to security that encompasses new forms of economic cooperation and political dialogue. Only such a broad approach, which requires considerable vision, energy and thought to implement, could lay the basis for a new set of transnational and regional institutions which could also provide a framework for resolving economic and ecological problems.

Choices about the future direction of security policy cannot be separated from choices about the future direction of economic development. In the security field, different concepts of security based on alternative scenarios for Europe and the world include a West European bloc, a pan-European security system, a Europe of nation states, and so on. All these scenarios are, in fact, variants of the cold war model. They are merely extending the trajectory of cold war thinking, in which the advanced industrialized world, through a series of security arrangements, is thought to be able to insulate itself from the more or less chaotic and disorganized 'third world'. The main question is how far the model extends: who is to be part of 'Europe'.

This kind of insulation is no longer possible, for a variety of reasons, not the least of which is the astonishing revolution in global communications which has taken place over the last two decades. If the process of fragmentation in the East and South continues, Western Europe and, indeed, other advanced industrial regions will be caught up in it. It is extremely unlikely that these rich parts of the world can hold out against the onslaught of problems of tragic proportions that arise from this process of fragmentation.

At the level of values, this dualism between integration and fragmentation can be observed, on the one hand, in the rise of identity politics, the claim to power on the basis of ethnic, religious or linguistic identity and, on the other hand, the re-emergence of a global humanist vision, based on the values of European enlightenment, the sense of belonging to a common global community with an accumulated heritage of civilization that surfaced so dramatically in the 1989 revolutions. At the level of policy, our case-studies showed, in both East and West, on the one hand, a retreat to the national – a renationalization of foreign, security and economic policies – and, on the other hand, a growing commitment to international responsibilities, including peace-keeping and humanitarian assistance. In terms of Western security policy, the shift from partial to global integration or, perhaps more accurately, from inward-looking to outward-looking integration, is expressed in the abandonment of the distinction between military operations within NATO territory and 'out of area' operations. In the case of the East European countries, particularly Hungary, the Czech Republic and Slovakia, all of them combined the redefinition of a broad range of policies on a national and often divisive basis, in the aftermath of the collapse of the Warsaw Pact and Comecon, with strong pressure to join international institutions, especially NATO and the European Community.

The dualism can also be observed at the level of institutions and indeed of society. In terms of security institutions, one dominant trend is the fragmentation of military units: the creation of new units at national and subnational levels, the emergence of private armies or paramilitary groups often, paradoxically, resulting from cuts in military budgets which release onto the market-place unemployed soldiers and weapons. Another trend is the new emphasis on multinational military units both within NATO and for peace-keeping operations. The defence industry is also undergoing a radical restructuring; in both East and West, this is characterized by a combination of privatization and trans-nationalization. Transnationalization consists of the creation of transnational defence companies (traditionally defence companies were 'national champions') and of a proliferation of joint ventures, international collaborative projects and transnational networks, mainly focused around the development of technologies.

Finally, at the level of society, it is possible to observe a phenomenal growth in interdependence: the fax, telephone, computer, television and cheap travel have opened up all societies to the outside world in a way that would have seemed inconceivable only 20 years ago. Yet at the same time the establishment of new semi-autarkic states and mini-states has led to the breakdown of trade and communication and the closure of ideas and attitudes, and even existing states are introducing new forms of protectionism, for example in the field of immigration policies.

In our view, the tendencies towards fragmentation are stronger than the tendencies towards integration. The latter have to be reinforced by conscious efforts at institution building. In effect, integrative tendencies have to be managed through new institutional arrangements. In Chapter 2, we argued that the cold war framework had profoundly shaped the pattern of economic development in the post-war period. The problem now is how to establish a new integrative post-cold war security framework that is compatible with a new phase of economic prosperity – how to shift economies away from national or bloc-based military priorities.

In both East and West, the dominant response to the crisis of the international system established after World War Two has been neo-liberal. That is to say, it is generally assumed that the sphere of state activity has to be diminished and that competition has to be encouraged through a range of measures that include public expenditure cuts, deregulation and privatization. By and large, military expenditure reductions have taken place within this overall policy framework and there has been no compensation in terms of increased civil spending or tax cuts. These policies can have the effect of destroying obsolete institutional and industrial structures as well as vested interests that constitute an obstacle to restructuring, but they also undermine the possibilities for constructing new institutions. They contribute to the re-emergence of mass unemployment, extreme social inequality and the vicious circles of deflation and deficits – an extremely unfavourable environment for institutional and industrial innovation.

The reintroduction of Keynesian policies is, however, difficult to envisage at a purely national level, both because of the internationalization of economies and because of the internal biases of national states, including the influence of the military sector. Such an approach could not solve the problems of unemployment and inequality and would most likely result in tendencies towards closed-in authoritarian expansionist and militaristic states. This is illustrated in an extreme degree by the new nation states of the former Yugoslavia, but similar tendencies can be observed in other countries, such as Slovakia.

Clearly, it is desirable to introduce at an international level rules of regulation similar to the Keynesian policies that used to operate at a national level. The commitment to the construction of a transnational civil society has to be reflected in new transnational mechanisms for regulating economies. These mechanisms have to incorporate agreed norms which might include the redistribution of resources on a transnational basis, respect for autonomous economic initiative, protection of the environment, and so on. But any such co-ordination of international economic policies would have to be complemented by measures which favour the emergence of new configurations of production and distribution at national, regional and local levels. In other words, global reflation cannot alone solve current problems. What is important is not just an international expansion in public expenditure but a change in the composition of expenditure and in the regulation of markets. Without such adjustments, reflation would just reinforce current imbalances and exaggerate heterogeneities between East, West, North and South and even between countries belonging to the same geopolitical zone; this would ultimately render any global economic policy inoperative.

This argument applies, in particular, to the security context. If we reconceptualize the problem not as too much or too little state intervention but as a problem of replacing the cold war framework, the institutions of the post-war period, then the possible directions for economic development can be more easily identified. On the one hand, neo-liberal policies are rather effective at dismantling the institutions of the previous period, but they do not create new institutions and they result in a dangerous spiral of deflation and unemployment. On the other hand, any increase in public expenditure at a national level is likely to include military spending of a traditional kind – a return to national war economies. This would constitute an obstacle to the reformulation of security policy at an international level as well as the adoption of alternative economic and political approaches to security and the reorientation of military forces towards international peace-keeping. It would also constitute an obstacle to industrial restructuring and to badly needed changes in work organization, skill profiles, technological priorities and so on. In fact, few if any national governments can afford a return to national security policies.

Keynesian-type policies at an international level would need to cover new types of expenditure and new regulations aimed at the creation of markets that are not yet saturated and the solution of pressing problems; these might include environmental spending, the eradication of poverty or the reconstruction of war-torn regions. In other words, they would have to be linked to a new set of political priorities which would include a new internationalist approach to security. The redistribution of tasks and responsiblities between national, regional and international levels would imply the definition of new forms of articulation between the different levels, since such policies would also need to be complemented by appropriate policies at the national and local level.

It is worth mentioning what cosmopolitanism might mean for the use of economic means as an instrument of coercion. In so far as economic policies have been used in the past, they have been based on Clausewitzean assumptions of conflict. Economic sanctions have been used to inflict maximum damage short of war, with very little discrimination; in effect, they identify the government with the people. This can easily have counter-productive effects by harming those groups in society that are victims or opponents of those against whom sanctions are directed. While there is a strong case for using economic means to settle conflicts, they have to be much more differentiated. Economic policies directed against states would include arms embargoes, for example, but should probably exclude cultural or scientific exchanges or humanitarian assistance so as to support opponents of the regime.

Some conclusions about what, in our view, needs to be done to reinforce integrative tendencies in the security and related economic fields have emerged from our studies of the problems experienced since the end of the cold war in defence conversion.

In Eastern Europe, where there was always a rigid international division of labour within the Warsaw Pact and domestic armies tended to specialize in one aspect of war preparations (arms production was, in contrast to the situation in the West, the most internationalized sector of the economy), conversion policies are part of the package of policies aimed at constructing a market economy. The problem of defence conversion is thus more or less the same as the problem of restructuring the overall economy. If we characterize these economies as typical cold war economies, the challenge is how to implement a transition to a peacetime economy.

In Western countries where, by the same token, the problems of defence conversion are very similar to the overall problems of transition faced in East European countries, there were always efforts to organize international collaborative projects of R&D and production in order to spread costs and encourage economies of scale, but these were organized along national lines, based on the principle of *juste retour* to each country, and therefore very wasteful. In these countries, conversion policies are part of an effort to cut public spending and improve the management of public services through introducing quasi-market principles linked into the wider efforts at deregulation. In Britain and France, for instance, even the oldest state-owned arsenals and dockyards have been or will be privatized. In the wake of the post-cold war cuts, there has been a rash of transnational mergers and takeovers and a dramatic restructuring on transnational lines. Everywhere, the growing importance of electronics in military engineering has led to a growing dependence on international technology networks. No individual country can any longer claim national self-sufficiency in defence.

Taken together, these phenomena amount to the break-up of national or bloc military–industrial complexes. Cuts in military spending which are not accompanied by measures to cope with the consequences of the cuts may merely displace military activities. Without a coordinated international response, the effect is to weaken democratic control over the behaviour of military units which can increasingly act as autonomous economic agents, thus exacerbating fragmentative tendencies. On the other hand, if there were a coordinated international response, this would constitute an opportunity to break free of the treadmill of continuous armament which was inherent in the logic of the cold war military–industrial complexes.

What policy conclusions about defence conversion can be drawn from our study? First of all, conversion has to be demand-led. There needs to be increased spending at a global level and there need to be new regulatory frameworks that stimulate spending in new civil fields, especially in the area of collective goods, such as the environment or education, and not on markets which are already saturated, such as private consumption. In Eastern Europe, in particular, spending on infrastructure and investment, especially in extractive industries, would be important in pulling skills and technological potential away from the defence sector. Our Russian case-study emphasizes the importance of developing medium technology sectors like agricultural or oil refining machinery.

New needs have to be defined by the users and not the producers. Undoubtedly, the skills and technological knowledge possessed by the defence sector could be applied to a range of currently unfulfilled needs, especially in the field of the environment and other collective goods. However, the content of spending should be based on criteria determined by those most affected by the problem and not by engineers and scientists in the defence industry. If not, there is a danger of developing large-scale inappropriate products and of excessively technological approaches to these problems. Such a demand-led approach may well mean that existing defence enterprises are unable to adapt to the new demands. But the new demand should ensure the redeployment of human capital.

Secondly, there need to be regional development policies for the worst affected defence-dependent regions, since there is no guarantee that increased public demand would assist specific regions. These should be focused on the needs of the regions and not on the dominant defence enterprises. The aim would be to maintain local employment, especially the employment of scientists and engineers, without necessarily sustaining the dominant defence enterprises. The involvement of local communities, especially trade unions and local non-governmental organizations (NCOs), would be important in ensuring a demand-led strategy.

Thirdly, international organizations have a key role to play in assisting conversion strategies. National demand-led strategies will tend to reflect national vested interests; it will be difficult for national governments to avoid supply-led enterprise-based conversion strategies, which would be much easier at an international level. In addition to conversion policies incorporated into existing institutions, such as the EU's PHARE programme or TACIS programme, it could be worth considering the establishment of a new agency which would combine regulation of the arms trade, especially the black market and the sale of surplus weapons, with technical and financial assistance for scrapping weapons, cleaning up defence-dependent areas, and conversion.

Thus the main conclusion of our studies of defence conversion is that cuts in defence spending have to be accompanied by appropriate forms of economic adjustment that are led by new political priorities formulated at an international and regional level. Otherwise, there is likely to be pressure for renewed military spending at a national level. Without appropriate defence conversion policies which would need to be linked to a reformulation of security policy, the tendency will be towards the spread of fragmented national or subnational war systems. There is thus a need for a range of policies which address both security and economic issues in new ways and which can no longer be confined to the purview of nation states. New institutions which act as agents for integration at regional and global levels will evolve through the adoption of such policies. Any new approach to the issues we have discussed has to be comprehensive. The new types of conflict, the spread of disorganized violence, the problem of dismantling and/or redirecting the resources currently locked up in the military sector, as well as economic turbulence and pain and the return of exclusivist political demands are all interconnected. What is needed, above all, is new guiding principles and globally accepted values. Nevertheless, such guiding principles cannot be estabished in the abstract – rather they will be the result of practical action. A virtuous circle of practical action, ideas and integration has to be set in motion to replace the vicious circle of laissez-faire, apathy and fragmentation that will otherwise lead towards catastrophe.

Index